Shadow Quilting with Marjorie Puckett

OTHER BOOKS BY MARJORIE PUCKETT

Lighter Shades of Pale
Flowers Are Forever
Hearts All Around
Monograms, Softly Yours
Patchwork Possibilities
Primarily Patchwork (with Gail Giberson)
String Quilts and Things
Sweaters, Softly Yours
Animal Makers, Series 1
Animal Makers, Series 2
Animal Makers, Series 3
Animal Makers. Series 4
Scotties, Scotties and More Scotties

SHADOW QUILTING with Marjorie Puckett

MARJORIE PUCKETT

Illustrations by Mieko Tsurimoto
Photographs by Dick Gould

CHARLES SCRIBNER'S SONS NEW YORK

Library of Congress Cataloging-in-Publication Data

Puckett, Marjorie.
Shadow quilting with Marjorie Puckett.

Bibliography: p.
Includes index.
1. Quilting. I. Title.
TT835.P795 1986 746.46 85–30261
ISBN 0–684–18339–0

Published simultaneously in Canada
by Collier Macmillan Canada, Inc.

1 3 5 7 9 11 13 15 17 19 Q/C 20 18 16 14 12 10 8 6 4 2

Printed in the United States of America.

CONTENTS

How I Got Started

Among my earliest memories, I recall Sundays after church. My father's entire side of the family got together. In the early 1940s, the Sunday drive from Seattle, where I lived, to my grandparents' large country home on the outskirts of the small town of Edmonds, Washington, took well over an hour. I usually became car sick somewhere along the winding road, so as a small child, I did not enjoy the lengthy drive. But the rest of those Sunday afternoons was heavenly. All the adoring aunts and warm, hugging uncles, the cousins, nephews and nieces, some with husbands or wives, added to the already large family. In their eyes, I could do no wrong. There were lots of other children to play with, to excitedly take up where we had left off the week before. Occasionally, sharing—and some fighting—would ensue over a favorite toy from Grandmother's closet, which she kept well-stocked with treasures of every size and shape. Just opening the closet doors and seeing the stacked cardboard boxes with their hidden contents was enough to make any child push and pinch to get a better view.

The sit-down supper was served at 2:00 P.M. sharp, and each week a few children were allowed to sit at the main dining-room table with the adults. This, of course, meant that you had to act like an adult and stay seated during the entire meal. After the splendid supper the men would retire to the drawing room with its grand piano while the women went about cleaning up. Small children were excused from assisting once the table was cleared because, as the women said, they were so easy to step on. Even that huge country kitchen started to feel crowded with more than eight adults in it.

With the dishes done and all the fine serving pieces returned to the right glass-enclosed china cabinet, the women would then turn to their needlework, which usually varied from huck weaving to knitting, embroidery, and needlepoint. The older girl cousins tried to outdo each other with the fancy argyle socks they would knit for their boyfriends. The men would discuss business, their voices gradually rising until the ladies would ask them to try to keep the shouting down. It was not a rare occasion for an elderly uncle, or even Grandfather himself, to become completely absorbed with the comments of the younger men. Grandfather would look sideways at those innovative and self-proclaimed business experts and would listen silently for a while about their suggestions for running the family business, not to mention the economy and the ongoing war effort. Soon I would spy Grandfather quietly leave the room for a large dose of baking soda.

As the women stitched, they would try to keep an eye on the children, who by now were constantly in and out of the house, dripping wet either from the seemingly never-ending rain or from being unceremoniously pushed into the large outdoor fish pond. Sometimes we were encouraged to explore the trails in the surrounding woods. One of our favorite paths led to a jagged cliff from which we could view the late-afternoon passenger train winding its way between the base of the cliff and Puget Sound.

Amid all this predictable commotion were the ladies, their inevitable needles never idle. In my mind's eye, I can still see Aunt Genita. She would be stabbing into her needlework, or "fancy work" as they called it, with ever-greater force as the day progressed and the noise increased and the temperaments of the adults were put to their weekly test.

The most outstanding maverick in the family was on my mother's side. My maternal grandfather was a renowned physician and surgeon, and my favorite relative. Our birthdays were on the same day, so ours was a very special relationship. The fine doctor did exceptionally fine needlework, usually designing and stitching in needlepoint. He said it helped keep his fingers limber and nimble for surgery. I am sure it also took his thoughts away from surgery and the medical problems he faced and coped with daily.

This was before the era of television, but that doesn't mean life was boring. Far from it. Every time the doctor and Grandmother would visit us, we would engage in a game of canasta. After Grandfather had beaten all challengers, he would turn to his needlepoint. He'd continue to work into the early hours of the new day. I know because I often awakened at three or four in the morning, needing a glass of water, and there he would be, sitting in the lamplight by the table, totally absorbed over his lovely shades of crewel yarns. The intricate shading he developed within his designs is still recorded in the set of twelve dining-room chairs now in my parents' home. It's difficult for anyone not to be impressed with their beauty as well as the quantity of needlework applied to each chair. The seats are not only stitched on 18-mesh canvas, but so are the inside and outside backs.

This energetic, distinguished gentleman passed on when I was nine years old. My thoughts didn't really focus on the needlework he did until much later, when I was a student at the University of Washington. Being a "good girl," I was expected to attend the university, and there was no room for discussion about it. I happened to be the youngest of all the nieces and cousins, with five older shining female examples to follow. Off to the university I was sent, there to blend in with thousands of other students and with the expectation that I would find a suitable course of study. Only as an educated woman with a college degree could I return home to become a respected homemaker. With no thought about a career, to me the college curriculum looked very bleak, a lot like an expensive prison. I decided finally upon a major in textile design in home economics. Grandfather's needlepoint came back into my life when I had to do a research paper on European embroidery. I went through the linen closets back at my parents' home, searching for samples of design based on previous periods. I came across many pieces of the doctor's needlework, some finished, some incomplete, but all accompanied with matching yarns and notes on how he envisioned the finished piece. I wrote that paper based on my grandfather's interpretation of traditional European needlepoint and how to adapt it to present-day use. My instructor was most impressed with my grandfather's stitching and color-blending abilities. She marveled over the samples of his work and showed them to the entire staff. All the instructors, assistant professors, and professors were women, and they joined in the hailing of his work as "quite extraordinary, especially for a man." Early discrimination in reverse.

It seems that all of a sudden the memories of those Sunday afternoons back in Edmonds flooded my senses, and I was never quite the same again. I strained to remember the details of Grandfather's work, as well as the work of my other relatives. If only I could go back and share experiences and techniques with them today and show them what I have done with their inspirations. They started me along the path that has brought me so much satisfaction and enjoyment.

Designing and teaching have given me the opportunity to develop and expand my interests and personhood. Because I grew up without much sense of identity, the whole world was left open as a playground for my renaissance. I've been able to put my needlework techniques, designs, and patterns into practice and print while lecturing and conducting workshops across the continent.

As an author and designer, a mother, and a searching adult, I feel it is no accident that some women find and center their creative identities around needlework, turning the humblest of fabrics into creations of real value and deep meaning. The simplest idea or design worked into fabric and stitched becomes entirely yours and unique. At the same time, something useful has been created, accompanied every stitch of the way by the joyful feeling that comes with doing pleasurable work. Whatever the degree of complexity, whether the selected project requires only a short segment of time or several sessions spread out over many days, needlework is bound to offer great reward to its maker. It is her very own creation.

I have learned to see needlework as a very strong expression of many feelings, including pain, boredom, disappointment, loneliness, love, joy, and, sometimes, tremendous exuberance. Needlework is more than a decorative medium. It is a vivid statement that reflects the needleworker herself (or himself!) at the very moment of creativity.

Shadow quilting brings us the much-needed personal warmth sometimes lacking in homes today. Our living areas tend to be filled with manufactured products that seem to say, "Untouched by human hands." One's personal living space can become identical to another person's, filled only with look-alike, mass-produced items. On the one hand, we want these products, and they do fill a need. Sometimes, however, these manufactured goods leave us unsatisfied, especially when they impart an impersonal feeling. A manufactured blanket may give us physical warmth on an evening when the air turns extra chilly, but I have never found that it produces quite the inner warmth and satisfaction of a handmade quilt. A handmade quilt spreads us with the comfort of emotional as well as physical warmth so that while it is functional, it also serves as a channel of love from its maker.

Shadow Quilting

With its soft curves and flowing lines, shadow quilting creates a far different effect from the geometric appearance inherent in traditional quilting patterns. Shadow quilting has the look of appliqué, but with shadow quilting, there is no need to turn under the raw edges of the fabrics used, as is the case with appliqué.

Shadow quilting is sheer enough to be worn as a garment and soft enough to be used on a pillow or tea cozy, yet sturdy enough for a quilt and beautiful enough for decorating a home. Because of its special look, it gives the illusion of demanding great skill, infinite patience, and many hours of devoted stitching time.

Just what is shadow quilting? It is a method of sandwiching colored fabric cutouts between a fabric foundation and an overlay of sheer fabric such as organza, batiste, or voile. Small outline running stitches hold the cutouts permanently in place. Further embellishment is sometimes added with embroidery stitches.

The end effect can run the full range from crystal clear and bright down to extremely delicate and muted. The more vibrant the colored fabric cutouts and the sheerer the top fabric, the brighter the final design. The more opaque the top sheer, the softer the underneath colored fabric pieces will appear. With the simplest experimenting and changing of fabrics, the needleworker can create a bright bolero vest of sunny yellows and sunset oranges or a parasol of pale baby blues. The soft tones of a christening gown come to light through shadow quilting, as do the lovely pastel colors of an heirloom-quality baby quilt.

Because a simple running stitch, or in-and-out stitch, is the basic skill needed for shadow quilting, a feeling of freedom can find expression. The needleworker can be inventive and playful, and the sensation of personal involvement can quickly surface. As the colors of the fabrics form patterns, sometimes abstract in shape, wonderful new ideas may spring forth to those who view the emerging creation. Shadow quilting designs can be simple or complex, therefore allowing for a great variety of expression. It can range from the flowing to the rigid. Skills and ideas are found to grow concurrently, and often they determine and alter the original design in mind. Shadow quilting can bring a feeling of joy, of challenge, and of great satisfaction. Teachers or group leaders will enjoy this new medium because the materials, the time required, and the amount of work space necessary are extremely flexible. And this needlecraft form can give pleasure to all ages; children respond enthusiastically to the cutting of the fabric and show great pleasure in the awareness of creating something permanent.

Fabric seems to be a highly logical material to adapt to one's creative needs because we touch and handle fabric every day. We are familiar with fabric; it doesn't appear threatening. It's easy to work with, and almost everyone has used scissors, needle, and thread. With these simplest of tools, shadow quilting offers something new for everyone.

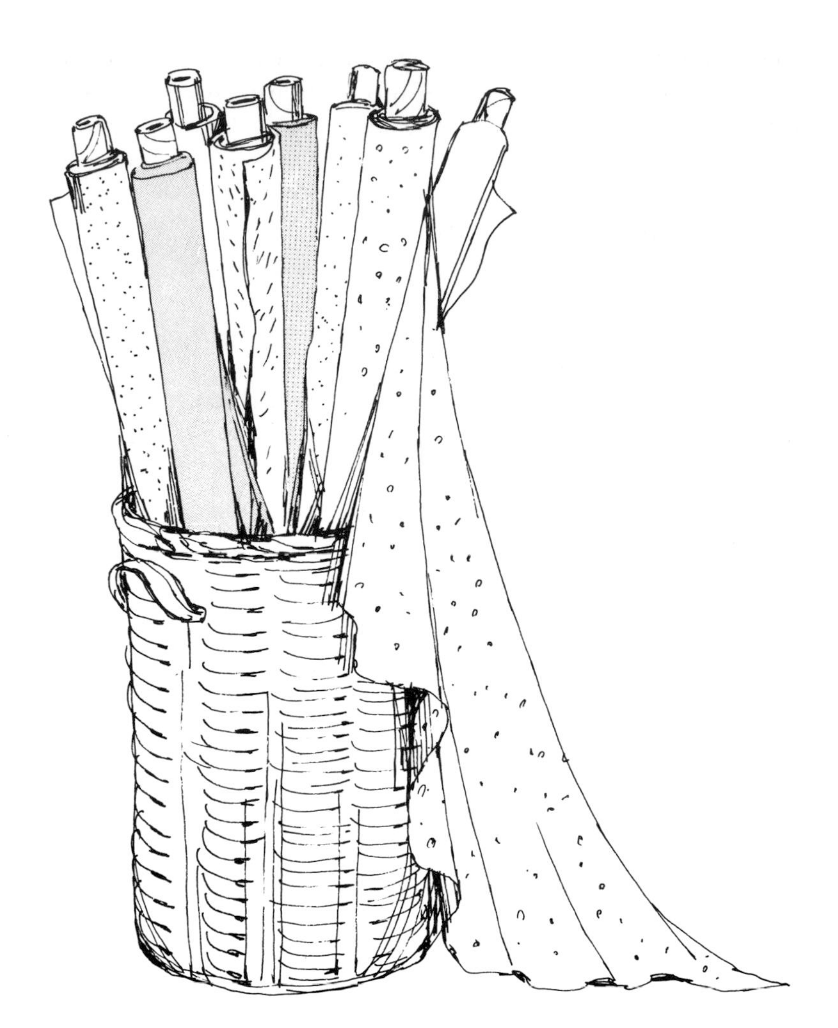

For Great Beginnings

If you believe the old saying, "You are what you eat," you understand the importance of the selection of fabrics for your shadow work. You always want to start any needlework project with the highest-quality materials available. After all, it takes the same amount of hours to do the designing, cutting, positioning, and stitching, so why invest in inferior products? An end product will never be better than the lowest quality of its materials.

THE FINE ART OF FABRIC SELECTION

As you begin to work with shadow quilting, you will become familiar with most of the fabrics suggested in this book. There's nothing like actually working with various fabrics to learn their individual characteristics. You will soon develop your own preferences for certain fabrics, blends, and colors and become increasingly aware of manufacturers and mills. In the meantime, use the ideas here as a guide for your first fabric purchases.

Try working with fabrics that are a blend of cotton and polyester, usually 65 percent cotton and 35 percent polyester or 50 percent cotton and 50 percent polyester. These blends produce easy-care fabrics that are strong, durable, and resistant to wrinkling. Their washability is superb, and they're usually colorfast. Information about the fiber content and whether the fabric is colorfast and shrink-resistant should be printed or labeled on the end of the bolt, along with the care directions.

Colorfastness

To me, colorfastness is the most important feature of a fabric. Unfortunately, we can't put 100 percent trust in the information found on the ends of the bolts. Yardage is often rewound by fabric stores and placed on a bolt other than the original one. Sometimes a fabric chain will purchase one yardage only to rewind it onto several different bolts to send to its various stores. The information given in the label on the end may no longer be true, or the label may carry insufficient information about the fabric on that bolt. I've also found that if I've purchased, let's say a green fabric, and need more of it two weeks later, it may be sold out. "Don't worry," says the concerned store owner. "I have a new bolt of that green from the same manufacturer." Later I sadly discover that the second bolt was not colorfast. Even though it was from the same manufacturer, it came from a different dye lot, had a different dye formula, or had been treated with a different finish.

It's always better to be safe than sorry, so test each length of fabric for colorfastness before you cut into it or store it away. To do this, cut a swatch about 4 inches by 4 inches (10 cm by 10 cm) square. Place this in a teacup, cover with boiling water, and allow to sit for five minutes. When you do this, be sure not to place several swatches in one teacup. Each fabric needs its own teacup. Besides, it's kind of fun seeing your teacups all lined up, almost like having a tea party.

If a fabric swatch was heavily loaded with loose dye, the color of the water will change, and the loose dye will be very obvious. Any swatch of fabric that does not pass the teacup test is going to be risky to work with. Your friends might suggest that you try a saltwater solution or use vinegar to set the dye. Personally, I have found nothing that completely stops the bleeding of loose dye from a fabric.

Sometimes a fabric will have only a small amount of loose dye, and the water in the teacup will remain clear. Even if the water in all your teacups is clear, give each swatch one more test. Remove them, one at a time, from their teacups, and place each between two sheets of white paper toweling. Press with a hot iron until the paper towels with the swatch inside are dry. If there was any loose dye in the swatch, the white paper towels will show some discoloration. Because this faint discoloration might be hard to detect if you use pastel decorator towels or paper toweling with a border print, I suggest that you use the plain white paper towels. When your fabric swatch passes both the teacup and the towel tests, you can be reasonably certain that it is safe to use.

However, if there is still light bleeding in a fabric, if the cup of water from a red swatch looks clear but there is a slight pink mark left on the white paper towels, the loose dye might be flushed out by machine-washing the fabric. Use soap or detergent and the hottest water possible. Be sure to wash the yardage by itself. Machine-wash three or four times, then test again for colorfastness, using the teacup and paper towels, all the while keeping your fingers crossed.

When new yardage continues to lose color even after several machine washings, consider it useless for your purpose and give it away. Donate it to a charity, with a note firmly attached warning that it bleeds.

Shrinkage

The fabric-care directions on the end of the bolt of fabric will usually indicate whether the yardage is preshrunk, Sanforized, or to what extent it might shrink. Generally, blends such as cotton/polyester will have little if any shrinkage, while 100 percent cotton may shrink from three to five percent. I consider any percent of shrinkage too much and not desirable.

No matter what the label indicates, all new yardage to be used in shadow quilting needs to be put through the washer and dryer several times after having been tested for colorfastness. Heat, moisture, and movement are what cause shrinkage, so this procedure assures shrinkage of the fabric while it is still in yardage form.

FABRICS TO PURCHASE

Foundation Fabric

Just as a house is built upon a foundation, so is the technique of shadow quilting, and the bottom layer of fabric that you are going to build upon is called the foundation. Choose a light- to medium-weight broadcloth for this, usually of a solid color but sometimes a stripe or small print will work. Broadcloth is a closely woven fabric. Think of a pillowcase and you can almost instantly visualize what broadcloth is like. Percale is similar to broadcloth but of a finer weave. Then there is batiste, which is very fine and light in weight. Lawn is another lightweight cotton cloth, made from combed or carded fiber and often given a crease-resistant finish. It has a nice drape and feel but is more expensive than the previously mentioned fabrics. Linen, denim, and oxford cloth are really not suitable for the foundation; the first two are too heavy, while the weave of oxford cloth is too loose.

Design Insert Fabrics

The colorful designs used in shadow quilting are cut from the same fabrics as the foundation. My favorites are lightweight broadcloth or batiste, which are easy to handle and stitch and come in a wide selection of colors. A tight weave to the fabric is important. You will later appreciate this when you find a fabric you like, perhaps a yellow, that is loosely woven. That lovely yellow may take on the appearance of greenish yellow if placed over a blue foundation fabric. When this happens, the fabric will need to be lined or have a fusible facing added. In contrast, a closely woven yellow fabric placed over a blue foundation will still appear to be very intense and bright.

Colored fabrics that are slightly dulled or grayed will tend to become even duller, or diffused, when a sheer fabric is placed over them. I find that bright, pure colors work best for the design inserts. They usually end up appearing as clear pastels in the finished project.

Top Sheer Fabrics

A wide variety of fabrics can be used for the top layer, or sheer. My favorite is voile, a blend of cotton polyester woven with a plain weave. Voile has a slightly crisp feel and wonderful drapability. It's readily available in white, solid colors, and sometimes prints. Most of my designs are worked with a top sheer of white voile. A low grade of voile will have slubs or blotches in its weave, while a fine quality will be very smooth and free of these annoying lumps. Always check the bolt by unwinding the voile right there in the store and placing it over a dark fabric. This will make it easier to see how consistent and even the weave is.

Organza is another of my favorite fabrics for the top sheer, but it shouldn't be mistaken for organdy, which has a very crisp finish and tends to wrinkle badly. Organza may be purchased in either 100 percent nylon or 100 percent polyester; you can also find it in silk, but I find this too expensive for my budget. Organza has a soft drape, and again, white is the color I use almost exclusively, although you shouldn't overlook the other available shades.

With its tiny dots, dotted swiss is a crisp, sheer fabric that you may find desirable. Chiffon and georgette should also be considered. Both are very sheer and transparent, which are desirable features, but they tend to be shifty or slippery, presenting problems in handling while being stitched.

In a nutshell, you must really find two types of fabrics: a sheer fabric to be used for the top and a light- to medium-weight, closely woven broadcloth for both the foundation and the design inserts. The next question you'll ask is, "Where do I find these fabrics?" For the sheer fabric, try a fabric store with a large bridal section. Solid-colored broadcloth is available at most fabric stores. If you live in a remote area or want to choose from 200 to 300 color swatches, refer to "Mail Order Sources" in the back of this book for a list of suppliers from whom you can order fabric samples and other notions.

HOW MUCH FABRIC TO BUY?

If there is one piece of wisdom that can serve as the golden rule, it's "a little goes a long way." I recommend that you buy ⅜-yard (0.3 m) cuts of fabric for the design inserts. Also, look at what the quilting stores call "fat quarters." These measure 18 inches by 22½ inches (46 cm by 57.5 cm). For the foundation and the top sheer, you need a piece of fabric only as large as required for the project in mind.

BASIC COLORS

One design may require only two colors for the design inserts while another design may need as many as eight. If there were such a thing as a beginning stock of basic colored fabrics for shadow quilting, it would have to contain sixteen clear, strong colors. These can be purchased as you find it convenient, to be kept on hand.

The Most Frequently Used Fabric Colors

Pure red	Peacock blue
Hot orange	Dresden blue
Shocking pink	Light blue
Bright yellow	Lime green
Light rose	Emerald green
Lavender	Light green
Melon	Cocoa
White	Light beige

OTHER MATERIALS

Bonded Sheet Batting

Cotton or polyester batting comes in a variety of weights and thicknesses and is used behind your finished shadow work to give body and texture. It's available by the running yard or in large, precut quilt sizes. I use only bonded battings or those that hold into a tight sheet and have to be cut rather than pulled apart. Bonded batts have less tendency to shift, lump, or migrate within the finished project. I also prefer working with thin batts as the hand stitches can be made smaller and will therefore be less likely to snag.

Fusible Interfacing

Fusible interfacing is used in shadow quilting to give support and density to fabrics. Light-colored fabrics used for the design inserts may need a fusible ironed to their back side to prevent the color of a darker underneath fabric from showing, or shadowing, through.

Sof-Shape by Pellon is the fusible I prefer, but there are many other comparable products available. Do not use a fusible interfacing that makes your fabric feel stiff, like cardboard. Follow each manufacturer's suggestions for cutting and fusing.

Loose Fiberfill

This loose filler is made of a fine-filament polyester. It is used to pack and stuff pillows, animals, dolls, and other craft or decorative items.

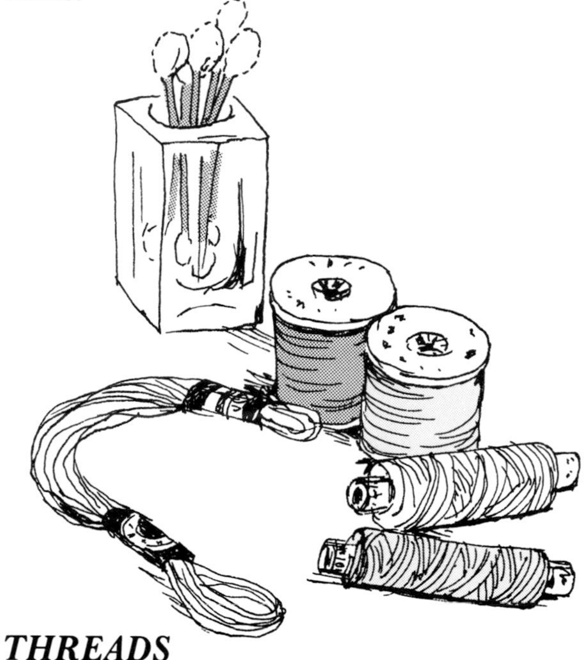

THREADS

The thread used in shadow quilting is second to fabric in importance. As a person who has sometimes literally stitched for twelve to fourteen hours a day, I've established a preference for certain types and brands of thread. You'll be able to form your own conclusions only after you expose yourself to various types of threads.

Try all the brands of thread available. You might like brand "A" with its twenty shades of red from which to choose but find that it's unavailable where you live and has to be mail-ordered. Another brand may "needle" beautifully but come in a limited range of colors. Another brand may draw or pull through the fabric with hesitancy, constantly tangling or twisting around itself, perhaps even fraying or breaking. Dressmaker's beeswax can help alleviate the problem of tangling. To condition your thread, pull it over the surface of the wax.

Thread Types

Sewing-machine Thread. This readily available type of thread comes in a wide range of colors. One store may carry one or two brands while another store may carry a different brand yet. Thread for general sewing-machine work is available in cotton, polyester, or a cotton-wrapped polyester core. Try hand sewing, using two strands of machine-weight thread versus one strand.

Cotton Embroidery Floss. Of all the needleworking flosses, cotton embroidery floss made from six plies, or strands, is available in the widest range of colors. I usually use one strand for my hand running stitches, but when I want to give a design area a bolder statement, I'll use two or more strands.

Pearl Cotton. A #5 pearl cotton is thicker than a six-ply embroidery floss, while the #3 pearl cotton is thicker than the #5, and so it goes. The smaller the number, the larger the floss. Large embroidery flosses are lovely, adding visual and textural accent to design areas through the use of decorative stitches such as featherstitching, buttonhole stitching, or french knots.

Thread Color Selection

When selecting the color of a thread for use in shadow quilting, never look at a spool of thread or a whole skein of floss for comparison. Instead, pull out one strand of thread and lay it across the surface of the fabrics where it would be used. One strand allows an accurate picture of how it would look stitched. Even so, remember that only half the strand of thread will show when stitched with a running stitch.

It's important that your hand stitching doesn't blend or disappear into the finished piece. Why would you do all that stitching and not have it show up? The hand stitching is half of the design and therefore extremely important to the overall appearance of your project. Take time to experiment; try using double strands of machine thread or two plies of embroidery floss. Remember, your lines of stitching *need* to show. The larger the thread or the more strands of thread or floss you use, the more apparent the stitching will be. Maybe part of the design needs to be worked with larger thread such as #3 or #5 pearl cotton. Perhaps a thread's color needs to be brighter, darker, or more contrasting, such as a bright blue thread worked over a hot pink fabric. When you view your work in these terms, you'll see why thread's color should be very intense or in contrast to the fabric.

THE SIXTEEN MOST-OFTEN-NEEDED COLORS OF THREAD

Six-Strand Embroidery Floss	*Coats & Clark's Royal Mouliné*	*DMC*	*Bates' "Anchor"*
Red	2405	666	046
Hot pink	2225	600	065
Bright pink	2720	603	068
Hot orange	7230	900	0333
Pumpkin	7045	971	0316
Yellow	6155	444	0298
Emerald green	5365	700	0227
Lime green	5285	906	0256
Spring green	5330	702	0258
Peacock blue	4710	995	0410
Bright blue	4700	996	0433
Lavender	3370	552	0101
Wisteria	3420	—	0110
Purple	3360	553	098
Cinnamon	8330	918	0352
Wood	8445	301	0356

BASIC SUPPLIES

Tools for Designing

Pattern paper
Lead pencils
Pencil sharpener
Light box
Transparent ruler
Commercial patterns
Paper-cutting scissors
Fine-pointed felt-tipped pens with black permanent ink

Tools for Marking

Fabric-marking pencils
Water-soluble fabric-marking pens
Air-disappearing fabric-marking pens
Dressmaker's carbon
Masking tape
Tweezers
Glue stick
Transparent ruler

Tools for Sewing

Needles
Thimble
Pins
Dressmaker's beeswax
Sewing machine
Cotton swabs
Scissors
Pincushion

Tools for Pressing

Steam iron
Distilled water
Ironing board
White paper towels
Coat hangers
Garment rack

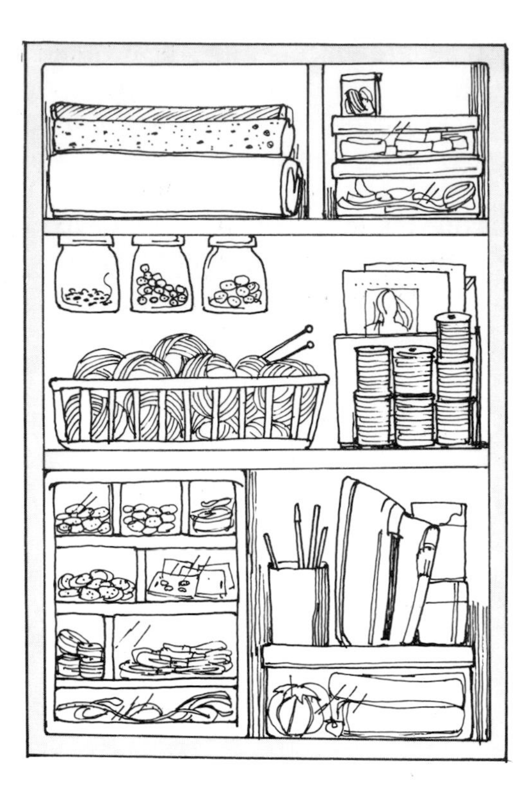

Air-Disappearing Fabric-Marking Pens

As the name suggests, these felt-tipped pens leave a mark that gradually, over a period of hours, disappears. In other words, their marks vanish without having to be purposely removed or washed out. The brands available vary greatly. Some will last for twelve hours, others up to forty-eight hours. Be sure you can identify which marking pens in your supplies are air-disappearing and which are water-soluble. Be forewarned not to use air-disappearing pens for signing checks or other legal documents, for the signature will fade or disappear completely.

These pens are valuable for marking a short-term project. You wouldn't want to use them if you had an extensive amount of marking to do and couldn't get all the cutting or sewing done before they faded.

Coat Hangers

Available in a wide variety of colors and styles, coat hangers are decorative as well as practical. Look for those especially designed to hang scarves, skirts, blankets, or other large bedding in addition to the more common hangers for blouses, shirts, jackets, or skirts and slacks.

Commercial Patterns

Any store-purchased pattern such as a Simplicity is referred to as a commercial pattern. Choose from the pattern brands available or use any pattern you find attractive. Always be aware of the seam allowance called for by a pattern. On garment patterns, ⅝-inch (1.5 cm) seams are generally used, while ¼ inch (6 mm), 1/3 or ⅜ inch (1 cm) are used on craft or decorative patterns.

Cotton Swabs

With a cotton swab, apply a light stroke of water to the cut edges of the design inserts to remove dark, water-soluble marking-pen lines. This leaves the edge of the colored design insert more clearly visible for hand stitching. Work sparingly with the water or the cut fabric edges will act like a sponge and feather out. I enjoy using my favorite china teacup or a finely cut crystal bud vase to hold the water. There's nothing like combining needlework with beautiful accessories.

Distilled Water

The removal of harsh minerals from water gives added life to your steam iron and prevents water marks on freshly ironed projects. You can find distilled water at your supermarket, usually in one-gallon plastic bottles.

Dressmaker's Beeswax

Beeswax strengthens thread and acts as a lubricant, making it easier to do hand sewing. Purchase dressmaker's beeswax in a plastic holder that has grooves through which the thread is pulled for waxing. The holder also keeps the wax clean when not in use.

Dressmaker's Carbon

Test your dressmaker's carbon on each fabric you plan to use, checking to see that the marks are removable. Many of the brands on the market today are not.

Fabric-Marking Pencils

White, silver, or pastel marking pencils may be needed for marking on dark fabrics. Some of the new marking pencils can even be wiped off with a damp cloth; others have to be washed out. If you use a pencil with a chalky type of lead, you can sometimes remove the marking with just a light brushing. Unfortunately, this can mean that even the motion of your hand as you work on your fabric may cause the marking to disappear before you want it to.

Fine-pointed Felt-tipped Pens with Black Permanent Ink

Keep both red and black fine- to medium-pointed felt-tipped pens on hand. These are applied only to paper, never to fabric. Use them to darken your selected design or to trace designs onto paper. The permanent ink will not lift from the paper or transfer to the underside of your fabric when you are tracing a design.

Garment Rack

This can be found at most department or variety stores. Projects in progress can be hung over coat hangers on the rack, keeping your work out of the way but within easy line of vision. A garment rack also helps to eliminate wrinkles and therefore the need for additional pressing.

Glue Stick

The glue stick is a fairly new tool, available through needlework, quilting, and fabric stores. Also, variety or dime stores often sell glue sticks in their stationery or school-supply departments. When buying a glue stick, read the label to make sure the glue is water-soluble and recommended for fabric use. Do not substitute other glues or white craft glues for a glue stick as they are not the same.

The glue stick is similar in size to a tube of lipstick. The glue is in stick form, with a consistency like paraffin wax or lipstick. It will soften or melt if placed in the sun or close to a heater. In hot, humid climates, it may support the growth of mold; store infrequently used sticks in the freezer to eliminate this.

With a wet paper towel, keep your glue stick clean of the tiny fiber specks that can cling or stick to its surface. You don't want any colorful fibers to transfer to your work, where they can become permanently embedded between layers of delicately colored fabrics.

Also beware: Glue sticks rapidly disappear in the middle of the night. Who knows where they go? You might find them later under your son's bed or in your daughter's crayon box, so be forewarned. Better buy one for every member of the family. Then maybe yours will be left alone.

Lead Pencils

A Number 2 soft lead pencil is necessary for tracing and for drawing designs on paper. Never use a lead pencil directly on fabric as the marks may smear and be next to impossible to remove. The same holds true for ball-point pens.

Light Box

Once you use a light box, you won't know how

you managed without one. A light box can be purchased at quilt or needlework shops, or you can check an art-supply source, although their prices tend to be higher. Light boxes are usually constructed of wood, with a surface of glass or Plexiglas. A fixture for a cool fluorescent bulb, placed on the inside of the box, makes tracing out your patterns a cinch. Information on making you own light box is given on page 158.

Masking Tape

A roll of 1-inch-wide (2.5-cm) masking tape is a vital tool in your sewing supplies. It helps to secure fabric or paper in place when tracing or transferring designs. The 2-inch-wide (5-cm) roll of masking tape is useful for removing lint, tiny threads, or bits of loose fiber from the surface of a project. You might also want to invest in a good lint roller.

Do not use adhesive tapes for any part of a project as they can leave a sticky residue on fabric. This is difficult to remove, and the fabric may require dry cleaning.

Needles

The needle is probably the needleworker's best friend. That's where we get the word "needleworker." I don't really understand why needles are numbered the way they are, but the higher the number, the thinner or finer the needle. The type and length of the needle are distinguished by words such as "Sharps," "Betweens," "Embroiderys," "Chenille," even "Darning." A variety pack of "Sharps" may contain sizes 7 through 11. Or you can buy a package of "Sharps" containing only Number 7. Chenille needles are large and needed for six-ply embroidery floss and pearl cotton. Embroidery needles have a long eye, and as their name implies, they are used for embroidery.

For shadow quilting, try using "Betweens," "Sharps," or "Quilting Needles" in sizes 8, 9, 10, or 11. If selecting from an assorted package, look for a thin needle. When I'm teaching class, I walk among the students looking at their work. When I find a student taking large, irregular stitches, I usually find that she's using a thick, fat needle. Now, if you haven't done a lot of sewing, you won't know what a thick needle is. Nevertheless, select thin, fine needles. To sew with a fat needle is almost like trying to brush your teeth with a carrot. It will be cumbersome and bang around, doing a poor job.

Paper Towels

I use white paper towels to check the colorfastness of fabrics. Pastel decorator towels and those with border prints are not good for this purpose as their coloring and design interfere with your ability to detect dye bleeding from the fabrics being tested.

Pattern Paper

Wide rolls of paper are now available to the home sewer for pattern drafting and design development. Small dots are printed on the surface, marking off 1-inch (2.5-cm) spaces to assist in drawing straight lines and establishing angles.

Pencil Sharpener

Many styles are available. I prefer those that give a sharp point and have a container attached to catch the cut shavings. A portable battery-operated model is a great gift item to put on your "want list."

Pins

It is probably time to treat yourself to a new box of pins. Mine have a way of just melting into the woodwork or showing up painfully in the soles of my feet. If you need to buy pins, look for the sharp, rust-free kind. Cheap pins can be inferior, even rusting in your fabric. They also tend to be thick, causing snags or leaving large puncture holes in your work. I prefer Angel Pins or Iris Pins. The latter come from Switzerland and are found in a round blue metal box shaped like a large checker or Oreo cookie. There are also some good Japanese pins available. Since I'm not prolific in reading Japanese, I don't know what they're called, but they are very fine and 1½ inches (3.8 cm) long, with a glass head. The glass head makes them easy to identify both in your work and in your carpet, which seems to be a favorite hiding or resting place for them. Some Japanese pins have pastel-colored flower heads, making them equally easy to locate. In some European countries, fine pins may be sold as "Lace" or "Bridal" pins.

Pincushion

I prefer to store my pins in a pincushion rather than in a box, which could allow the pins to scatter if it falls to the floor. Stay away from a magnetized pincushion. It tends to transfer some of the magnetism to the pins. When this happens, the pins become hard to work with, jumping or pulling toward each other.

Scissors

I collect scissors in almost the same way as I collect cats: They just sort of fall into my life. Some I purchased, others were given to me. A few are orphans, left behind. Scissors, like cats, come in all sizes and shapes. If you were to look over my collection, you would see one pair of brushed stainless steel and another pair of shiny chrome, with very fine points. Then there is one pair with broken tips, which I use as a screwdriver when repairing or working on my sewing machine. Another pair I keep handy to cut paper and batting, even heavy cardboard or sheets of plastic. Then there are the scissors that my family can use. I've tied bright red ribbons to these, and woe to the person who grabs any pair without a red ribbon. My best scissors are put away in my sewing area, because they're a very personal possession.

I've found through teaching and talking to my friends that each of us tends to like a different brand of scissor. It's almost as if scissors fit our hands differently. Maybe the structure of your hand or the bone size is what determines the brand of scissor that feels best to you. Jacki, for instance, likes the 2-inch (5-cm) blade available on the Fisker scissor. I always envy her for her tiny hands and bones. She's Vietnamese, and her bone structure is exactly the opposite of my big wholesomeness. I prefer using the Ginger. Another friend, Barbara, prefers the Marks scissor. However, these scissors all have one thing in common: The best scissors for shadow work have a 2-inch (5-cm) blade, and they are very sharp. Their total length is 4½ to 5½ inches (11.5 cm to 14 cm). Shorter scissors, such as manicuring scissors, won't work, and anything with a blade over 3 inches (7.5 cm) will tend to be cumbersome.

Keep your scissors in a sheath to protect them. The Ginger scissor #G5C comes in a wonderful leather sheath. You might even make a simple sheath for your favorite pair. It will help emphasize their importance to those family members who might grab them to open a bottle top, to cut electrical cording, trim the dog's tail, or pry loose a nail.

Several manufacturers make left-handed scissors as well as the universal scissor for both left- and right-handed use. The common right-handed scissor is always available. If you can't find left-handed scissors in your area, turn to the section, "Mail Order Sources," at the back of the book.

Sewing Machine

While the shadow quilting itself is done by hand, a sewing machine is needed for the final assembly of most projects.

A sewing machine cared for according to the manufacturer's manual can last for a lifetime.

If you are considering the purchase of a sewing machine, visit sewing centers maintained by the various manufacturers and try the machines under the supervision of a demonstrator. As a rule, the more things a machine can do, the more it will cost. When making your selection, remember that you will be using the machine over a period of many years and that your sewing needs will change along with your life-style and needs.

Steam Iron

Happiness is a warm iron. Keep your iron and ironing board set up and close at hand, if possible. Try not to iron over pins as they may scratch the plate of your iron. Keep the iron base polished, cleaning it from time to time with the manufacturer's recommended cleaning products.

When purchasing a new iron, select one that is a combination of steam and dry. Make sure the iron has a temperature control that indicates synthetic, wash-and-wear fabrics, cotton, wool, and linen. Always use distilled water for steam pressing; it is free of minerals that might otherwise clog your iron.

Thimble

This is a small but very strategic item, used to prevent sore fingers. It's an absolute must for hand sewing through thick or heavy fabrics. The thimble is generally placed over either the middle finger or the ring finger of the hand you sew with. When the thimble is in place, the sewer uses the front surface of it to push the needle through the fabric. I recommend that you learn to use a thimble by giving yourself two hours of practice with a scrap of fabric. Hold or pinch the needle between the thumb and index finger while pushing with the thimble finger, using the front surface of the thimble. It may feel awkward at first, but if you persevere, you'll find that your sewing goes more smoothly than ever.

An additional thimble is often worn on the opposite hand when quilting, the hand that is kept to the underside of the quilt. Quilt and needlework shops carry thimbles specifically designed for this purpose. They may be constructed of plastic, leather, or a sheath of leather wrapped around a metal splint.

Transfer Pencils

These pencils are permanent, making them touchy to use. The smallest trace or smudge from their lead will remain on your fabric forever. Embroidery stitches often fail to cover the marks. I advise against their use for sewing or fabric projects.

Transparent Rulers

These come in a variety of shapes and sizes. Try to have a short, 6-inch (15-cm) ruler as well as a 12-inch (30.5-cm) and an 18-inch (46-cm) ruler in your sewing supplies.

Tweezers

A 6-inch-long (15-cm) surgical tweezer will soon become one of your most often used tools for shadow work. With its extremely long handles and sharp point, it is useful for positioning the cut design inserts on the foundation fabric, for retrieving loose threads, and for reaching into those hard-to-get-to places. They can help you hold on to tiny pieces of cut fabrics that want to stick to your fingers once the glue stick has been applied. Tweezers are great for ripping, holding, and picking. They become doubly useful for people with arthritic hands or finger joints.

I've tried many types of tweezers and found the standard household type available in the drugstore unsuitable. Use them only until you can find the long surgical or sewing tweezers. Ask for them at your local quilting, needlework, or sewing-supply store, or check the "Mail Order Sources" in the back of this book.

Water-Soluble Fabric-Marking Pens

These pens would receive the highest marks if we took a poll to choose the most versatile and valuable new notion for sewing in the past five years. The water-soluble ink is easily removed from fabric by wiping over the design with a damp cloth or cotton swab, or by completely submerging the fabric in cool water.

Be sure to read the directions accompanying the pen you buy. As a precaution, always test a newly purchased marking pen on scraps of the various fabrics on which you will be using it to see how it reacts with the fabrics' finishes. It is often recommended that you never iron fabrics that have the pen's marks still on their surface; heat, hot water, and certain detergents may affect the removability of marking lines. Be sure that all marks have been flushed from the fabric before ironing or washing the finished product.

DEFINITIONS OF TERMS

I've defined several terms you'll need to know as you become acquainted with shadow quilting.

Design. The decorative element or shape, such as a flower, cat, or rainbow. This book contains many designs suitable for shadow quilting and related techniques such as cross-stitch, embroidery, stenciling, candle wicking, appliqué, and needlepunch. A design is selected and applied to an area within a pattern.

Design Insert. This is the decoration, or design, cut from a light- to medium-weight fabric. It is positioned over the foundation. Any colorfast broadcloth may be used.

Finger Press. The technique of applying pressure with the fingertips. This is called for when an iron should not be used for pressing.

Foundation. In shadow quilting, this is the bottom layer of fabric—thus the name, foundation. Other fabrics are placed upon the foundation, just as a house is built upon a foundation. A light- to medium-weight broadcloth of closely woven material is the fabric usually selected. Any color may be used, although white is the most popular.

Pattern. A pattern, such as a Simplicity pattern, can be purchased at your local fabric store, or you can construct your own pattern, usually from paper. The pattern has a twofold purpose: It presents a physical area or shape, such as a dress yoke, sleeve, or collar, and usually provides a plan of action or step-by-step assembling sequence. Each project—whether it be a pillow, dress, vest, or padded picture frame—requires a pattern.

Top Sheer. Just as the name implies, a sheer fabric, usually voile, organdy, organza, chiffon, or very fine batiste, forms the top layer of the sandwich of fabrics necessary for shadow quilting. White is the preferred color, but any soft shade may be used.

METRIC CONVERSION CHART

FABRIC LENGTH CONVERSION
(yards to meters; slightly rounded)

Yards	*Meters*	*Yards*	*Meters*
1/8	0.1	3	2.7
1/4	0.2	4	3.6
3/8	0.3	5	4.5
1/2	0.5	6	5.4
2/3	0.6	7	6.3
3/4	0.7	8	7.2
7/8	0.8	9	8.1
1	0.9	10	9.0
2	1.8		

FABRIC WIDTH CONVERSION
(inches to centimeters; slightly rounded)

Inches	*cm*	*Inches*	*cm*
25	65	50	127
27	70	54/56	140
35/36	90	58/60	150
39	100	68/70	175
44/45	115	72	180
48	122		

INCHES INTO MILLIMETERS AND CENTIMETERS
(slightly rounded)

Inches	*mm*		*cm*
1/8	3		
1/4	6		
3/8	10	or	1
1/2	13	or	1.3
5/8	15	or	1.5
3/4	20	or	2
7/8	22	or	2.2
1	25	or	2.5
1 1/4	32	or	3.2
1 1/2	38	or	3.8
1 3/4	45	or	4.5
2	50	or	5
2 1/2	65	or	6.5
3	75	or	7.5
3 1/2	90	or	9
4	100	or	10
4 1/2	115	or	11.5
5	125	or	12.5
5 1/2	140	or	14
6	150	or	15
7	180	or	18
8	205	or	20.5
9	230	or	23
10	255	or	25.5
11	280	or	28
12	305	or	30.5

So—Let's Sew a Project

I often tell newcomers to shadow quilting that the hardest thing about it is deciding what to choose for their first project. I suggest you do a pillow top for your initial learning experience. It's ideal for your first project because it can be completed in a relatively short time while still allowing you to go through all the basic steps of shadow quilting. This means that you would definitely rule out starting with a bed-sized coverlet, but it doesn't mean that you couldn't select a coverlet for your second project.

Although these are the steps used to execute a design for a pillow top, the same basics are followed for all the other projects in the book. The instructions may look lengthy, but great effort has gone into covering each point in thorough detail and illustration. You'll be pleasantly surprised at how quickly it goes once you start in with fabric, needle, and thread.

When I mention the word pillow, ten different people will conjure up ten different images of pillows. Pillows can be round, square, rectangular, or crescent-shaped, just to list a few. Their edges can be finished in various ways—

corded, flanged, knife-edged, or even boxed. One pillow might be huge—a floor cushion, for example—while another could be delicate and small—a boudoir pillow.

Just how big do you want your pillow? Rather than "thinking" of a size like 12 inches by 12 inches (30.5 cm by 30.5 cm), you need to be able to see what 12 inches by 12 inches really looks like. Do this by making a paper pattern. Cut out a piece of newspaper or use the paper from a grocery-store bag to give yourself an accurate visual. Place your cutout where the pillow will be used, such as on a sofa or a bed. In most cases, what you thought would be a good size isn't. Make another paper pattern, testing it in the same way until you think the size looks right. Remember to add seam allowances to all the outside edges.

Always begin every project with a pattern, whether it's a commercial pattern or one you draw up and construct yourself.

Find a suitable design for the pillow top, something relatively small. After all, you would like to get the project done today, wouldn't you? If you're like me or if you often find that your eyes are bigger than your stomach, you may have to force yourself to keep to a simple design, such as the one we're using. You'll find it on page 53. This design will give you ample

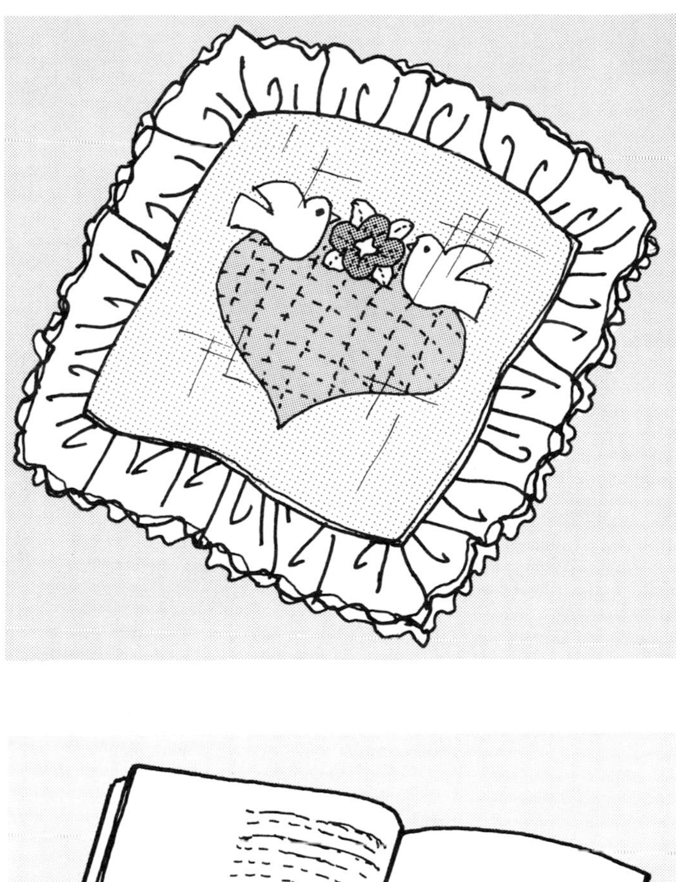

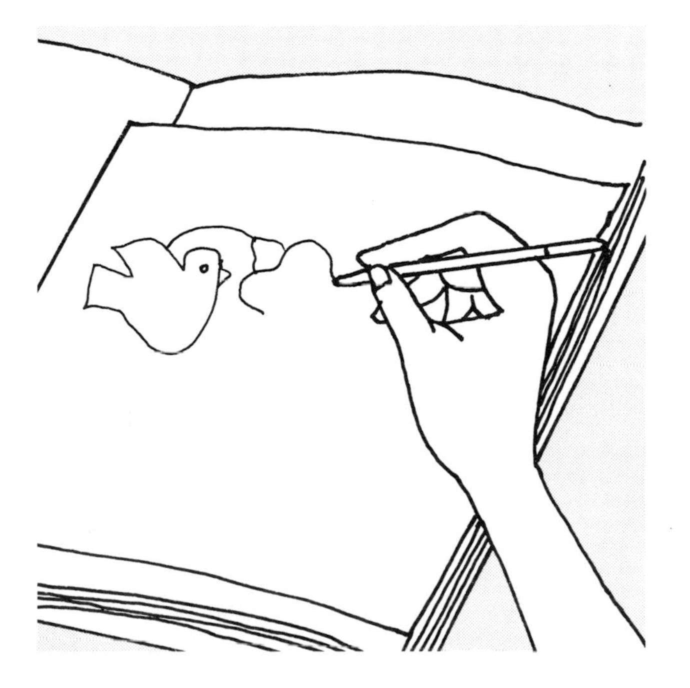

experience with color selection, cutting, and stitching, while requiring a minimum of time.

Place a sheet of tracing paper over the selected design, then trace it with a pencil. To steady your hand, rest your palm where it joins your wrist against the drawing surface or table

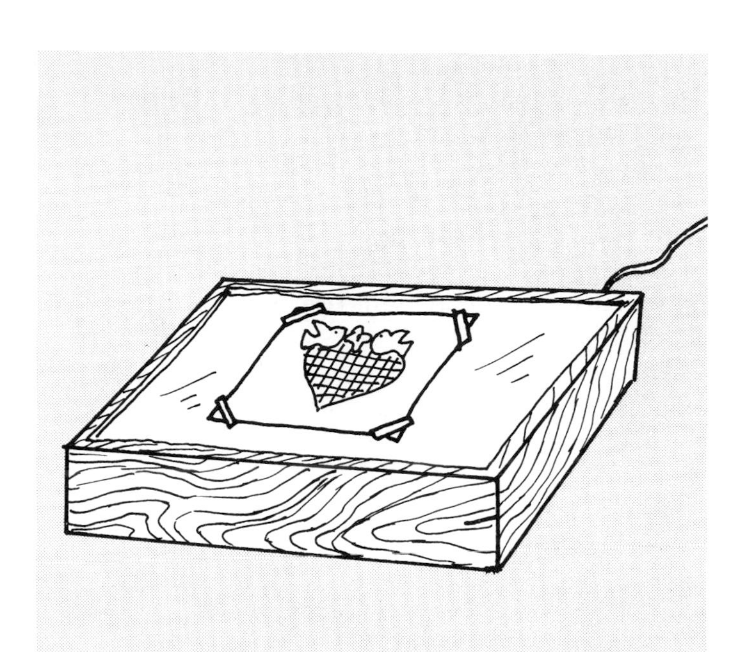

top. Remove your paper and darken the tracing, using a fine-pointed felt-tipped pen with black permanent ink.

Using masking tape across the corners, tape your traced drawing to the surface of a light box or against a windowpane through which a good light is coming toward you. Sometimes if you simply place a sheet of heavy white paper or cardboard behind the tracing, its lines can be seen more easily.

Cut your foundation fabric 2 inches (5 cm) larger on each side than needed for the finished project. Find the center of the fabric by folding the fabric in half, then in quarters. Finger press the folds so they can be seen; mark the fold lines with a water-soluble fabric-marking pen. Also mark the diagonals, working from corner to corner to establish them.

Center the foundation fabric over your design, using masking tape across the corners to

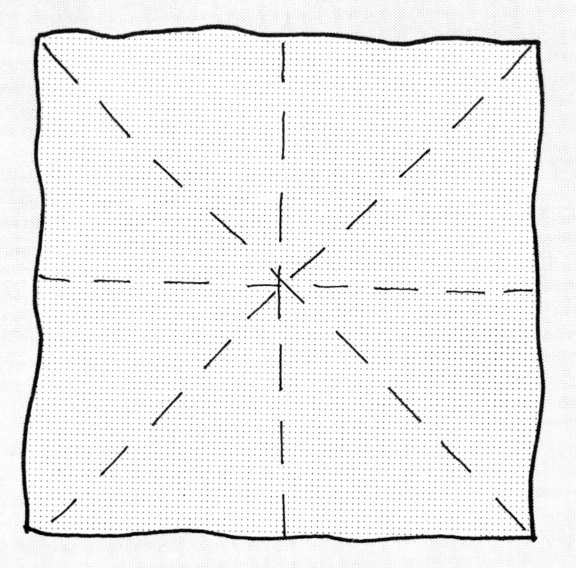

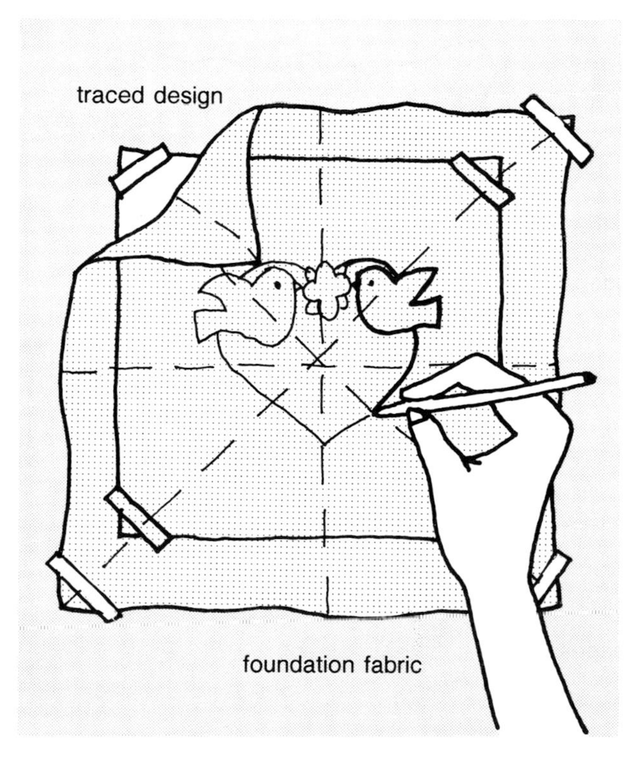

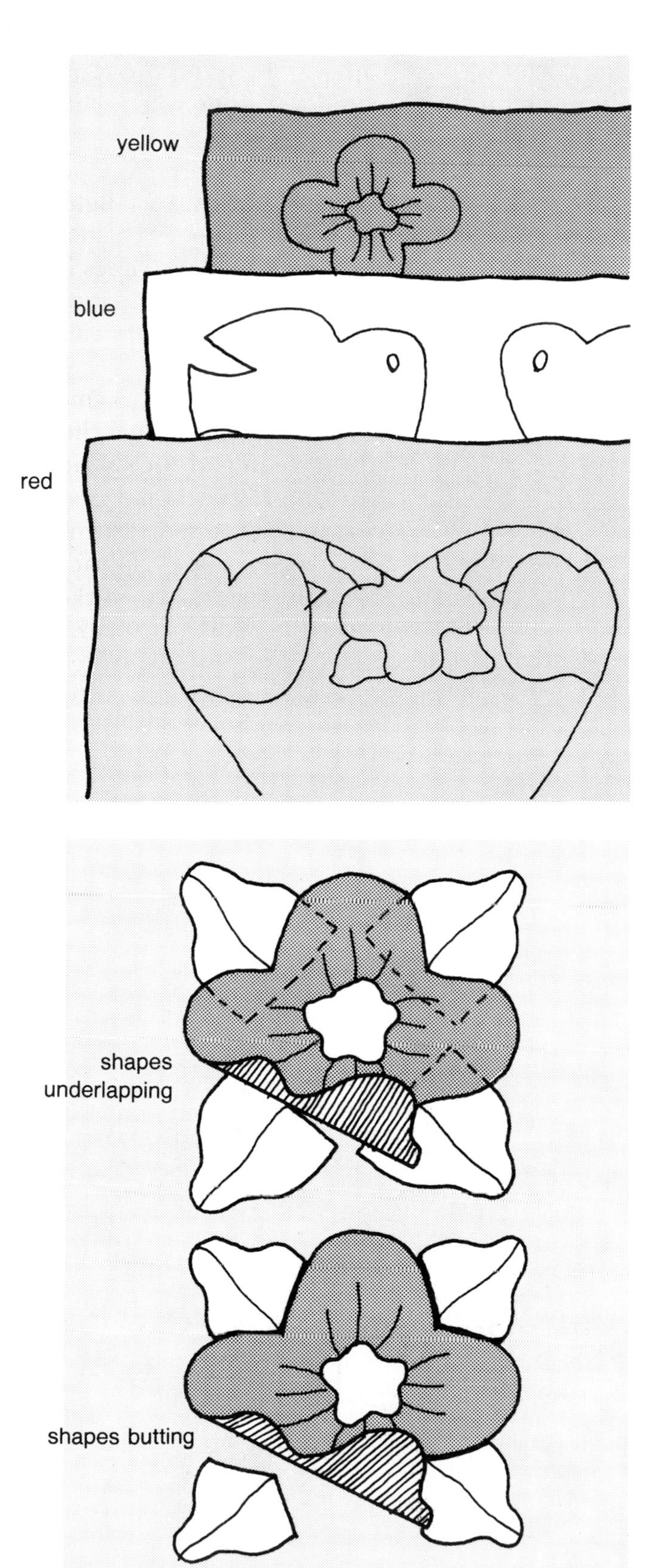

keep it from shifting. With a water-soluble fabric-marking pen, trace along all lines. Remove the foundation fabric.

Trace the design inserts, following the techniques used for the foundation fabric. Carefully trace each shape needed onto the colored fabric selected—for example, the birds onto blue fabric, the heart onto red, and the flower onto bright yellow.

Design inserts may be traced to allow their edges to butt, or you may add a small extension for underlapping. Be sure to trace the fabrics with the water-soluble marking pen.

When tracing onto a dark fabric, you may need to use dressmaker's carbon. This is placed over the fabric, and the design is positioned on top. Trace with a worn-out ballpoint pen.

When all the fabrics are marked, begin cutting out the design inserts, using scissors with

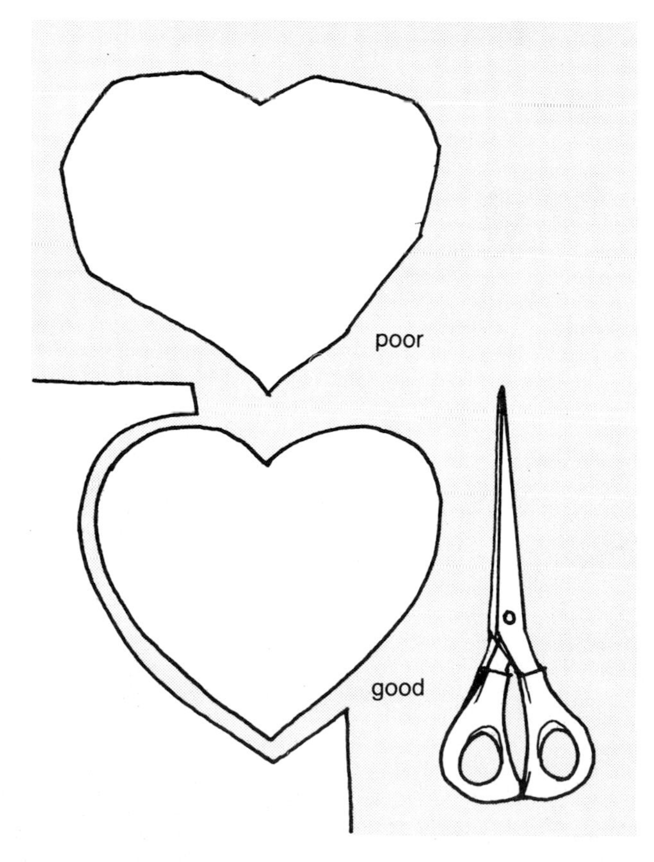

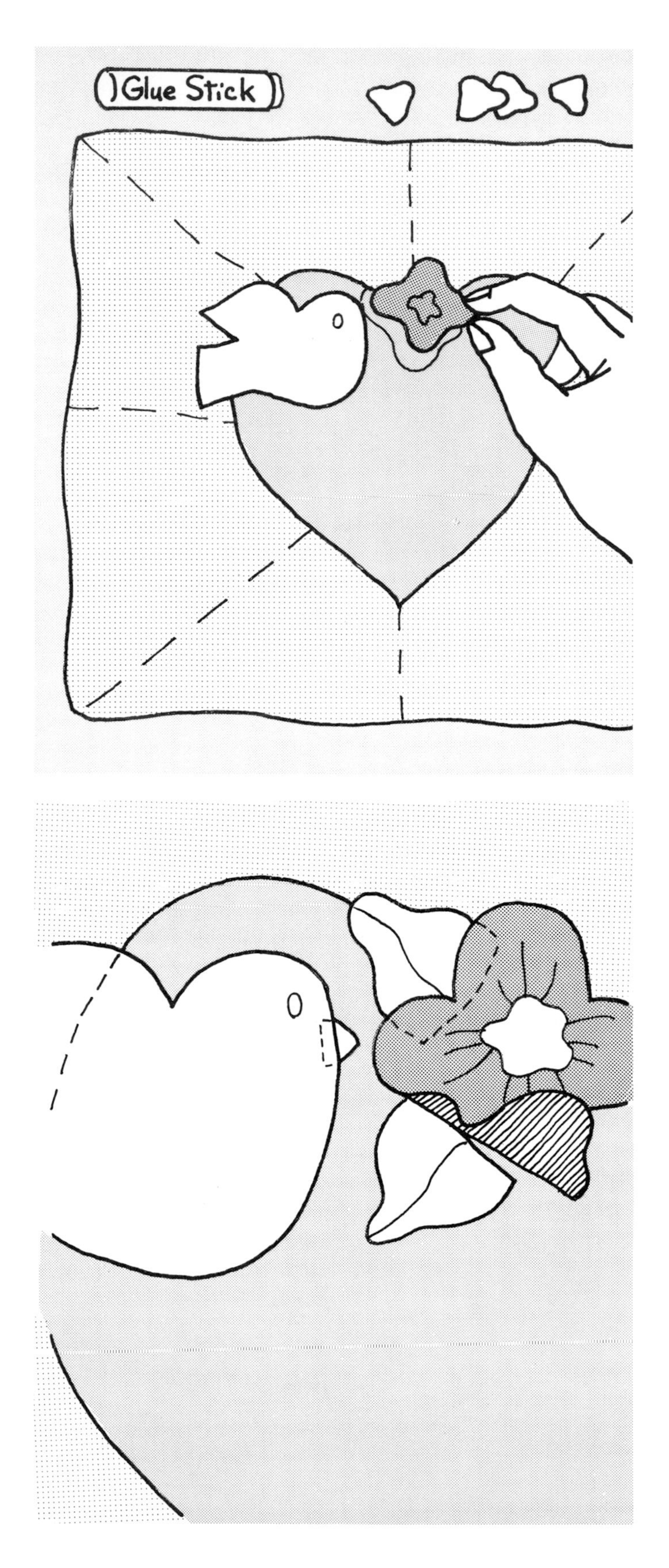

short, sharp, 2- to 3-inch (5-cm to 7.5-cm) blades. Cut on or just to the inside of the marked lines. The cut shapes should have smooth, jagged-free edges. To keep the cut design inserts free of wrinkles and their edges protected from fraying after they are cut, place them inside a folded-over sheet of heavy white or bond paper.

With a glue stick, apply a few light strokes of glue to the back side of the cut design inserts, finger pressing into place on the marked foundation. Always apply the glue stick to the largest piece of fabric first. In this example, the glue stick would be applied to the foundation; then the heart would be positioned and finger-pressed into place. Next, apply a fine line of glue to the heart where the bird will be positioned, putting the bird in place with a gentle pressing of the fingertips.

In the design shown, the leaves should be glued into position first, then the large flower added. The flower's edges will either butt the base of the leaves or they will be placed over the leaves' small extensions if these were added, as shown on page 23. The small flower center is then positioned over the flower. When doing the bird, the beak is positioned onto the heart; then the bird's body is put into place.

Sometimes when a light-colored design insert is placed over a darker fabric, the underneath color may shadow through. A fusible interfacing applied to the back of the lighter color will eliminate this. Bond the fusible interfacing to the whole piece of fabric before the design insert is cut from it. This is easier than trying to bond the interfacing to the small, individual cut shapes. Be sure to follow the manufacturer's directions for fusing or bonding.

With masking tape, a lint roller, or tweezers, clean any small threads or fine particles of lint from the fabric foundation and design inserts. Position the top sheer fabric over the design inserts and foundation. The top sheer should be cut to the same size as the foundation. Hold it in place with several straight pins. Then, to keep your fabrics from shifting, baste through

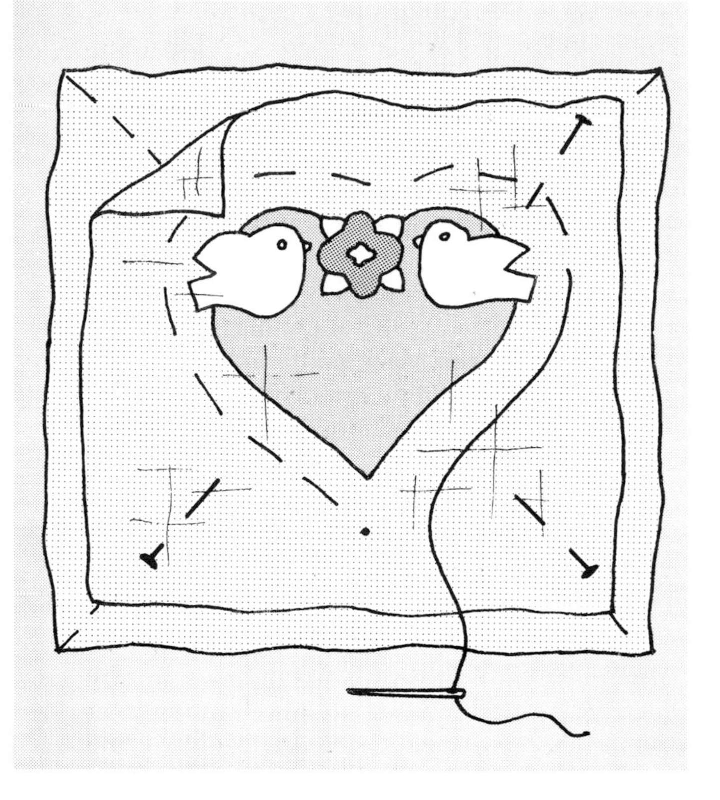

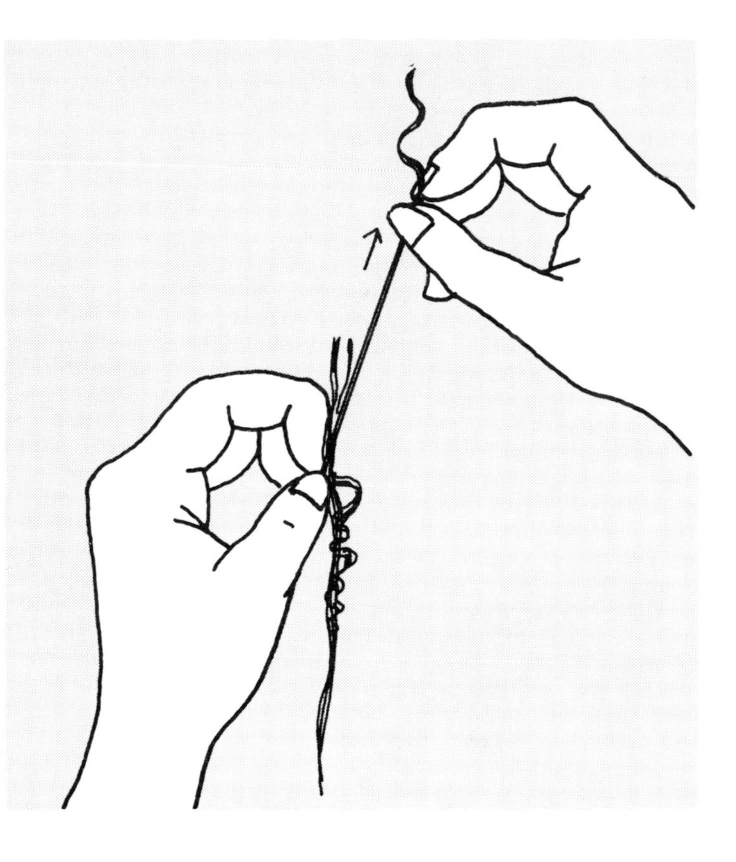

the top sheer and foundation with 1-inch (2.5-cm) stitches, using basting thread to match the color of the foundation. The stitches should lie approximately ½ inch (1.3 cm) outside the design inserts. Additional basting may be needed vertically and horizontally if the work is exceptionally large.

Select the highest-quality sewing-machine thread, or use the best cotton embroidery floss available, for hand stitches. You may use one to two strands of either thread, but avoid combining both types on one needle.

Cotton embroidery floss is made of six strands. You may choose to work running or decorative stitches, using a single or double strand of floss rather than all six strands. To divide the floss, cut a length 18 inches (46 cm) long, or approximately the distance from extended fingertips to elbow. Pull one strand loose by lifting it straight up while the other hand tightly pinches the other strands. Remove only one strand of floss at a time.

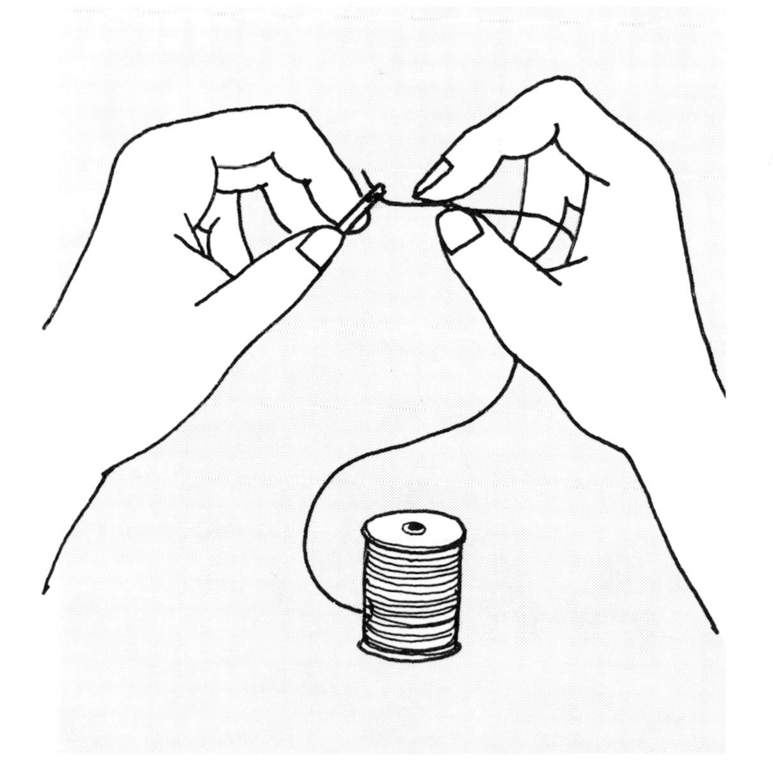

Step 1

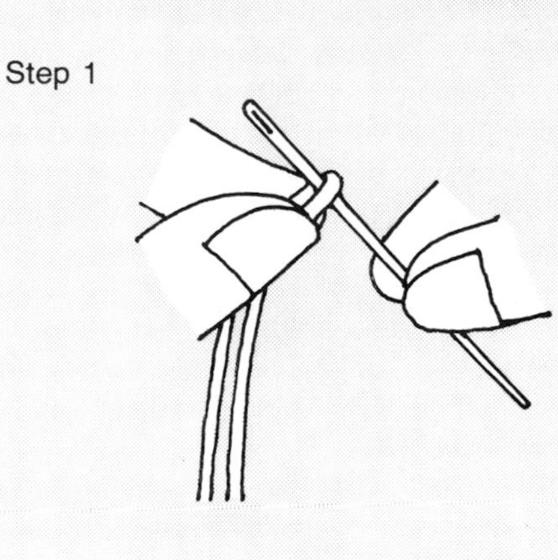

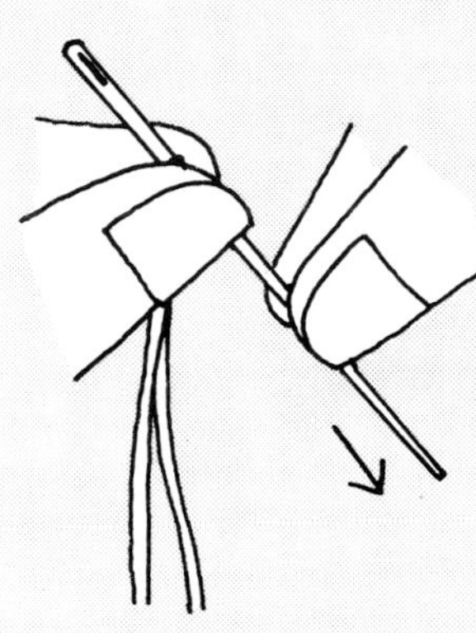

Step 3

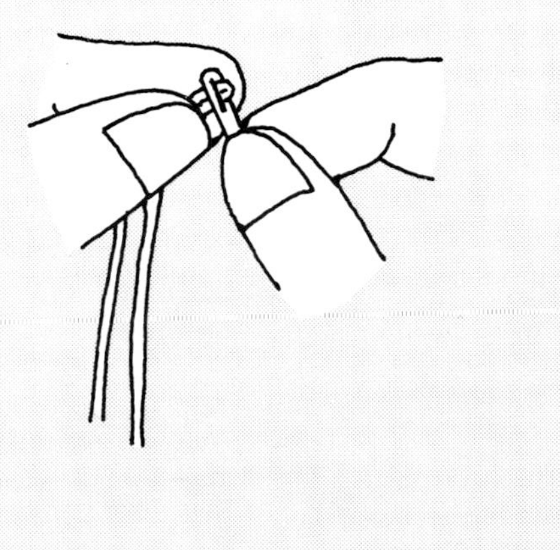

Cut across the tip of your thread at an angle. For hand sewing use a "Sharp" or "Between" needle in size 8, 9, or 10. A relaxed approach to threading the needle is to lick the cut end of the thread, then push it through the eye of the needle. This may work for smooth threads or floss, but it won't work as well with thicker yarns or multiple threads.

Here's a second method to try for threading a needle. *Step 1.* Loop and pinch the thread tight against the needle with your thumb and forefinger. *Step 2.* Remove the needle, keeping the thread tightly pinched. *Step 3.* With your free hand, force the eye of the needle down horizontally between your pinched fingers so it slips over the thread.

To make a knot in your sewing thread, use the end cut from the spool. Place this end between your fingertips and the needle.

Wrap the thread three or four times around the needle while holding the end between your fingers and the needle. Pull the wraps downward.

While pinching the wraps, pull the needle up with your free hand. A knot will form near the tail of the thread.

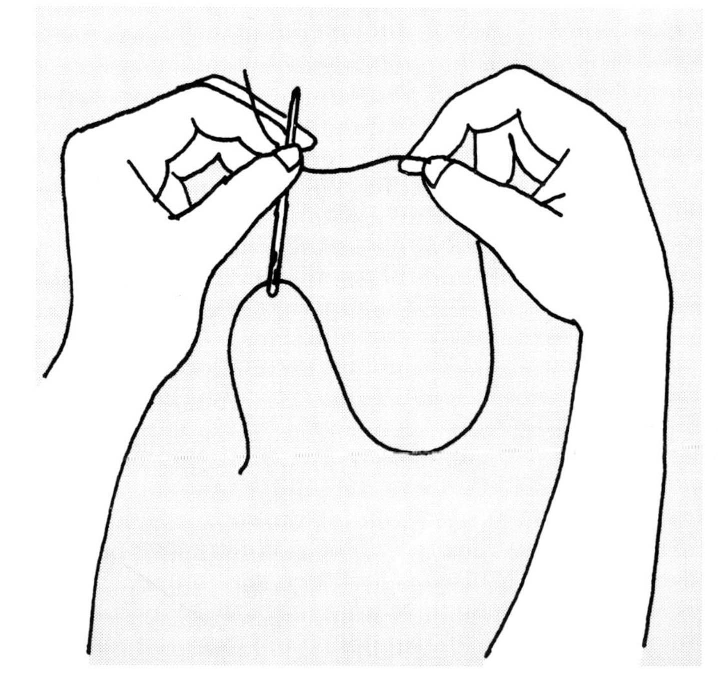

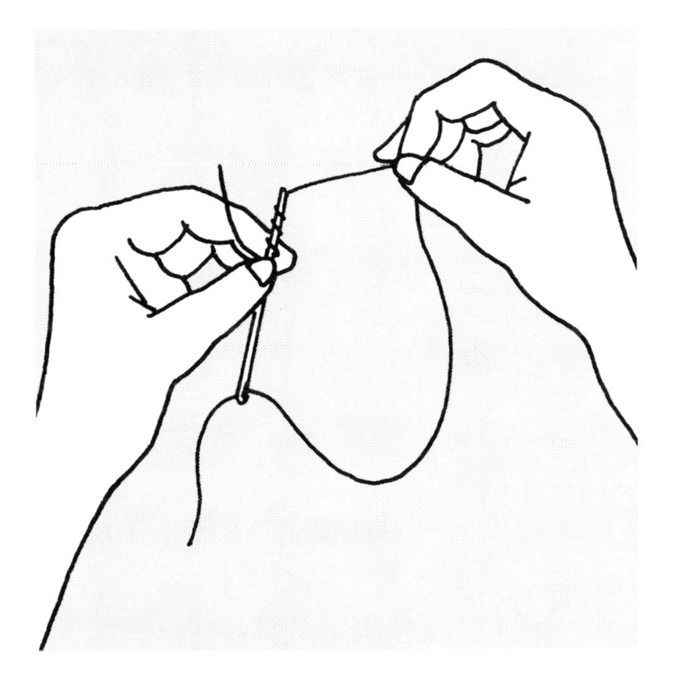

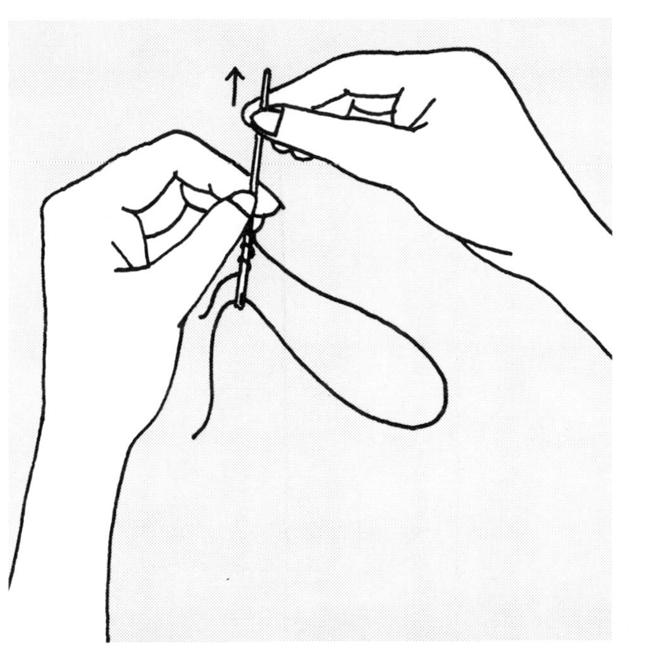

Trim away any excess thread behind the knot.

The layers of fabric forming shadow quilting are held in permanent position with the use of a running stitch. This stitch can vary in appearance, depending on how much of the thread is exposed, or floats, across the top surface. The running stitch is the simplest of all stitches, consisting only of an in-and-out movement. Experiment a bit on fabric scraps by bringing your needle up through the layers of fabric to the point where you wish to stitch and trying a practice row to see how evenly you can space the stitches. Next, try stitching several rows of running stitches, changing the stitches' length for each row.

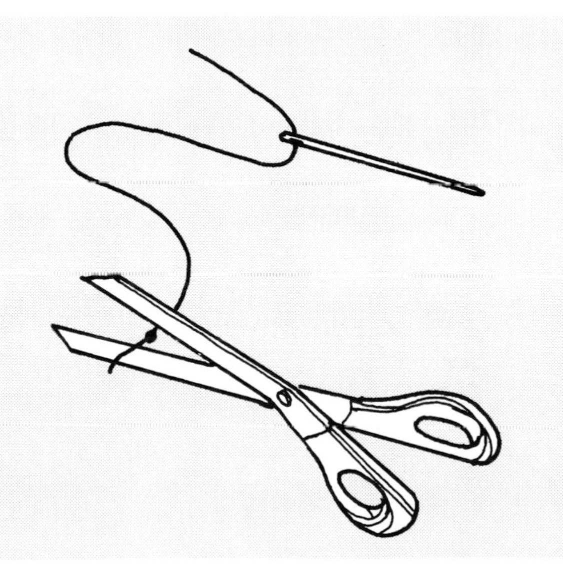

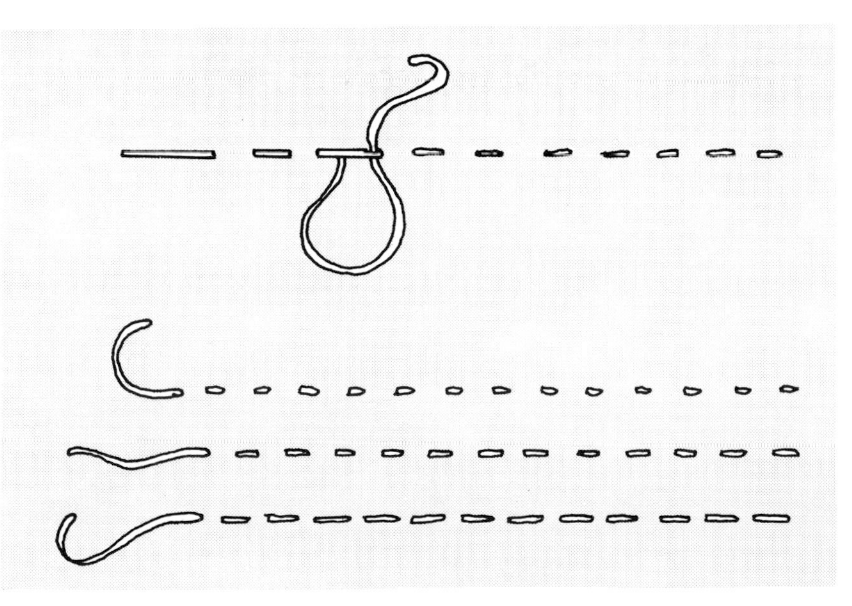

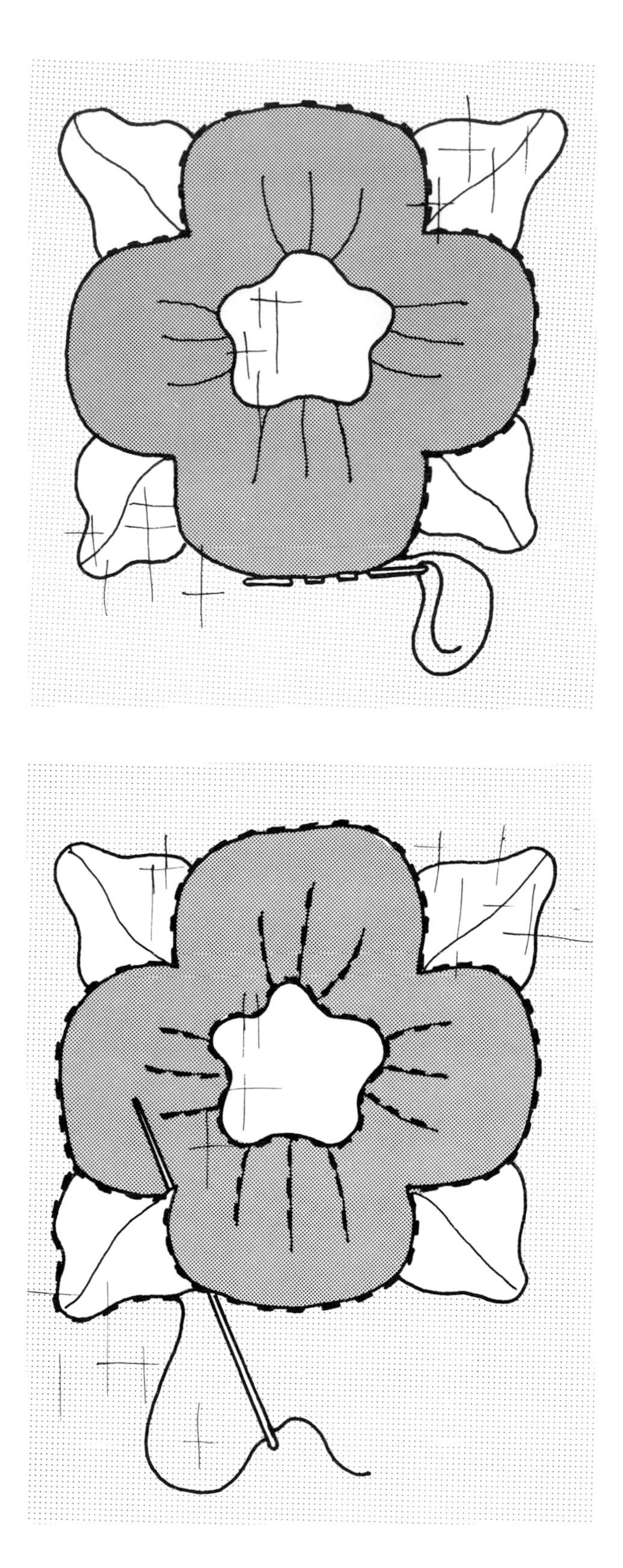

Begin stitching your project by bringing the needle up from under the design foundation fabric. Give the thread a light tug to pop its knot between the foundation and the design inserts. Sew with small, consistently spaced running stitches, working in and around the design inserts. The stitches should be placed on or just catching the edge of the design insert. When you are finished stitching with one color of thread, "fasten off" the thread on the back side by taking several small stitches in place on the back side of your foundation fabric, preferably under a deep-colored design insert so the ending place won't show from the top surface. Trim off the excess thread or tail. A new color of thread might be desired for sewing the leaf.

After the outside edge of the leaf has been stitched, proceed to stitch down the leaf center. The working thread is moved to the new starting point by bringing the needle up from the back side, as shown. This should be done only when the distance of the floating thread on the back side is no longer than ½ inch (1.3 cm).

This is what the back side will look like. Notice that the stitch floating across the surface is ½ inch (1.3 cm) or less in length. The floating

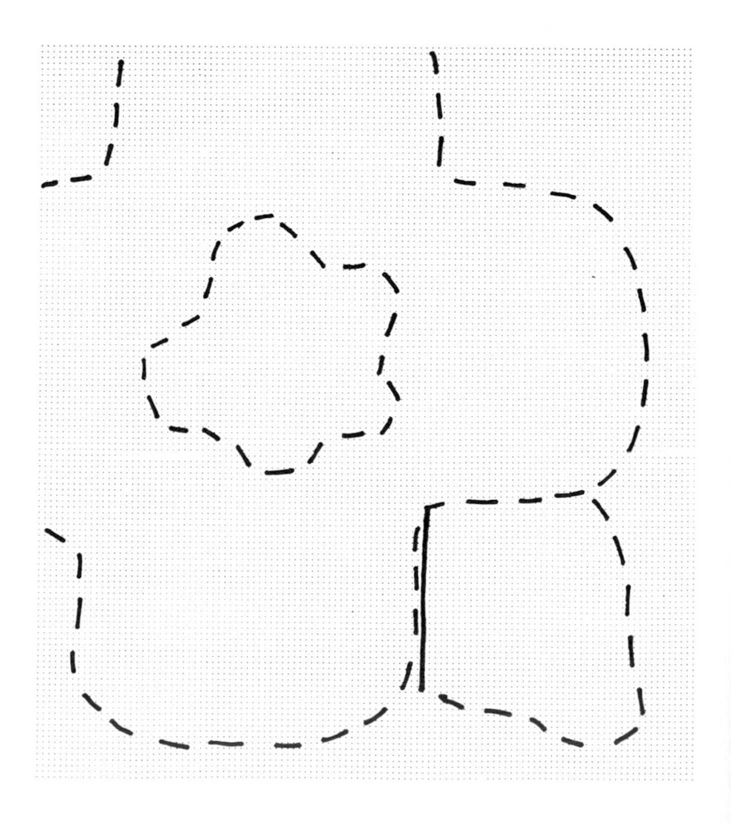

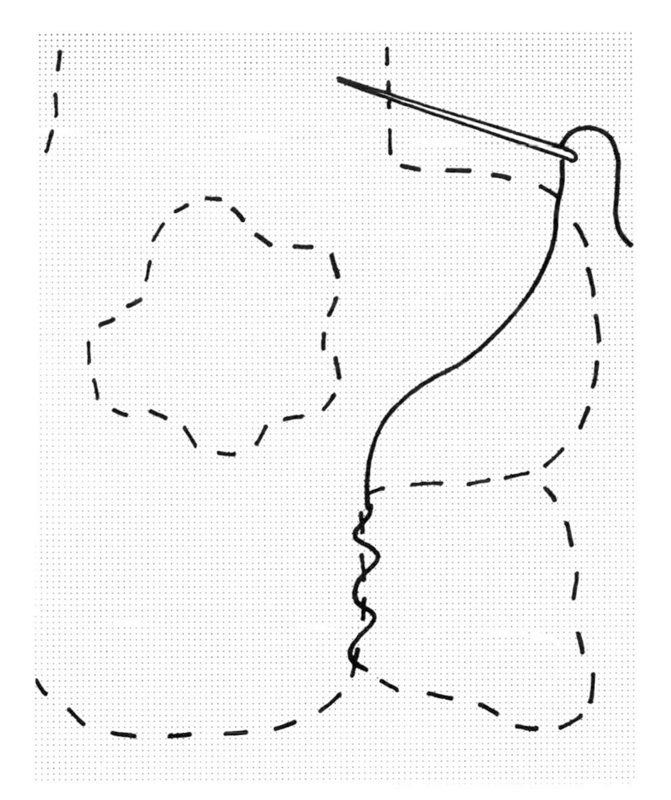

stitch should not "shadow" or show through to the front side.

Another technique, that of lacing your thread along the back side, is used when floats are longer than ½ inch (1.3 cm). This technique is also used when any floating stitch would shadow through to the front side or when a neat-appearing back side is especially desirable, as for unlined garments and decorative linens such as napkins.

Once the needle comes up at the new position on the front side, the stitching continues as previously described.

When your hand stitching is completed near the outside edge of a design insert, you should lace the working thread along the back side of your work. Fasten off the thread by taking several small stitches in place, preferably under a deep-colored design insert so the ending place doesn't show from the front surface. Be sure to trim off any excess tail of thread.

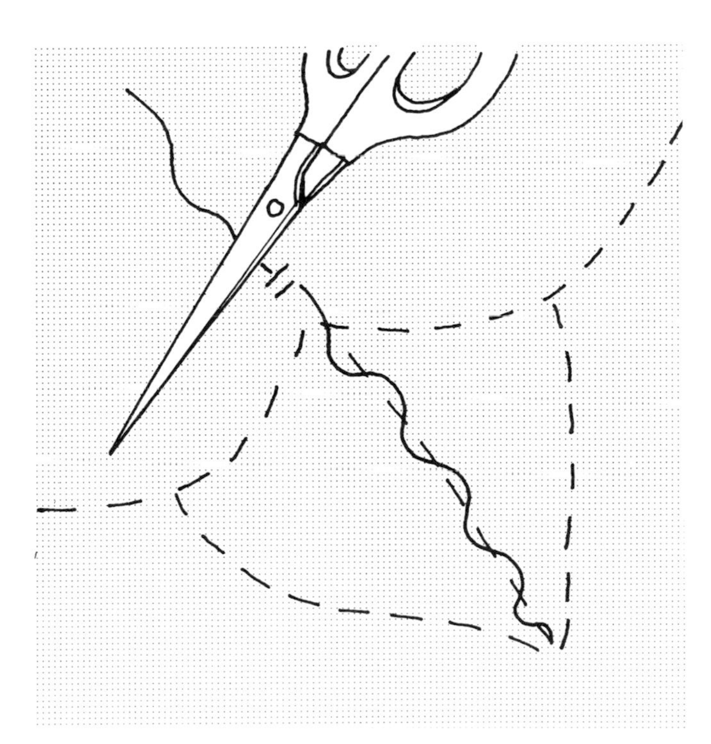

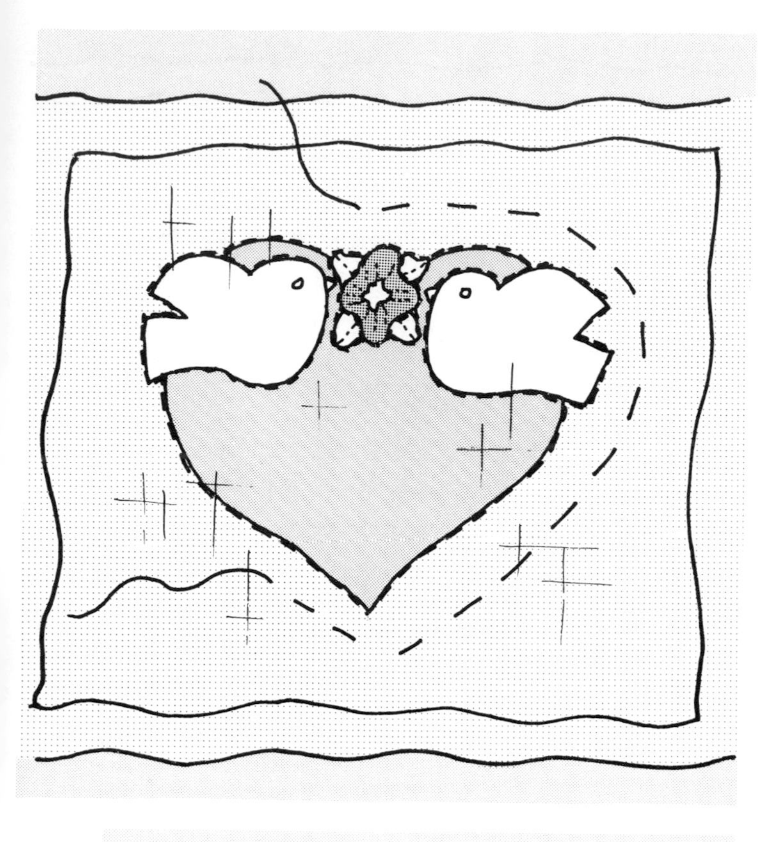

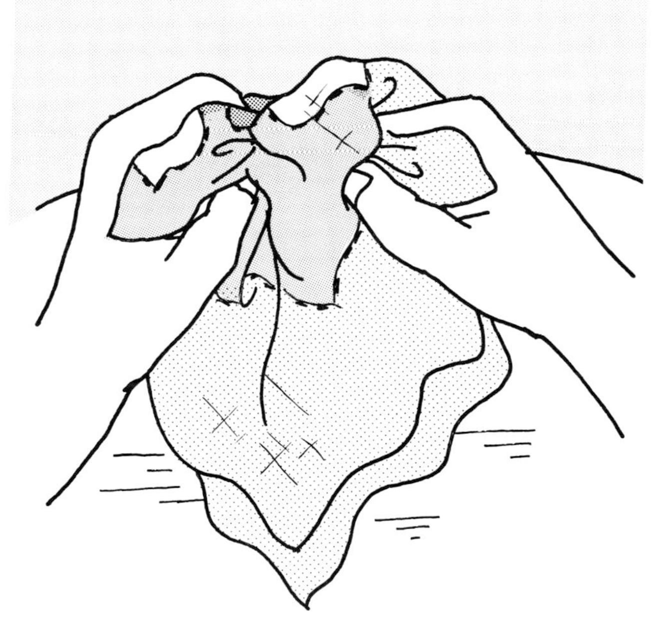

Stitch each of the design inserts until you are satisfied with the amount of stitching. You should stitch completely around each design insert, catching all of its cut edges. Remove basting.

Now place the stitched design in a basin of cool water, letting it soak for approximately five minutes. This will soften the glue and remove the marking-pen lines from the fabric. Gently rub your finished work between the palms of your hands to make sure that all the glue is loosened. Rinse well under cool, flowing water.

Towel dry for a few minutes; then press dry with a steam iron or let dry at room temperature. If powdery white spots appear after ironing, the glue was not completely removed, in which case, repeat the washing process.

Hand quilting will be needed if you want the design area to puff out slightly, becoming more dimensional. Hand quilting also adds a soft textural quality to the project's flat surface. Mark the proposed quilting lines on the finished top, using a water-soluble fabric-marking pen. Consider having the lines run

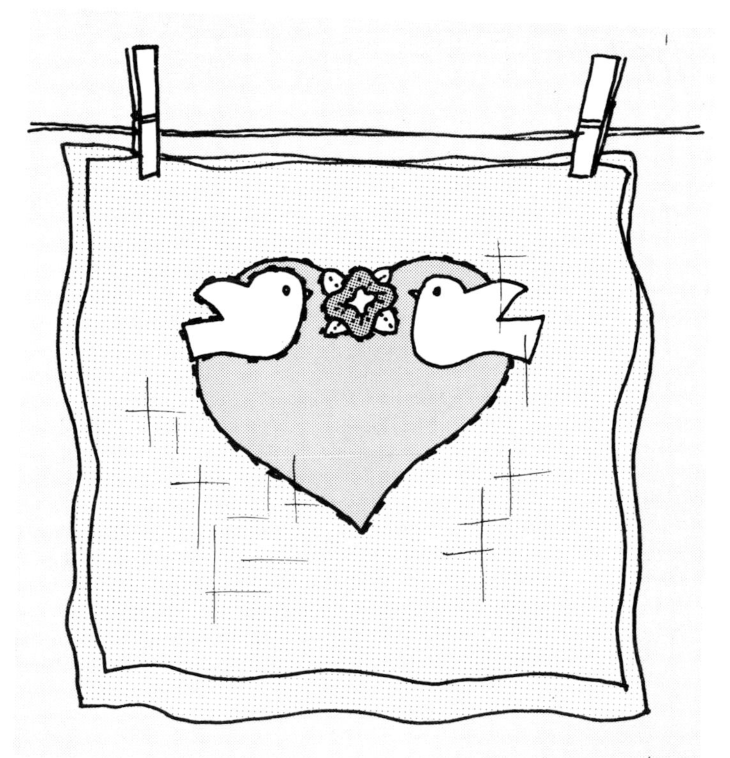

parallel with the design. For straight lines, use a transparent plastic ruler as a guide for marking. The designs in this book have light broken lines where quilting is suggested. Hand quilting is sometimes used to pull a surface area down, to flatten it, thus giving more contrast to the design; this is done by placing the rows close together.

Place sheet batting and a backing fabric of light- or medium-weight broadcloth behind your work, basting through all the layers. Baste 1 inch (2.5 cm) in from the outside edges and place additional basting within the design if needed to keep the layers from shifting. The basting stitches should be approximately 1 inch (2.5 cm) long, and the rows should cover the surface, allowing approximately 6 inches (15 cm) between each row.

Hand quilt using your favorite sewing needle, or try using a quilting needle. Using small, evenly spaced running stitches, quilt along the marked lines. You be the judge of whether you want to follow the quilting lines suggested with the book's designs or whether you want to design some quilting effects of your own.

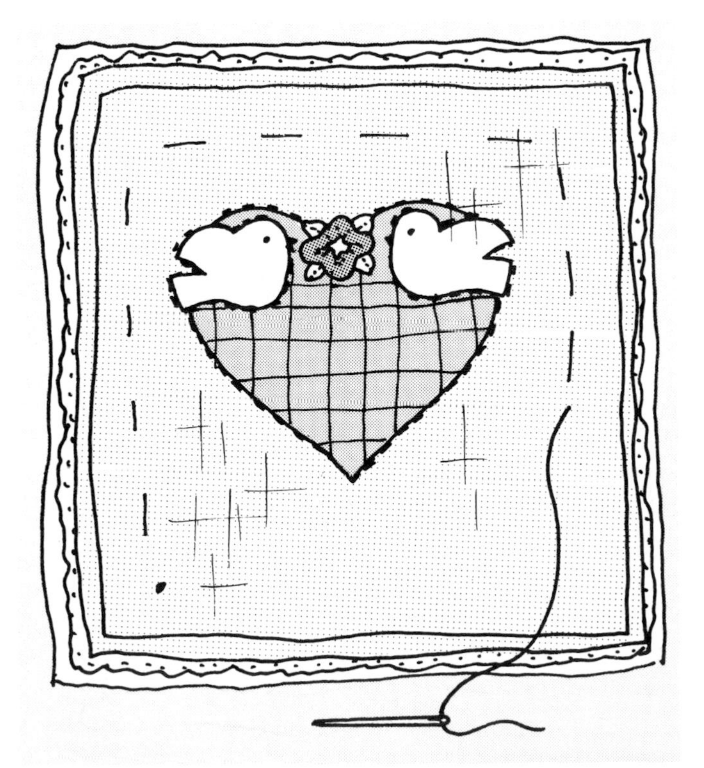

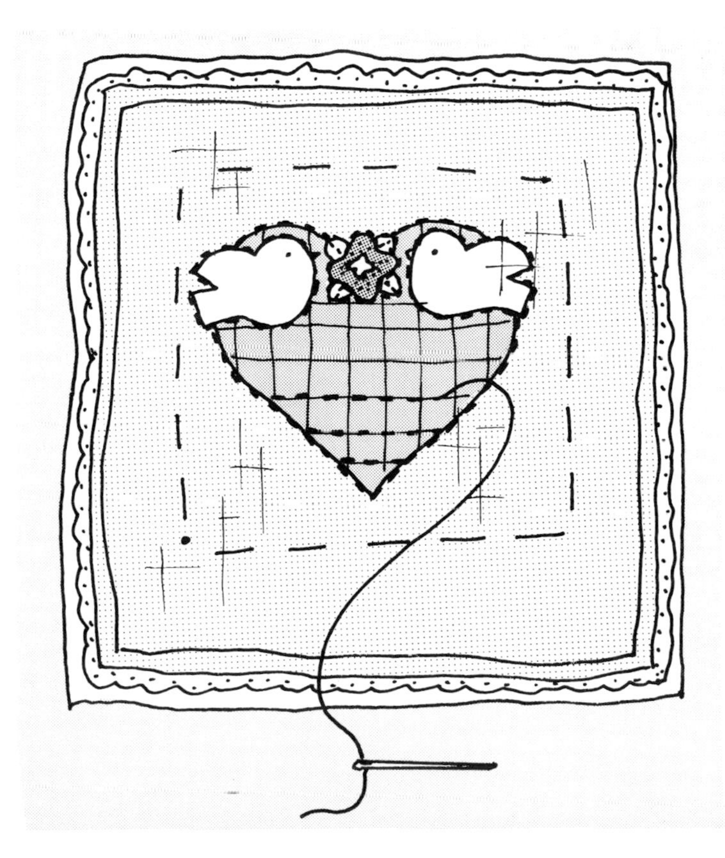

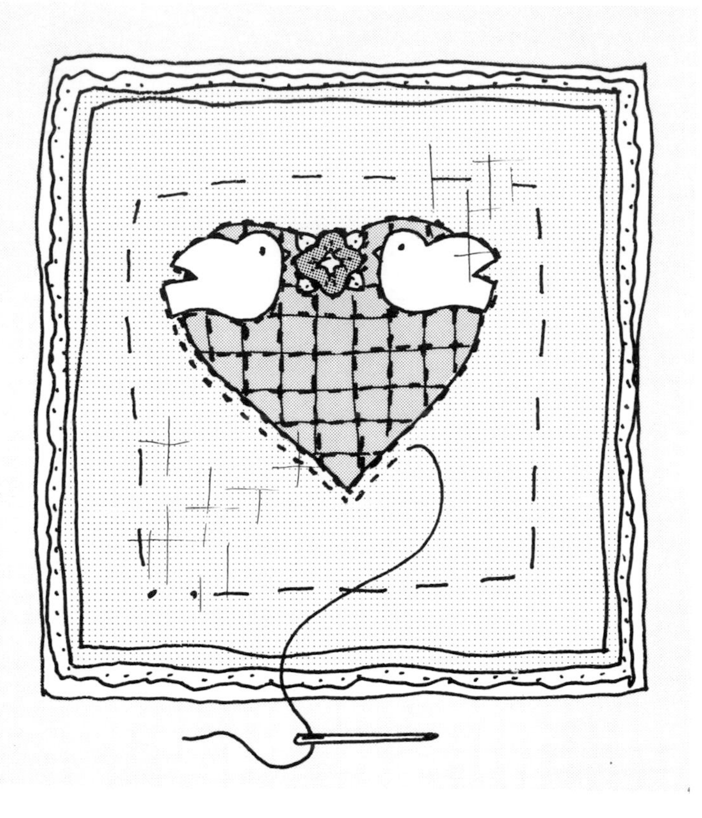

Quilting stitches can also be placed just off the edge of the design inserts.

When designing shadow quilting for a sweater or any other store-purchased garment, lay the garment flat and study its neckline, armholes, shoulder-sleeve seams, and total length. These are important factors in deciding where to position your design. Once you choose the position, select a suitable design from this book. Cut the foundation fabric from nylon, polyester organza, or organdy. Allow for 2 inches (5 cm) of extra foundation on all four sides. Using a water-soluble fabric pen, mark the area on the foundation fabric that the design is to cover. Follow the preceding steps, using only nylon, polyester organza, or organdy for the top sheer.

Position the washed and ironed finished panel over your sweater and secure it in place with a few pins. Re-mark the cutting line with a ruler and an air-disappearing fabric-marking pen. Remove the marked panel from the gar-

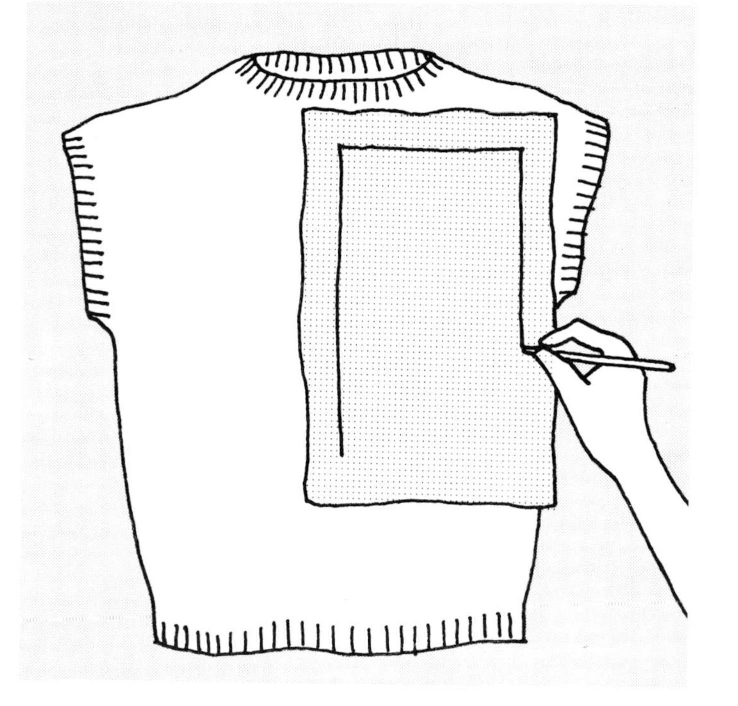

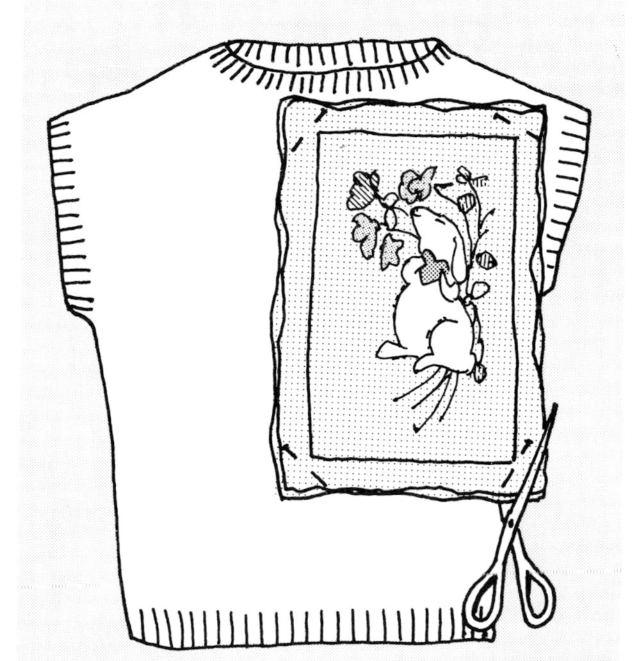

ment. Using sharp dressmaker's scissors, cut just a hair's width to the outside of the marked line. Hand-baste together the top sheer and the foundation, stitching ½ inch (1.3 cm) in from the trimmed edge.

The cut edges of the nylon or polyester panels will tend to fray. Eliminate this by forming a melted edge. Practice on a scrap first, and work in an area free from drafts. Light a tall candle; then hold the panel's edges firmly in your hands, which should be positioned about 5 inches (12.5 cm) apart. Pass the edges of the panel close to the bottom of the flame, near the top waxy surface of the candle. Watch closely, and you'll see the fabric's edges melt, forming a bead. For evenly melted edges, move the stretched panel quickly from side to side.

If you happen to have an electrically heated wood-burning tool or electrical stencil cutter, either one could also be used to melt and bead the synthetic fabric's edges.

Place the finished panel over the sweater, pinning, then basting it into place. To keep from stitching through to the back side of the sweater, insert a sheet of cardboard, tagboard, or flexible plastic or acetate between the front and back of the garment. Using the full six strands of cotton embroidery floss threaded on a chenille needle, stitch the panel to the sweater with a blanket stitch or a featherstitch, as shown on pages 34 and 38.

These step-by-step instructions are little more than recipes for success. Just as a beginning cook would follow a recipe closely, you will want to stay close to the original instructions with your first designs; however, as you begin to feel freer and more comfortable with shadow quilting, go ahead and branch out with some of your own ideas or ingredients. I would encourage you to try the techniques the way I show them here, taking your time to enjoy the experience. As you progress, you'll find that your methods and techniques change and combine as your needs change. What works well for one project won't necessarily work well for another. The final choice is up to you. Experience will eventually teach you what can and cannot be done.

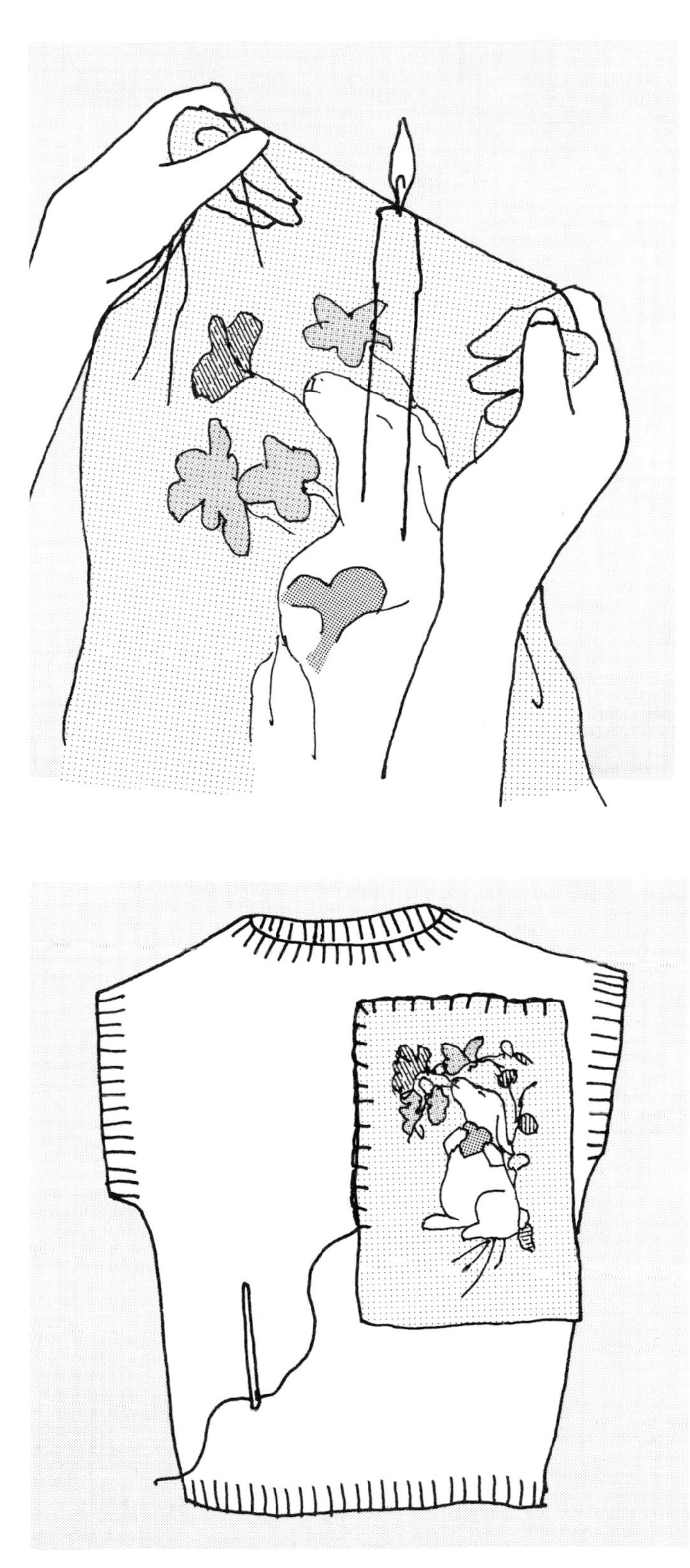

Stitches for Embellishment

Almost all embroidery looks better if it is worked in an embroidery hoop or a frame. Hoops are double rings or ovals of wood or metal. They come in many sizes. The best kind to use is a wooden hoop with a screw on the outer ring to adjust the tension. This is a desirable feature to have when your needlework varies in thickness as a result of layering or of textural embellishment. The hoop can easily be repositioned around the exact area you wish to stitch.

Frames also come in a wide range of sizes and can usually be adjusted to larger or smaller dimensions. Ordinarily the fabric's entire surface is suspended, or held, in the frame, even if only a small area is to be embroidered. At times this can make your stitching area somewhat awkward to reach. An advantage of a frame is that it will not leave pressure marks on the fabric as does a hoop. These pressure marks are only temporary though.

BLANKET OR BUTTONHOLE STITCH

The buttonhole stitch is worked in the same

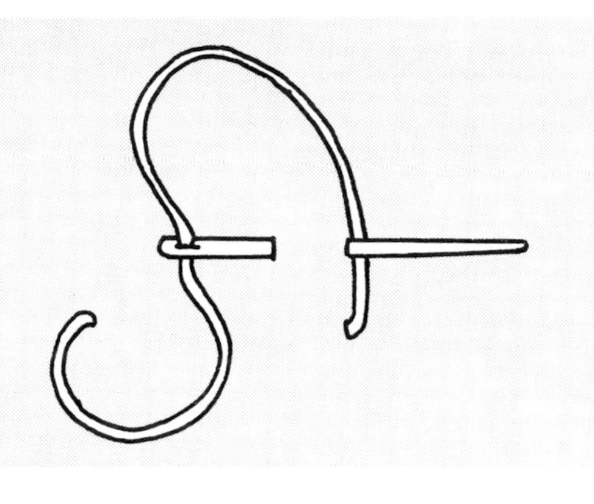

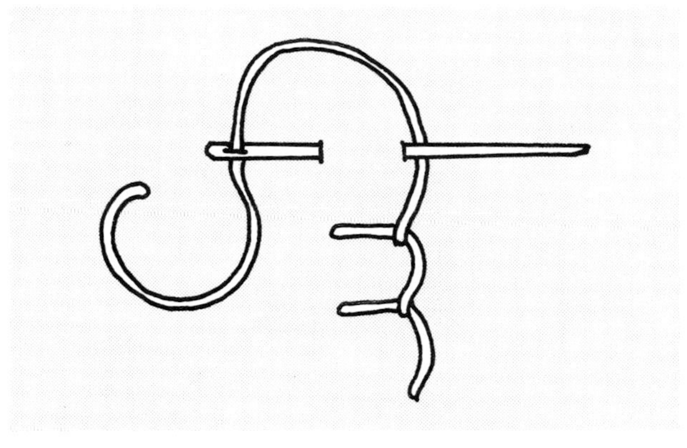

way as the blanket stitch except that the buttonhole stitches lie closer together. Bring the needle out on the lower line. Insert the needle in position on the upper line, taking a straight downward stitch. Be sure the thread remains under the needle's point. Pulling the needle, ease the thread into place. Repeat.

CHAIN STITCH

Bring the needle up through the fabric's surface to the top of the line to be stitched. Insert the needle close to the place where it emerged, bringing the point out a short distance below. Hold the working thread down and looped over to the left, using your left thumb if you are right-handed. Pull the needle through, easing the thread into place to form a chainlike appearance. Always keep the working thread under the needle point while stitching.

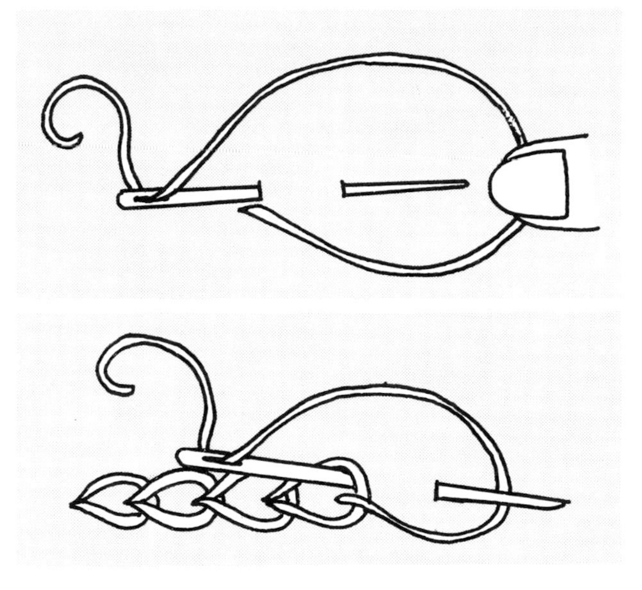

CROSS STITCH

When stitching horizontal rows, work one row of half-stitches, going from right to left; then stitch from left to right, putting in the second set of slanting stitches. All the top stitches should slant in the same direction. When doing vertical rows, complete each stitch before moving up or working down to the next row.

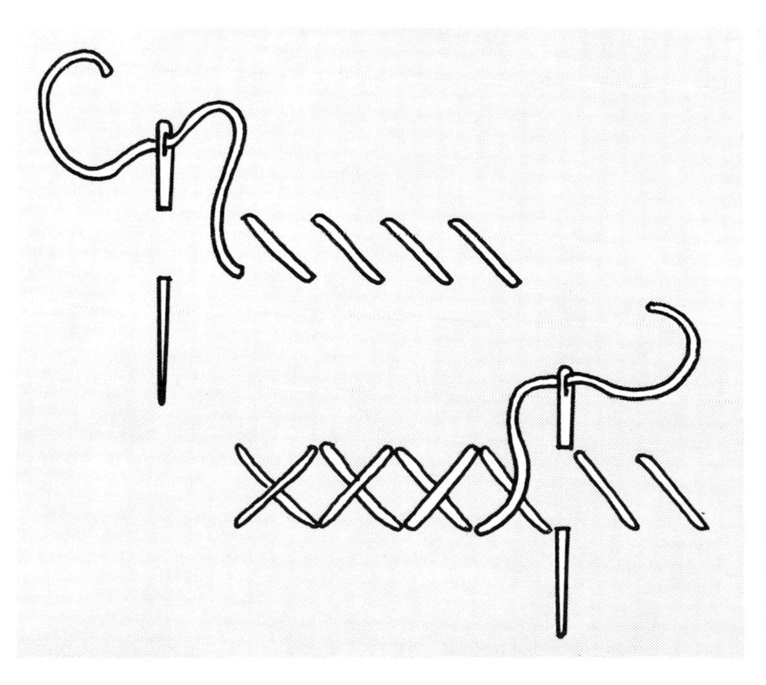

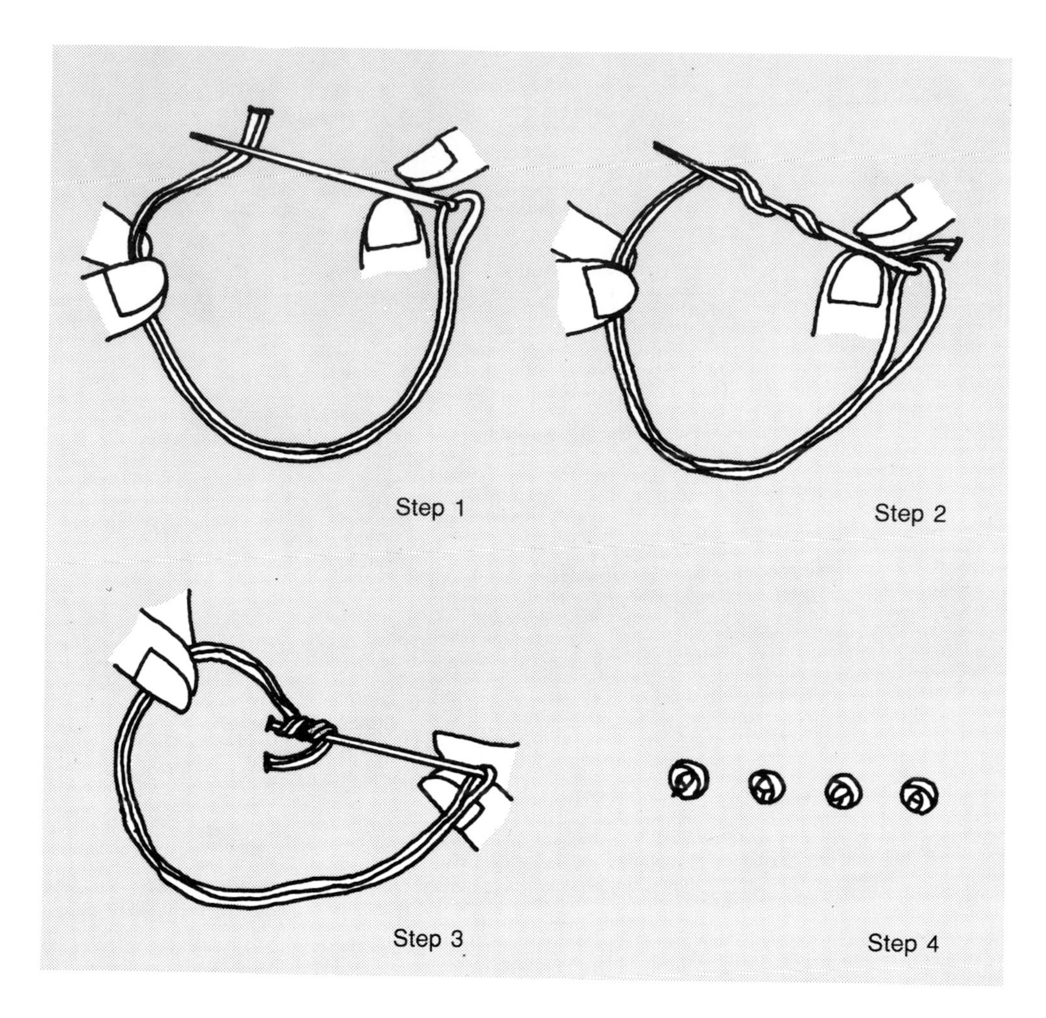

FRENCH KNOT

Step 1. Bring the needle up through the top surface where the knot is to be placed. *Step 2.* Wind the thread around the needle four or five times. *Step 3.* Insert the needle back into the fabric as close as possible to the spot where the thread emerged, but not through the same hole. *Step 4.* Gently pull the needle down and out to the underside of the fabric, and a french knot will remain on the surface of your work.

OUTLINE OR STEM STITCH

This stitch is worked from left to right if you are right-handed. Bring the needle up on the stitching line. Insert it to the right of the line and bring it out a little to the left of the line. Always keep the working thread falling below the needle.

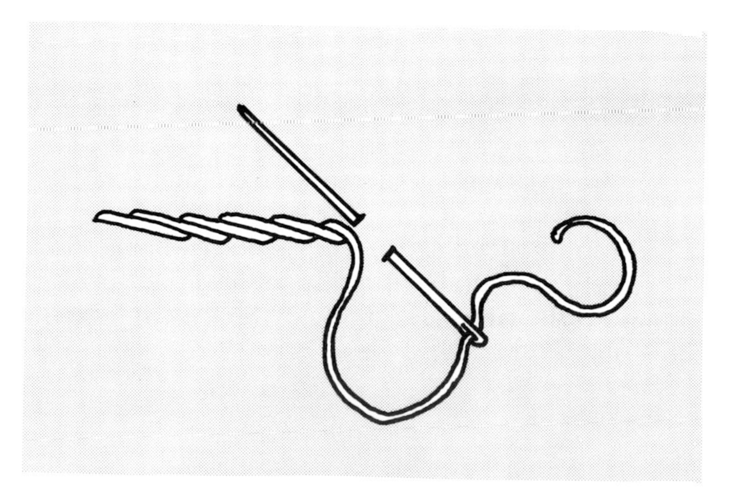

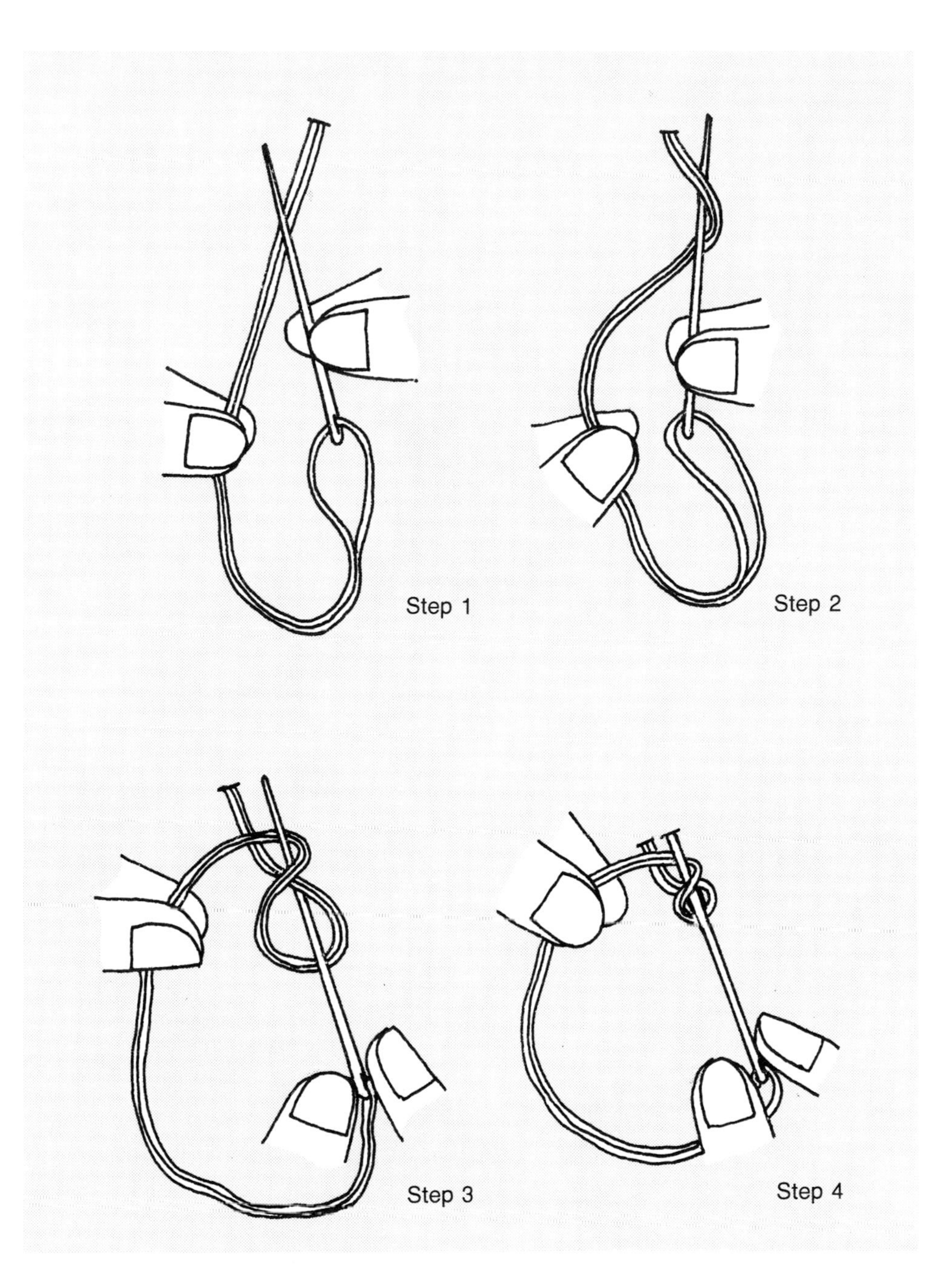

COLONIAL KNOT

Bring the needle up to the place where the knot is to be positioned on the fabric. *Step 1.* With your left hand, pull the thread toward you, grasping it approximately halfway between where it emerges from the fabric and from the needle. *Step 2.* Wrap the needle over to the left, under the thread, and back up toward the right. *Step 3.* Take the thread held in the left hand, wrapping it over the top of the needle, under, and back up to the left, forming a figure 8. *Step 4.* Reinsert the needle tip into the fabric, tightening the wraps, or figure 8, around the needle to take out the slack between the fabric and the needle. Pull the needle through, and your knot should be perfect.

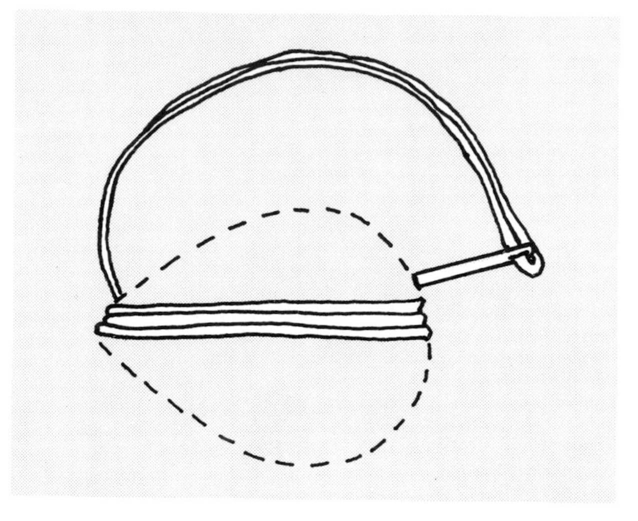

SATIN STITCH

Bring the needle up at one edge of the area to be covered. Insert the needle back into the fabric on the opposite edge and return to the starting point by carrying the thread underneath the fabric. The stitches should lie parallel and close together.

FEATHERSTITCH

Bring the needle up through the fabric at the top center of your stitching line. With your left thumb, secure the thread against the fabric. Inserting the needle to the left on the same level, take a small stitch down toward the center of the stitching line. Be sure the thread is kept under the needle point. Next, insert the needle to the right on the same level and take a stitch toward the center stitching line, again keeping the thread under the needle point. Work these two movements alternately down the length of your stitching line.

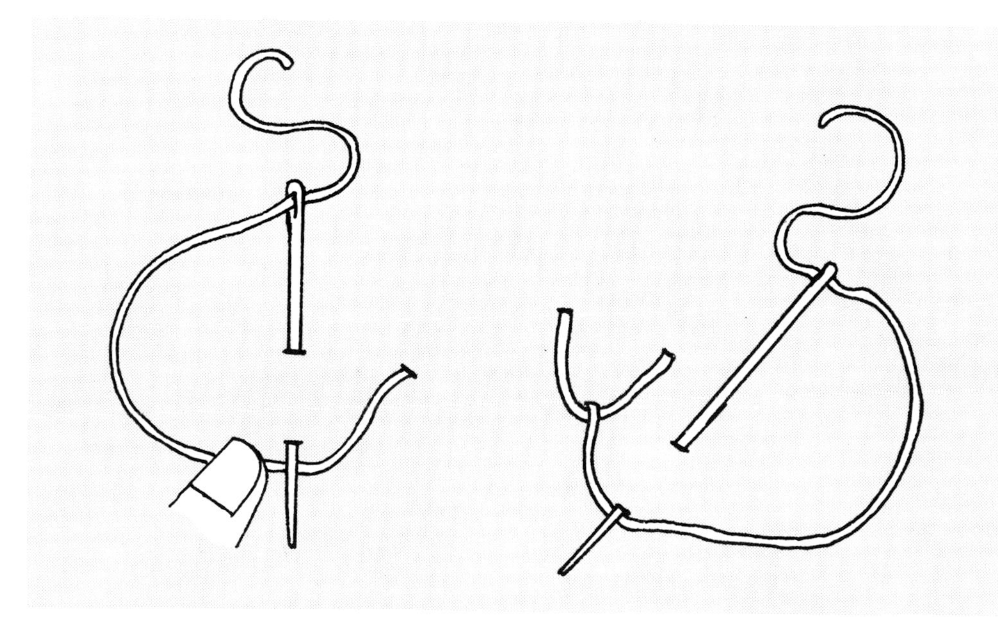

Ideas for Shadow Quilting

On pages 40–47 I've compiled a list of suggested projects that you might want to try, but the list is by no means limited only to these ideas. Be creative!

THE KITCHEN

Egg cozy
Tray liner
Towel trims
Apron

Framed picture
Tea cozy
Canisters
Casserole holder

Broom skirt cover
Plant sticks
Wall hanging
Hoop art

Putter around your kitchen in a pretty shadow-quilted apron of your own feminine design. Dip into canisters covered with shadow quilting and cook with casserole holders that have been decorated with quilted birds and hearts in muted shades. The kitchen is a natural place in which to use shadow quilting. Keep your eggs and tea toasty warm with specially designed egg and tea cozies. Trim your towels with shadow-quilted flowers. Framed pictures, hoop art, and wall hangings make the kitchen cheerful and bright. Even your broom becomes decorative when it is covered with a shadow-quilted skirt. And your favorite plants are prettier than ever when quilted sticks adorn them.

THE BEDROOM

Bed coverlet	Bed skirt	Neckroll pillow	Tissue-box covers
Dresser scarf	Decorative boxes	Boudoir pillows	Bed-tray scarf
Sachets	Stool cover	Book covers	Hatboxes
Pillow shams	Lampshade	Padded picture frames	

Shadow quilting can add charming touches to your bedroom. A lacy bed coverlet accompanied by a shadow-quilted dust ruffle looks inviting, especially when pillow shams, boudoir pillows, and neckrolls cushion the bed in unifying shades and designs. Dresser scarves can be sewn in pretty, bright patterns and accessorized with matching book covers, padded picture frames, bed-tray scarves and tissue-box covers. Lampshades and stool covers can carry the shadow-quilted design throughout the room, and quilted sachets and hatboxes make even the closet festive and fragrant.

THE OUTDOOR EATING AREA

Seat cushions	Plant sticks	Fabric-covered baskets
Table runner	Place mats	Napkin rings
Napkins	Chair backs	Table-top throw

A plain patio is transformed into a personalized dining area when shadow quilting is used on furnishings, decorations, and linens. With shadow quilting, you can create a beautiful covered basket that will make a stunning centerpiece, especially when accompanied by matching place mats, napkins, and napkin rings. Shadow-quilted seat cushions and chair backs make a unique statement when you use them with a same-design table runner or tablecloth. And live or silk plants look gaily festive when adorned with shadow-quilted plant sticks.

THE NURSERY

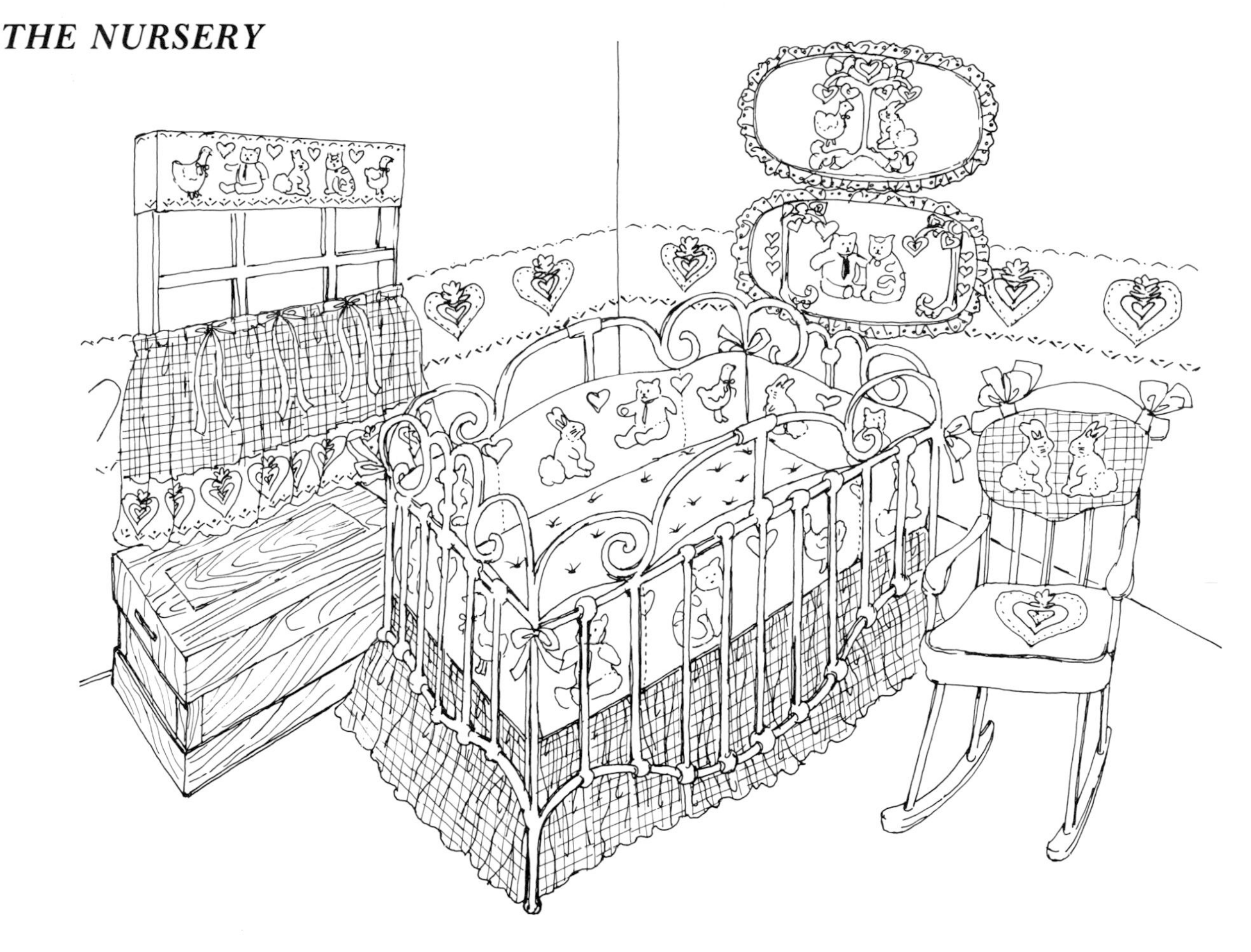

Framed verse
Stuffed animals
Bibs
Mobile
Dress yoke
Baby pillow
Christening gown
Door pillow
Crib quilt or coverlet
Baby book
Hoop art
Baby bonnet
Window hanging
  or sun shimmers
Tooth Fairy pillow or bag
Lampshade
Tissue-box cover

Cuddly bears and lovable geese, cute ducks and huggable bunnies make a shadow-quilted nursery warm and inviting to both Baby and Mother. Stuffed animals, baby books, baby pillows, and lampshades can be sewn in lovely pastel shades of pink, blue, yellow, and green. Cribs are made soft and downy with shadow-quilted coverlets. Framed verses, colorful mobiles, and hoop arts adorn the walls of Baby's room and can be created with hearts, lace, and adorable little kittens. Baby can wear a bib, christening gown, or bonnet in shadow-quilted designs, perhaps matching Mother's dress yoke or the Tooth Fairy's pillow. The cheerful room is even brighter when window hangings are added and the soft light shimmers in shadow-quilted shades.

FASHION, THE LARGE AND SMALL OF IT

Adults

Dress, wide borders
on sleeves, at hem,
or down the front
Jackets
Sweaters
Soft jewelry
Robe
Evening dress
Vest
Jogging outfits
Shawl
Jumper
Hostess apron
Handbag or tote bag
Sportswear
Blouse
Wide sash or belt

Ladies' fashions—from jumpsuits to jumpers and from jackets to evening dresses—have more flare and are more fun to wear when adorned with shadow-quilted designs. Dresses with lacy-looking borders on sleeves and hems can be worn with soft, shadow-quilted jewelry. Vests and robes go from plain to pretty with the bunnies and hearts you shadow quilt on them. Wide sashes and belts make a personal statement in your wardrobe, and they can be accessorized with handbags and tote bags in similar designs. Shawls, hostess aprons, and sportswear are empty palettes for the enthusiastic shadow quilter.

Children

Jumper	Book bag
Pinafore	Jacket
Jumpsuit	Vest
Pajamas	Dress yoke, hem border
Lunch sack	Sweater
Knapsack	

Shadow quilting can make a real fashion statement—even for the very young. Little girls will cherish shadow-quilted pinafores and jumpers sporting puffy clouds, cheerful little houses, and tall green trees. Little boys will proudly wear their shadow-quilted jumpsuits and vests, jackets and sweaters. Quilted pajamas make bedtime a treat. Lunch sacks and knapsacks—perhaps with bunny rabbits happily munching crunchy carrots—make mealtimes memorable. Dresses with pastel-colored yokes and lacy hem borders delight young ladies.

GIFT GIVING

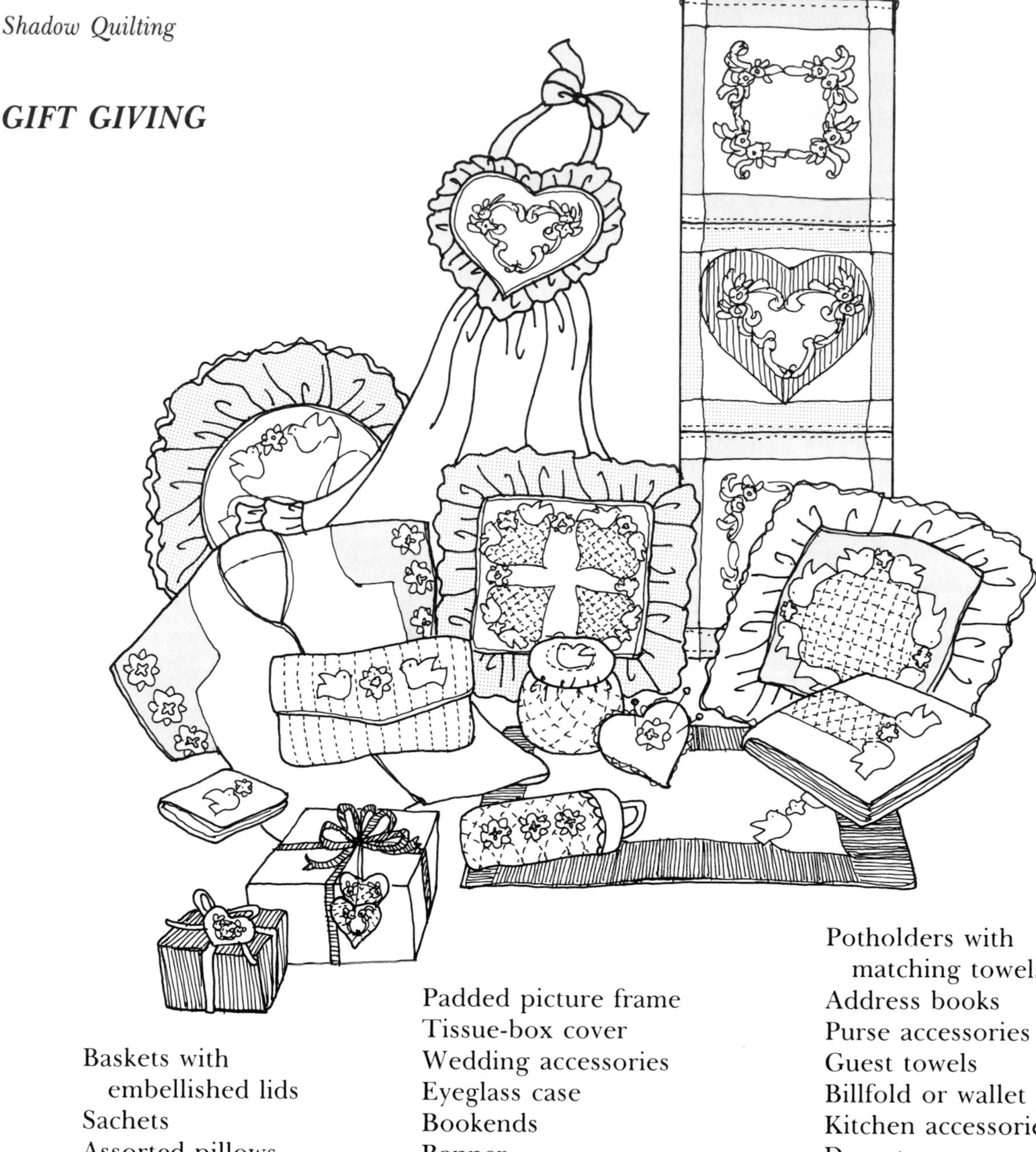

Baskets with
 embellished lids
Sachets
Assorted pillows
Guest book
Photo album
Padded picture frame
Tissue-box cover
Wedding accessories
Eyeglass case
Bookends
Banner
Place mats and napkins
Hostess apron
Potholders with
 matching towels
Address books
Purse accessories
Guest towels
Billfold or wallet
Kitchen accessories
Doorstop
Bed-sized coverlet
Wall hanging

When shadow quilting is used to create outstanding and unique designs, everything from doorstops to photo albums, from pillows and sachets to banners and bookends, will make beautiful gifts for all occasions. The range of themes can be as wide as your imagination and can be used on billfolds and wallets, coverlets, wall hangings, and address books. Potholders and matching towels make unique hostess gifts. Place mats and aprons with pastel-shaded patterns are perfect shower gifts. Brides will cherish wedding accessories and guest books accented with lacy shadow quilting as keepsakes. Purse accessories, with matching eyeglass cases, are both lovely and practical. Tissue-box coverings and baskets with embellished lids, ruffled and beribboned, are one-of-a-kind gifts with a personal touch. And your gifts will have even more impact if you wrap them with shadow-quilted hearts, birds, and flowers.

CHRISTMAS SHARING

- Tree ornaments
- Advent calendar
- Christmas tree skirt
- Teddy bear
- Package decorations
- Dolls
- Sewing accessories
- Family album
- Christmas tablecloth
- Christmas wreath
- Christmas socks
- Address book
- Pincushion
- Eyeglass case
- Mirror frame
- Christmas table runner

The creative shadow quilter knows that Christmas is the perfect time to use the art on tree ornaments, Advent calendars, tree skirts, tablecloths and runners. Quilted Christmas wreaths and stockings make delightful holiday treats. Packages can be pinned with shadow-quilted hearts, and quilted table runners add an air of festivity to the Yuletide fare. Teddy bears with bibs and dolls in dresses of tiny, flowered patterns will delight the young; sewing accessories, family albums, address books, pincushions, and mirror frames, all in pretty shades, make Christmas memorable for special someones of all ages.

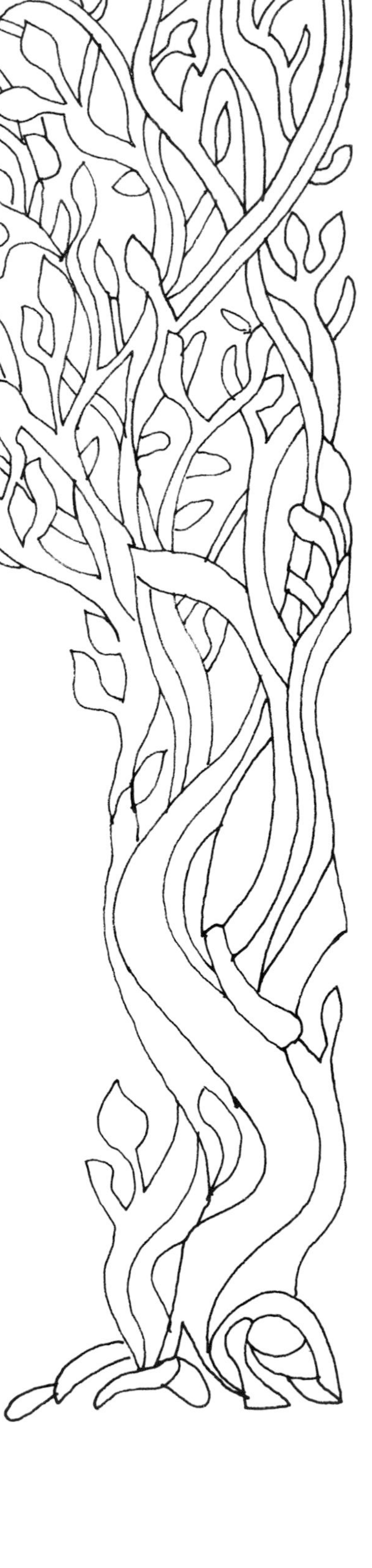

Designs

The designs used on the projects in the color plates follow. To find a design from a color plate, consult the Index.

On all the designs, this legend indicates the instructions for cutting, assembling, and stitching:

Solid line indicates edge of colored design insert. ————————

Dark broken line indicates small running stitches. - - - - - - - - - -

Light broken lines indicate suggested hand quilting. - - - - - - - - - -

Slanting lines indicate embroidery stitching. \\\\\\\\\\\\\\\\\\\\

TIME REQUIRED FOR PROJECTS

	Short (2-5 hours)	*Moderate (5-15 hours)*	*Long (15 or more hours)*
Heart Felt Birds	X		
Basket of Cats		X	
Cat Time		X	
Lily Delight			X
Frame A Loved One		X	
Soft Heart	X		
Contessa Border			X
Small Wonder	X		
Daisies—Uniquely Yours		X	
Elegant Daisies		X	
Daisies Forever		X	
Daisy Ring		X	
Duck's Delight		X	
Entwined Ribbon Place Mat	X		
Ribbon Bouquet	X		
Bunny Love		X	
Heart Bibs for Bears and Babes			
Heart Over Heart	X		
Feathered Hearts	X		
Double Hearts	X		
Hearts, Side by Side	X		
Gaggle of Geese	X		
Warm Hearts for a Special Doll			X
Exotic Ring			X
Exotica		X	
Exotic Pastel		X	
Small Bouquet	X		
Twisted Bow	X		
Bows and Bouquets		X	
Heart of Flowers		X	
Flowing Flowers		X	
Flowing Border			X
Soft Flow			X
Entwined Hearts		X	
Entwined Flowers and Hearts		X	

TIME REQUIRED FOR PROJECTS *(Continued)*

	Short (2-5 hours)	*Moderate (5-15 hours)*	*Long (15 or more hours)*
Square of Entwined Hearts			X
Entwined Hearts All Around			X
Flower Checkerboard with Entwined Hearts			X
Heart Cluster	X		
Rabbit with Flower	X		
Curly Lamb	X		
Medley of Hearts and Flowers	X		
Bearthoven	X		
Double Tulips	X		
Heart for Heart	X		
Checkerboard of Hearts	X		
Hen a-Nesting			X
Not for Animal Lovers Only Quilt			
Cat with a Bell	X		
Tree of Flowering Hearts		X	
Beribboned Goose	X		
Puffy-tailed Bunny	X		
Boysenbeary	X		
Corner Hearts		X	
Sunshine and Hearts			X
Beribboned Heart	X		
Pig O' My Heart		X	
Scribner Cat			X
Squared Flowers		X	
Elegant Scroll		X	
Small Monogram Alphabet	X		
Christmas Socks		X	
Christmas Tree Ornaments			
Christmas Hearts	X		
Christmas Roses	X		
Christmas Wreath			X
Christmas Hoops			
Noel		X	
Joy		X	
Christmas Table Top or Christmas Tree Skirt			X

Heart Felt Birds

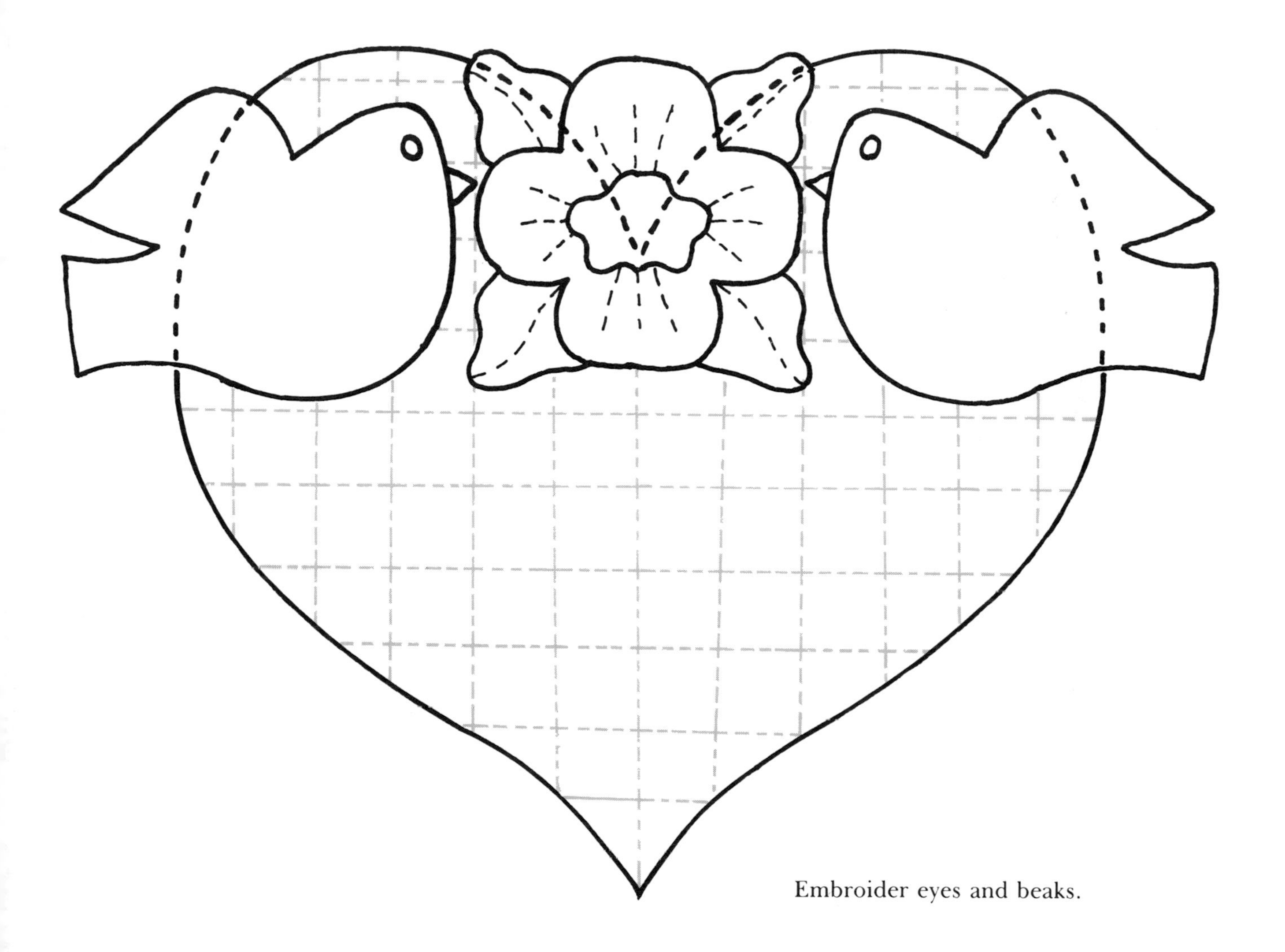

Embroider eyes and beaks.

Basket of Cats

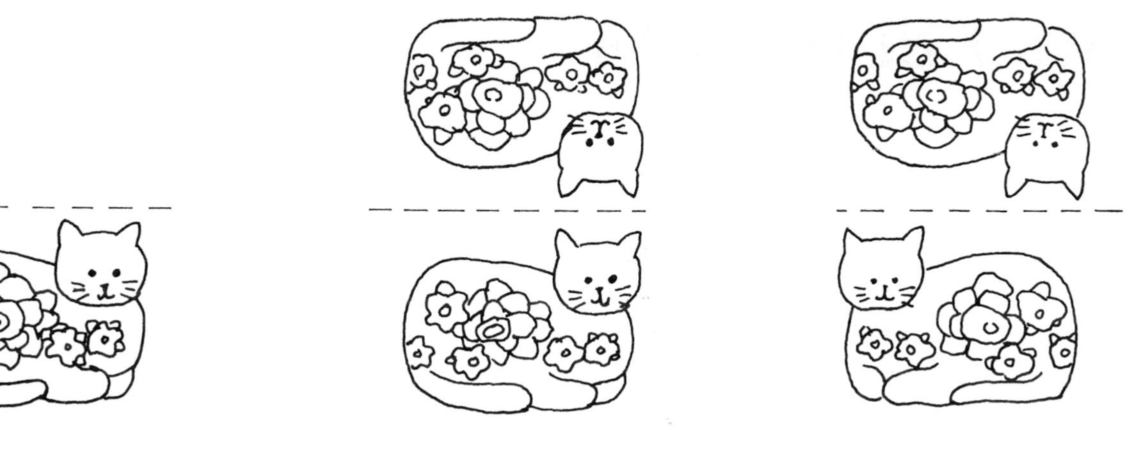

one half of design for basket lid

full design

or try this variation

Embroider the eyes, nose, mouth, and whiskers.

Cat Time

Lily Delight

Use this floral design with your favorite vest pattern.

Use part of this design with your favorite vest pattern, such as this one by Simplicity Patterns.

Combine parts of this design with your favorite dress pattern, such as this Simplicity pattern dress.

Heart Felt Birds

Basket of Cats,
Cat Time (sweater)

Lily Delight

Soft Heart,
Frame A Loved One

Contessa Border (tablecloth), Small Wonder (napkin)

Elegant Daisies (left), Daisies—Uniquely Yours (center), Daisies Forever (right)

Entwined Ribbon Place mat, Ribbon Bouquet (napkin), Duck's Delight

Note: An apron can be embellished with a border of Entwined Ribbon and Ribbon Bouquet added to one side

Heart Bibs for Bears and Babes: Heart Over Heart, Feathered Hearts, Double Hearts, Hearts, Side by Side (left to right)

Scribner Cat

Warm Hearts for
a Special Doll

Exotic Ring (left),
Exotica (center),
Exotic Pastel (right)

Small Bouquet (pincushion), Twisted Bow (scissor case), Bows and Bouquets (sewing doll and thimble holder)

Small Wonder (bottom), Heart of Flowers (left), Flowing Flowers (right)

Flowing Border (skirt and parasol), Soft Flow (dress top)

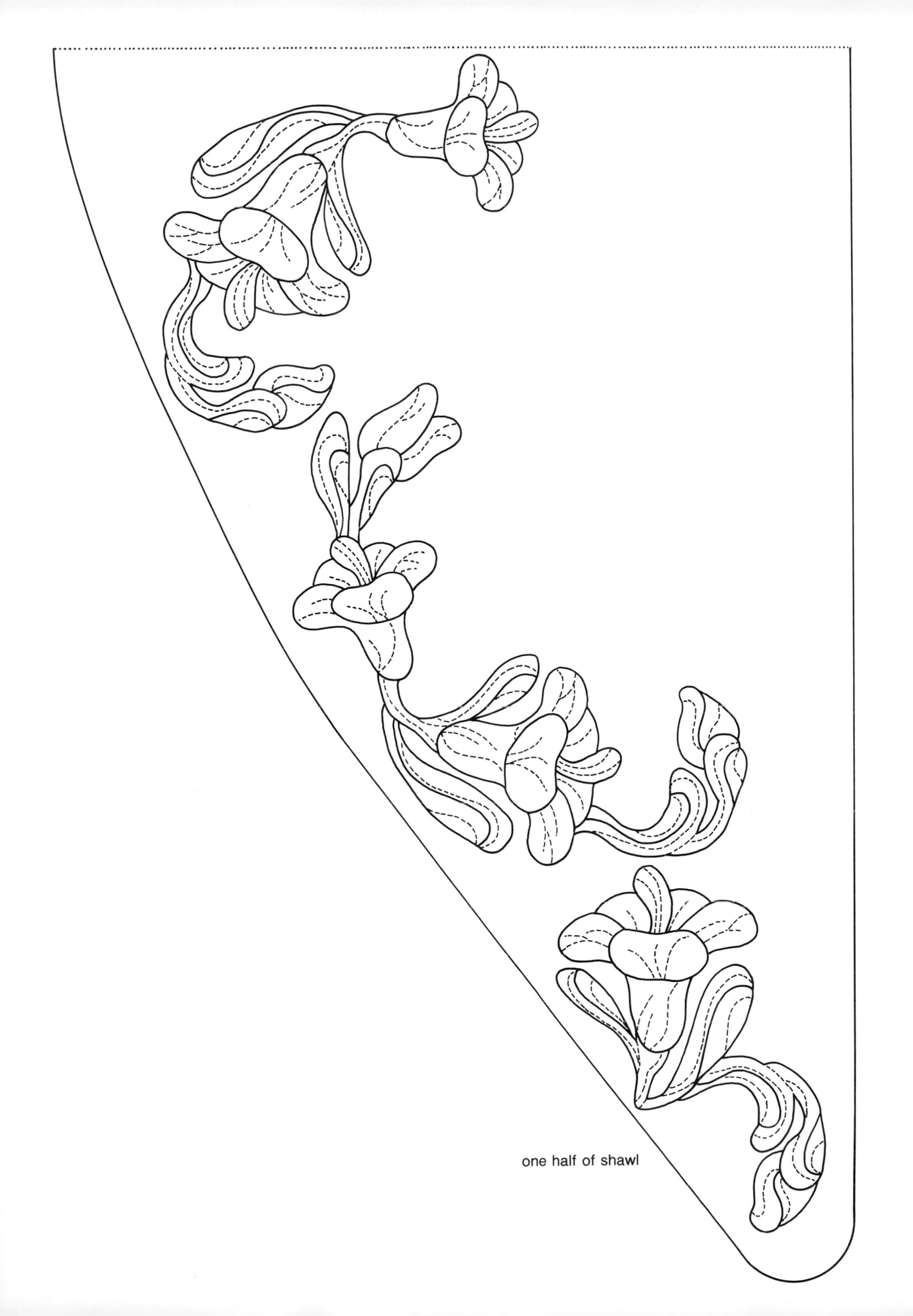
one half of shawl

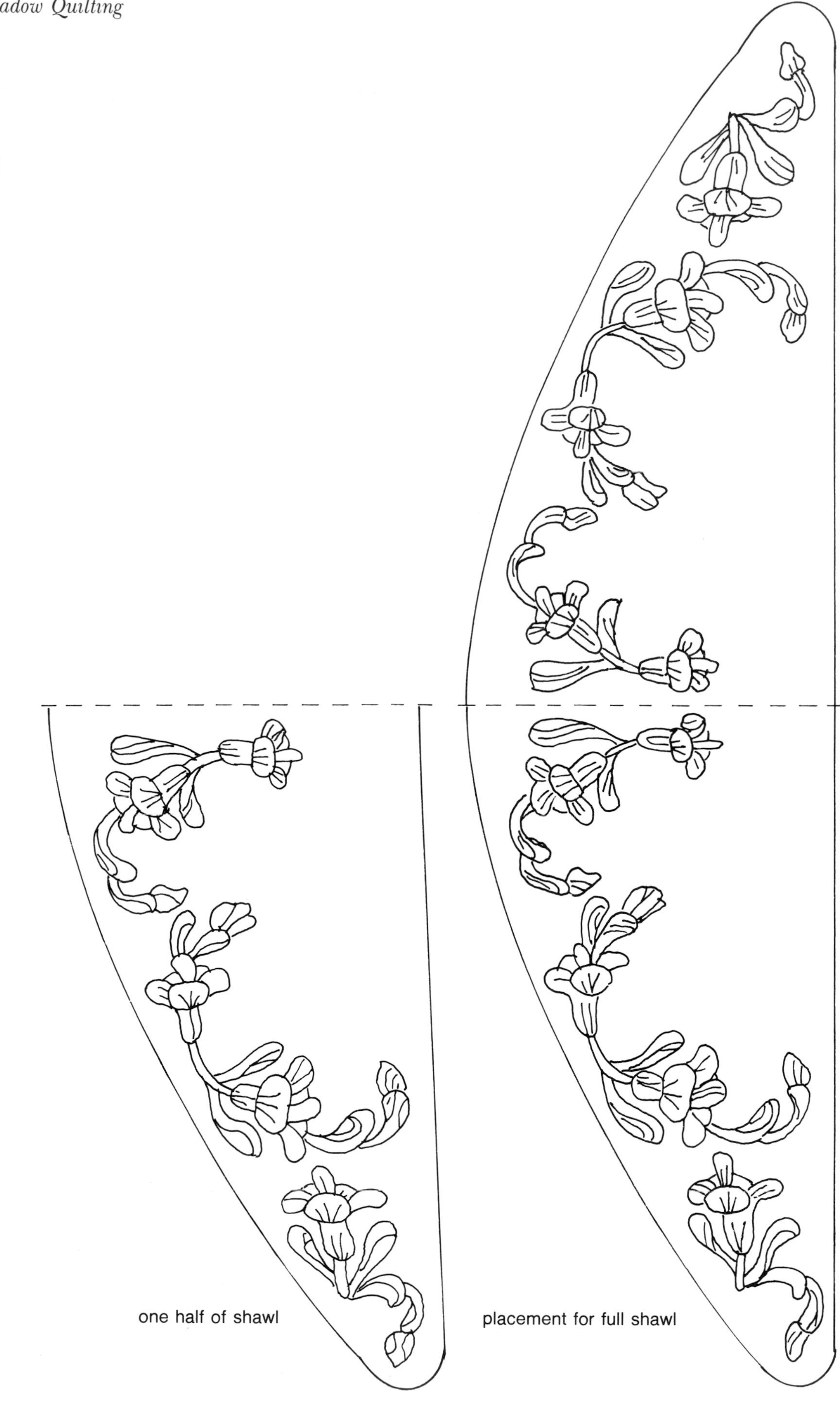
one half of shawl
placement for full shawl

Frame A Loved One

one half of design

full design

To make picture frame, cut two sheets of heavy illustration board, following the shape given. To assemble, follow directions for any frame pattern, such as this one by Simplicity Patterns.

one half of design

Soft Heart

quilt along broken lines

Contessa Border

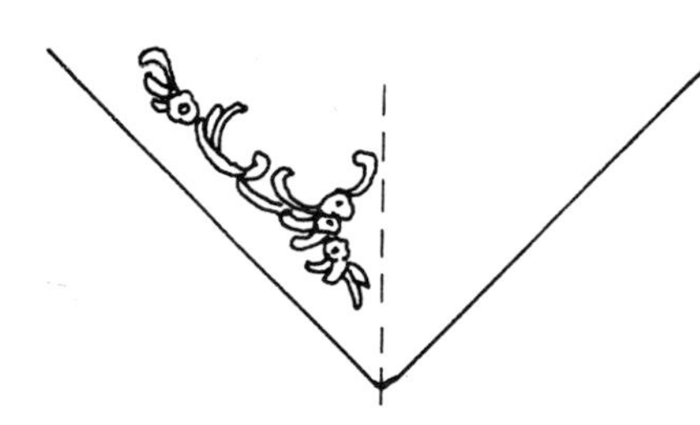

one half of a corner

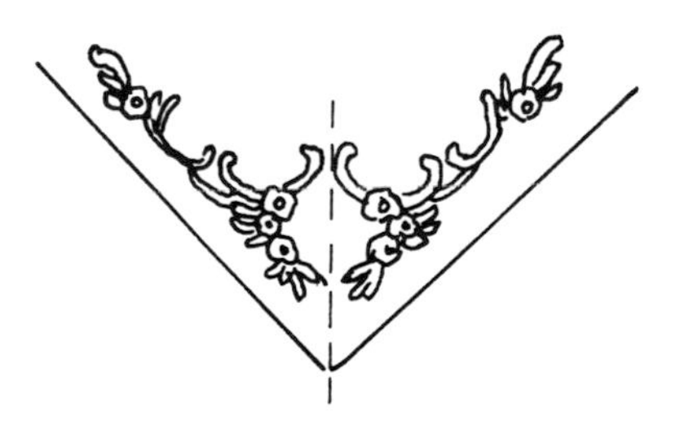

full corner

four corners

Small Wonder

trinket box

Daisies—Uniquely Yours

Apply this design to your favorite vest pattern, such as this one by Simplicity Patterns.

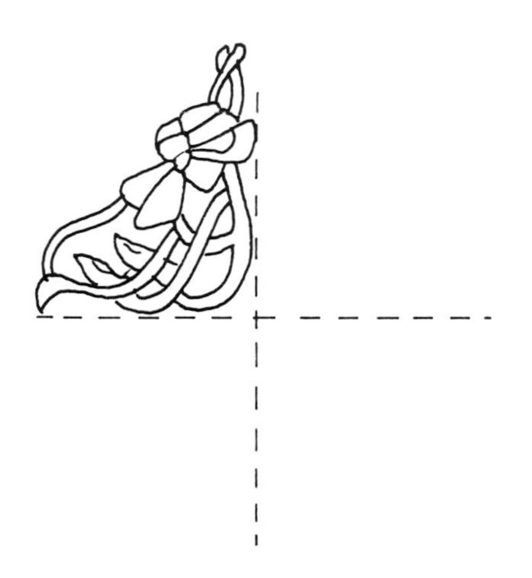

one quarter of design

one half of design

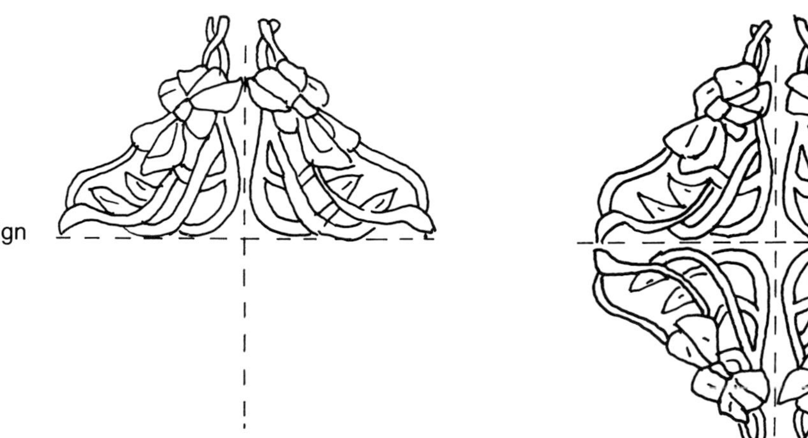

Change this border design into a block. Use for a quilt or pillow top.

full design

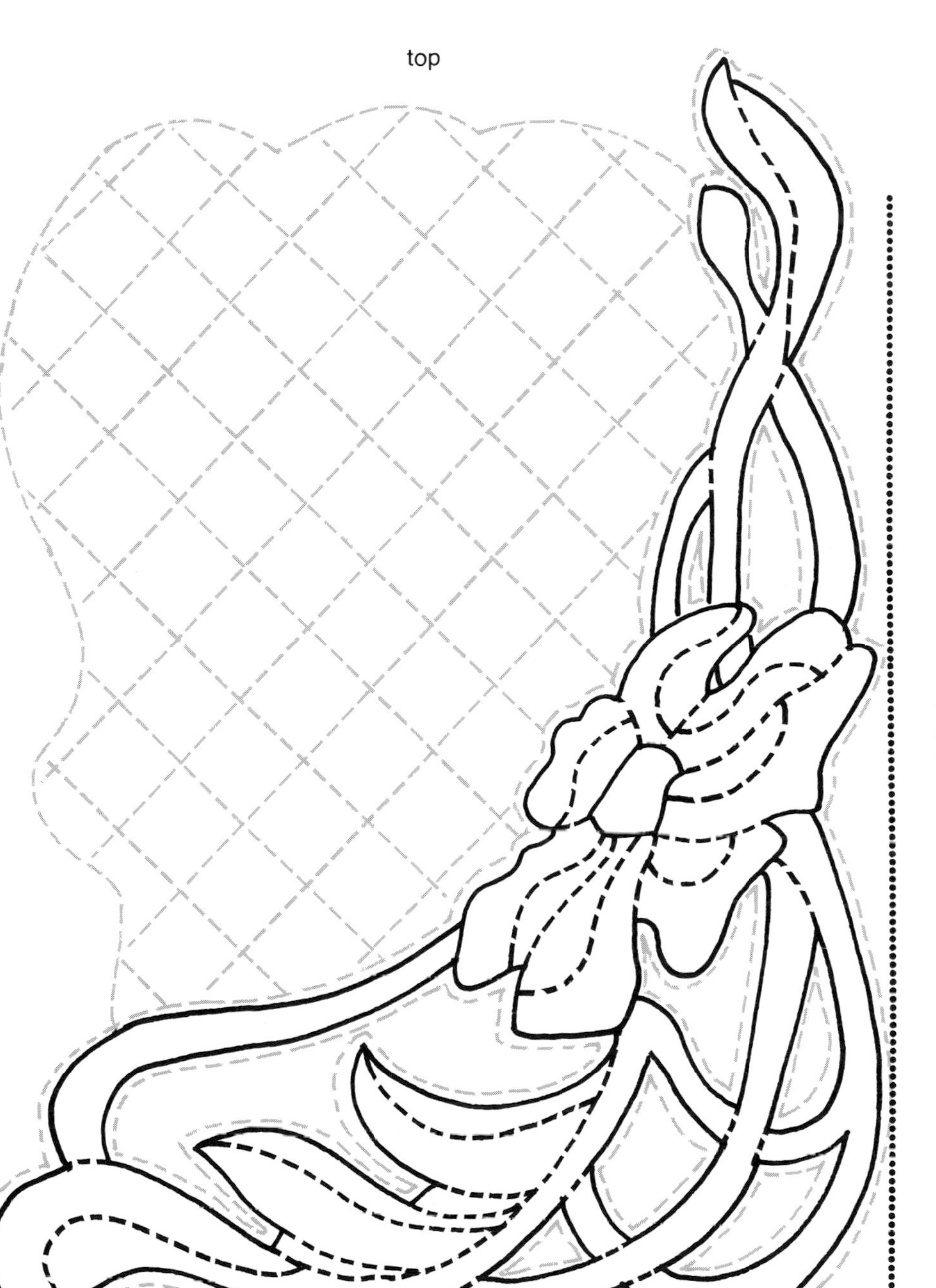
top
one quarter of design
one quarter of design

Elegant Daisies

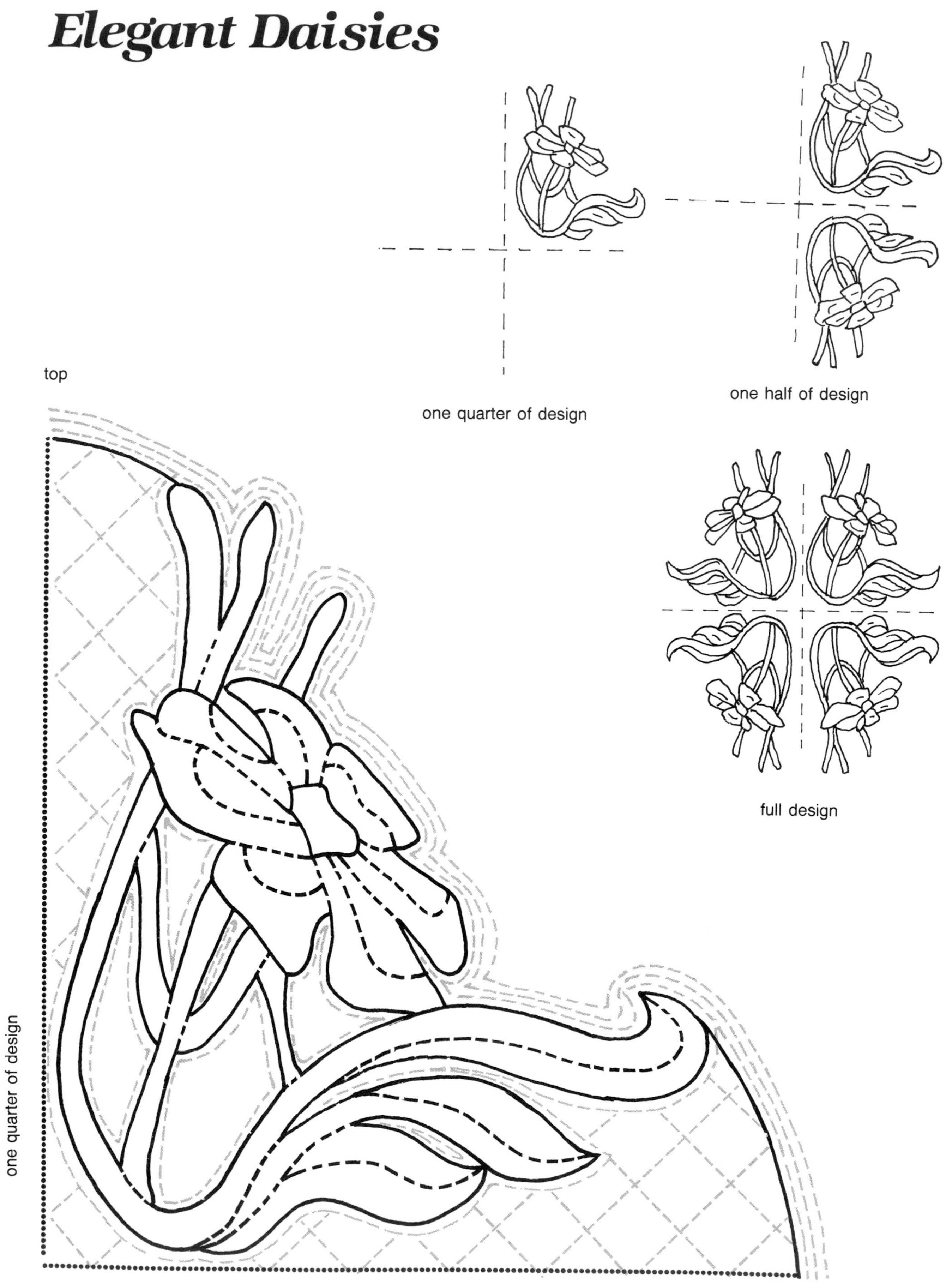

Daisies Forever

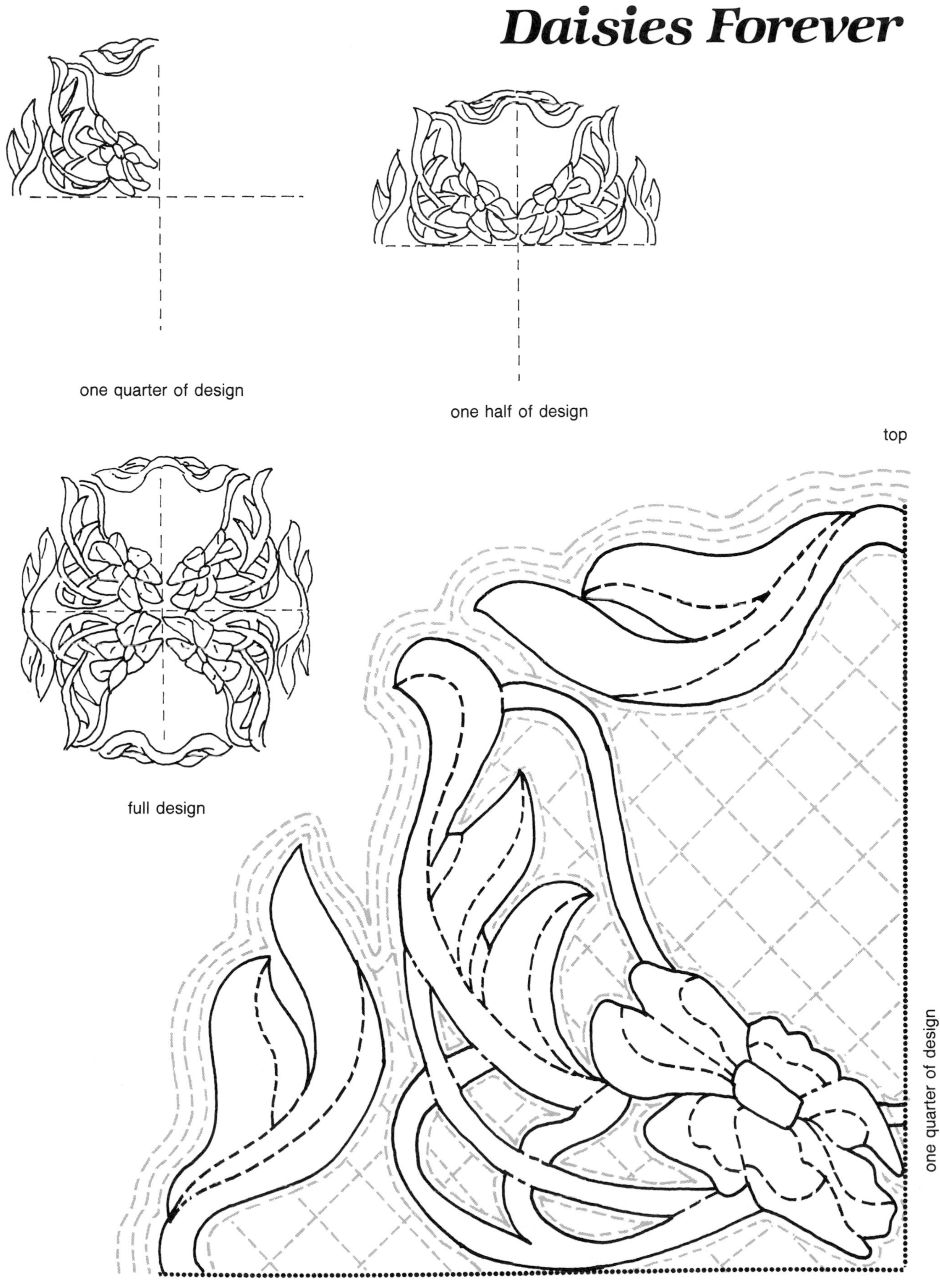

Daisy Ring

You can make this wall hanging or quilt from patterns for Daisies—Uniquely Yours, Elegant Daisies, and Daisies Forever. The patterns have been assembled into squares. Daisies—Uniquely Yours has been rearranged to form Daisy Ring.

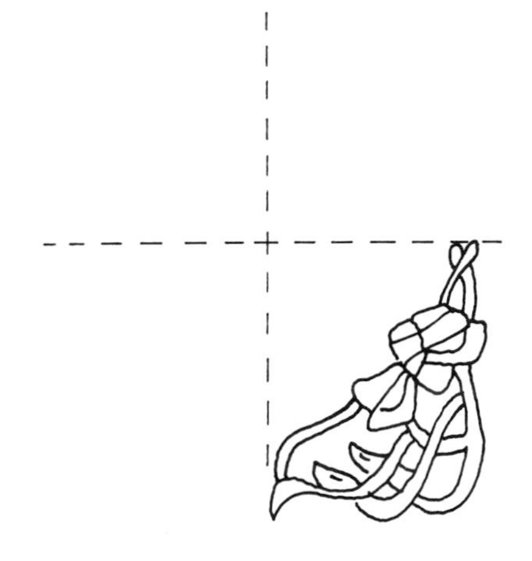

one quarter of design

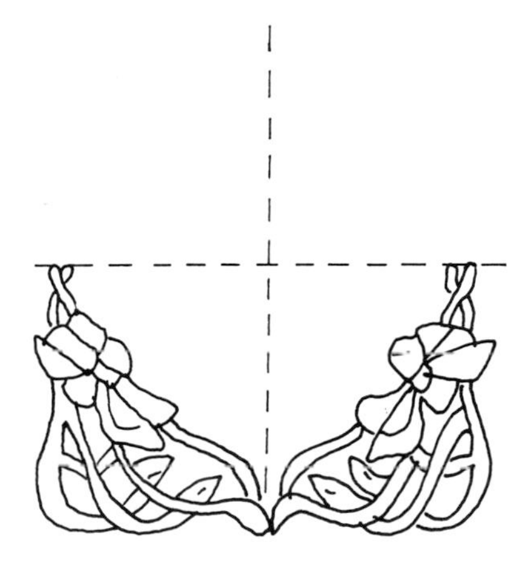

one half of design

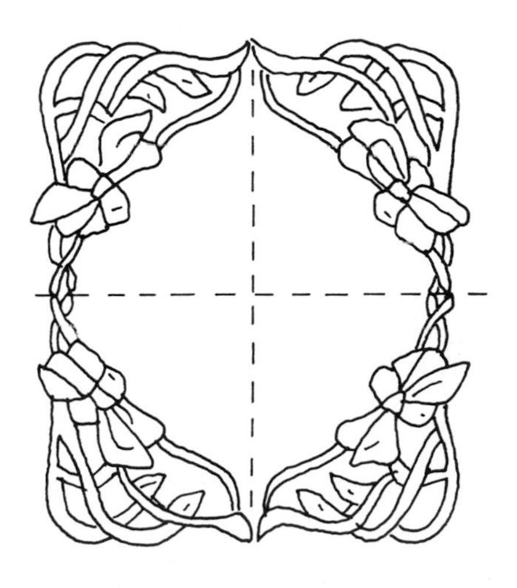

full design

Duck's Delight

Apply this floral cluster to your favorite commercial duck or goose pattern.

Entwined Ribbon Place Mat

one half of design

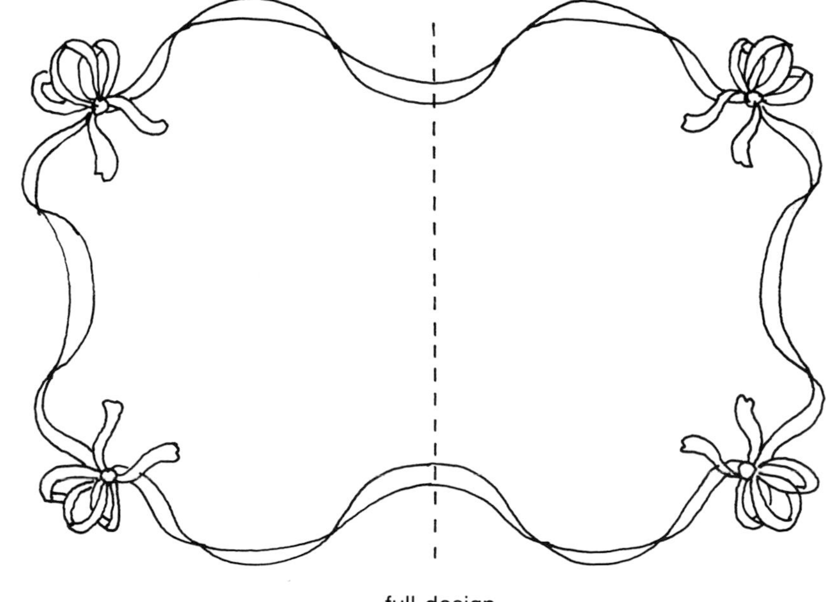

full design

one half of design

Ribbon Bouquet

Apply this bouquet to your favorite apron pattern, such as this one by Simplicity Patterns.

Bunny Love

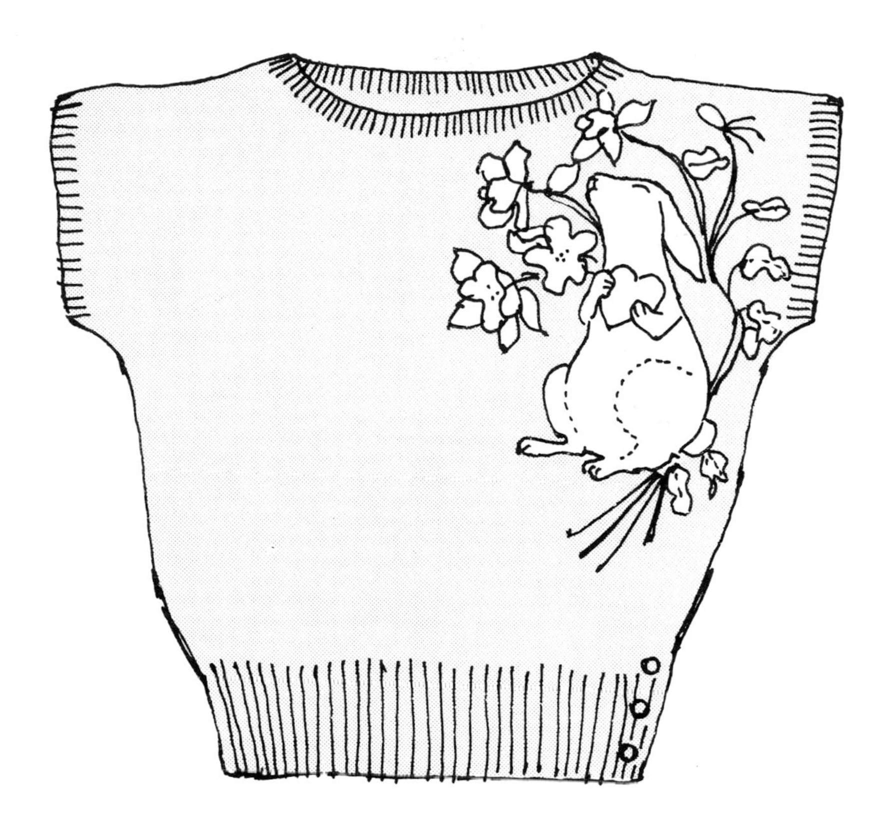

Heart Bibs for Bears and Babes

Heart Over Heart

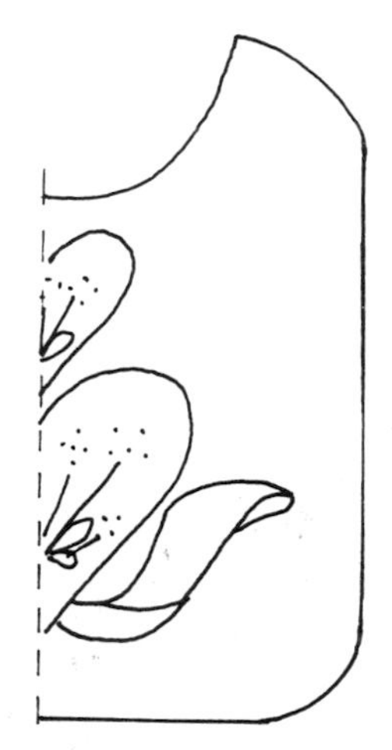

one half of design

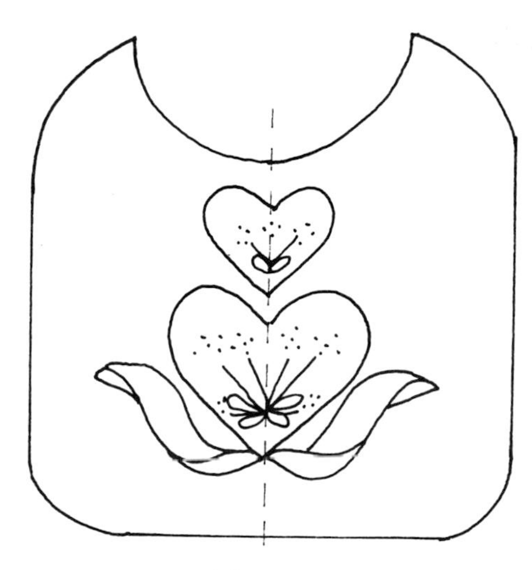

full design

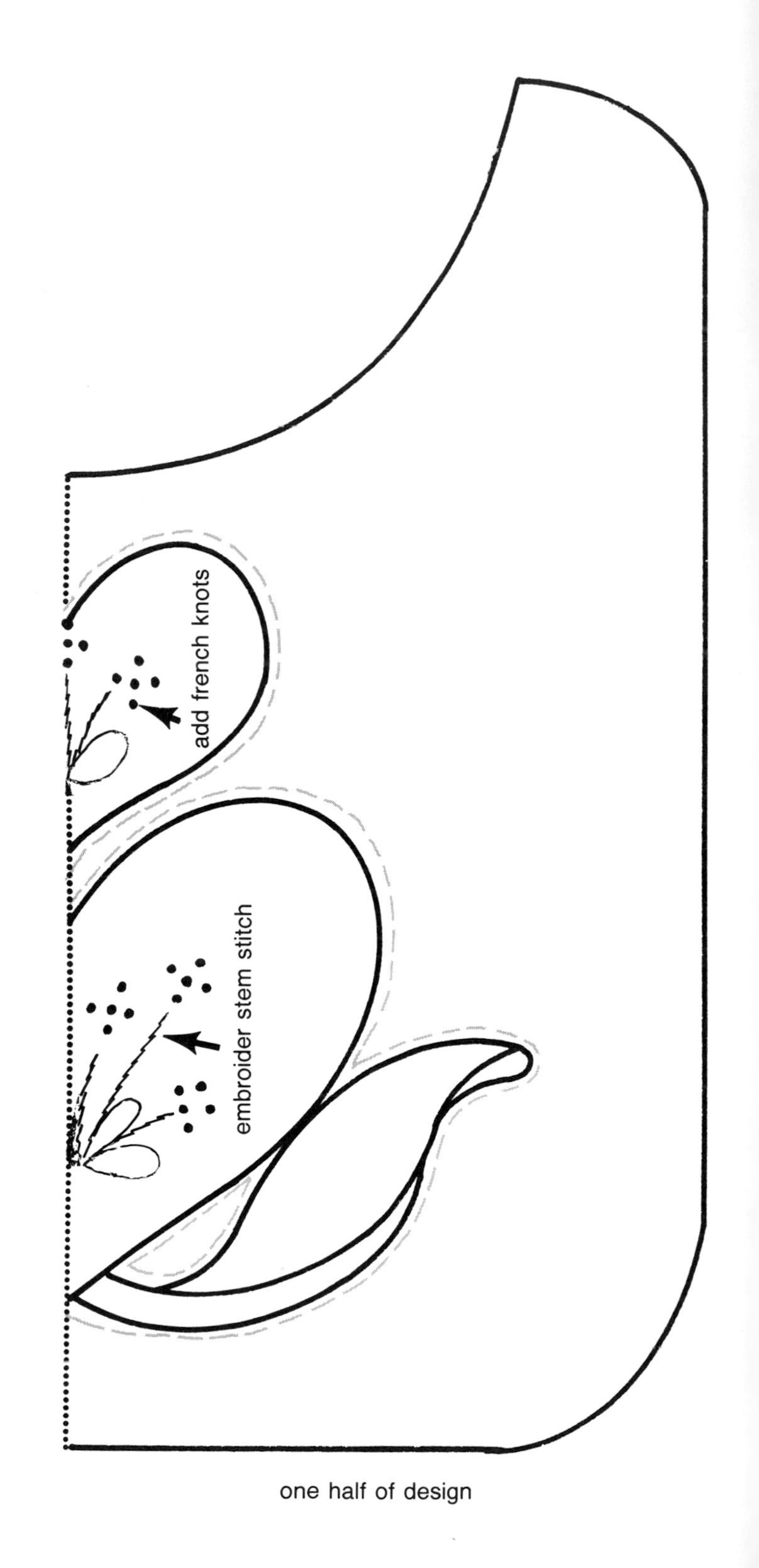

one half of design

Feathered Hearts

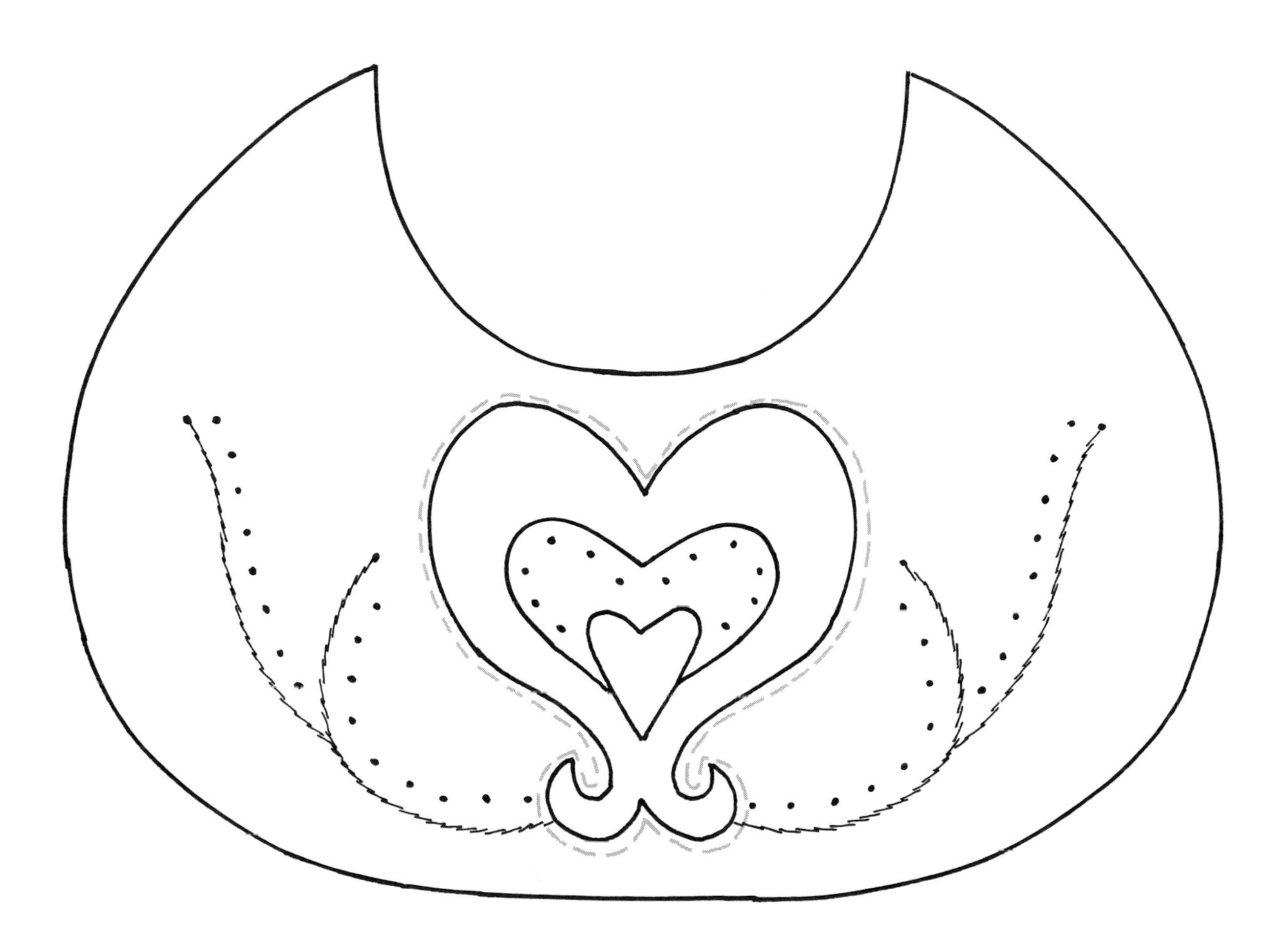

Double Hearts

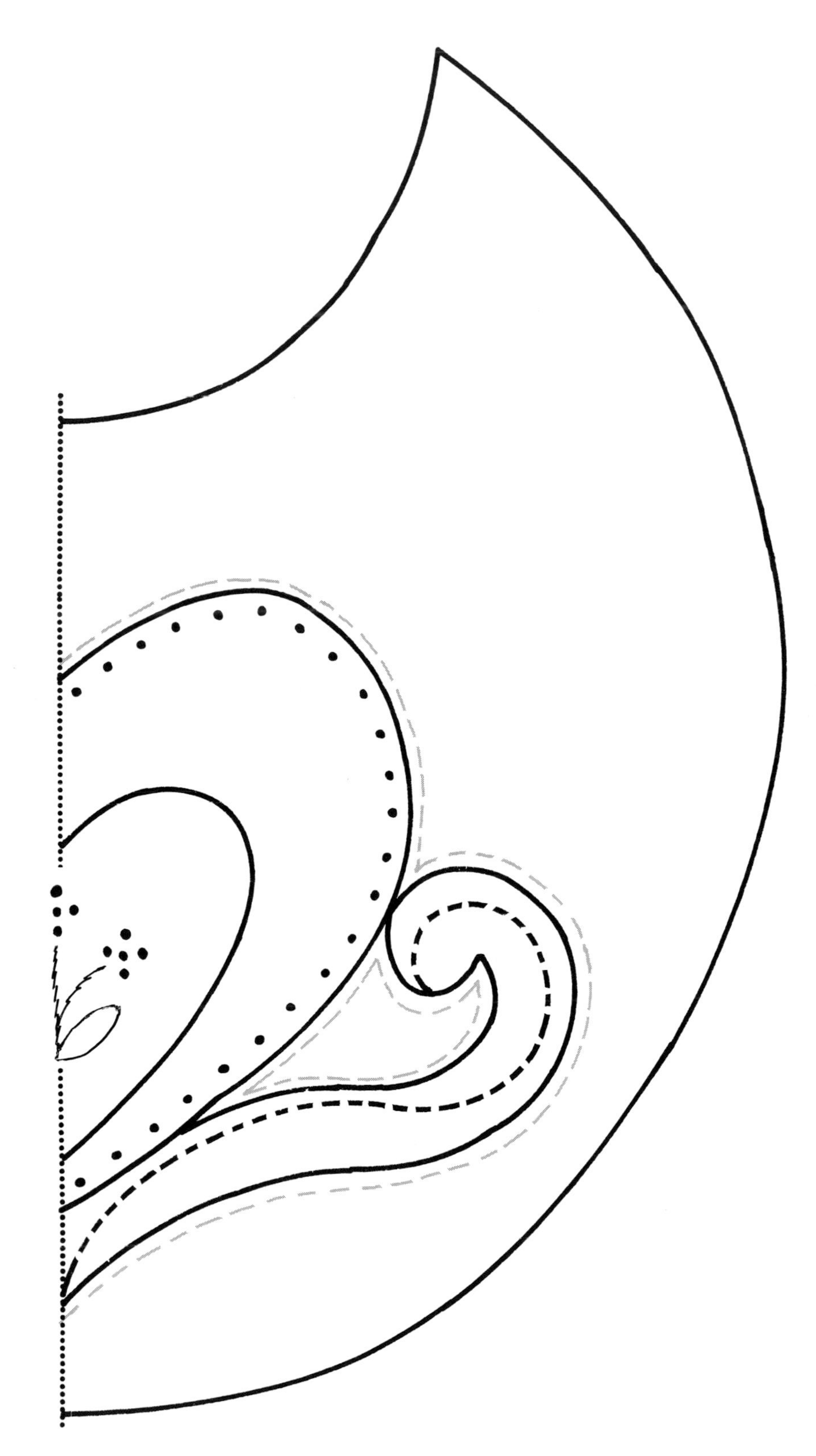

Hearts, Side by Side

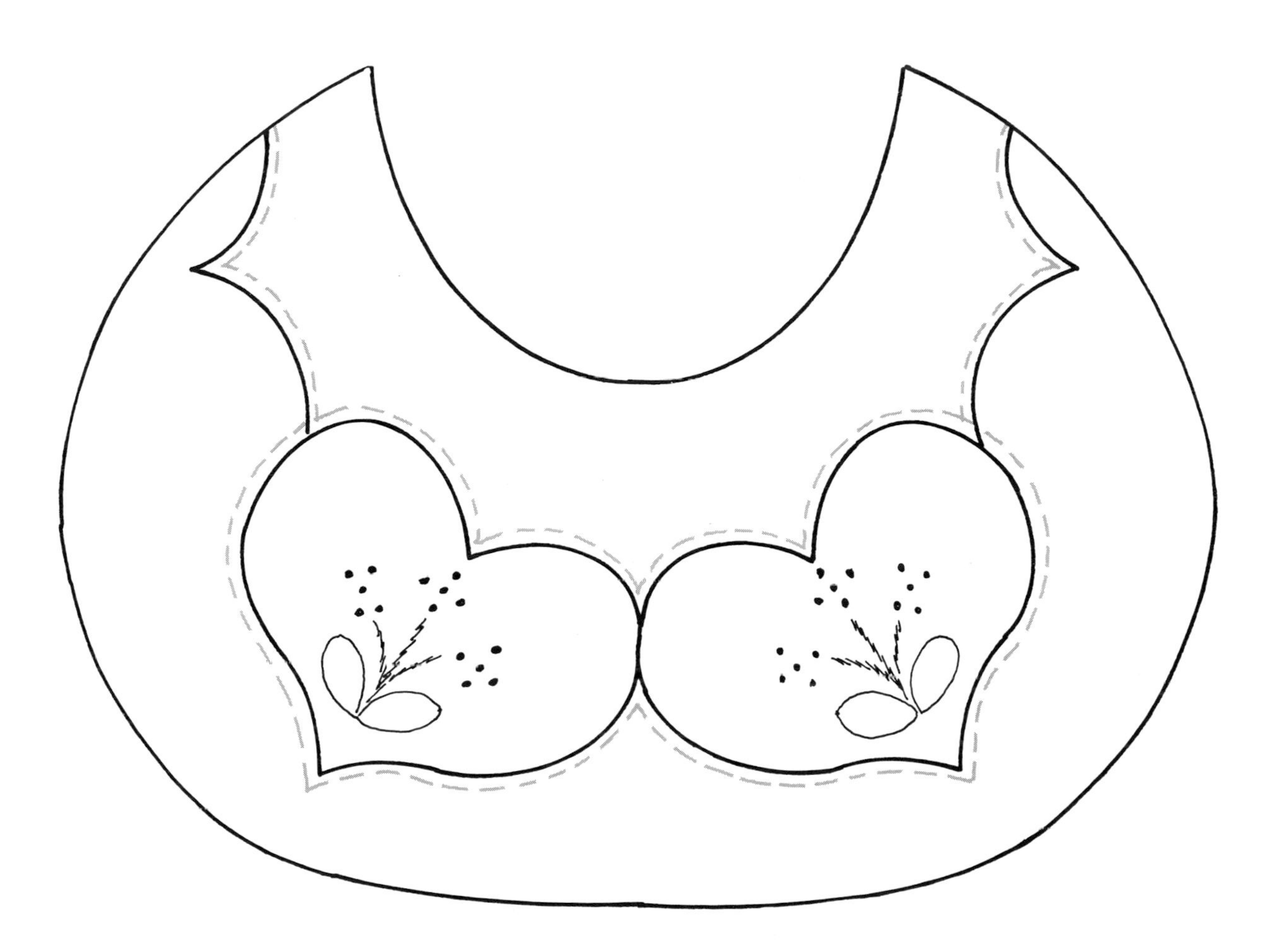

Gaggle of Geese

Warm Hearts for a Special Doll

1. Cut the background shapes from various fabrics following the sizes below. Measurements allow for ½-inch seam allowances.

	SIZE	
Block A	5 × 5 in.	(12.7 cm × 12.7 cm)
Block B	4 × 5 in.	(10.2 cm × 12.7 cm)
Block C	3 × 5 in.	(7.6 cm × 12.7 cm)
Block D	6 × 5 in.	(15.2 cm × 12.7 cm)
Block E	6 × 7 in.	(15.2 cm × 17.0 cm)
Block F	6 × 7½ in.	(12.7 cm × 19.1 cm)
Block G	5 × 4½ in.	(12.7 cm × 11.4 cm)
Block H	8 × 10 in.	(20.3 cm × 25.4 cm)
Block I	4 × 3 in.	(10.2 cm × 7.6 cm)
Block J	4 × 4 in.	(10.2 cm × 10.2 cm)
Block K	5 × 4 in.	(12.7 cm × 10.2 cm)

2. Follow the illustration to assemble the shapes into a doll quilt. Cut various sizes of hearts from fabric. Arrange over assembled background. Place sheer fabric over entire top. Baste well.

3. Shadow quilt along and through all heart shapes. Stitch along seam lines. Embellish with buttons, ribbons, trims, and so on. Embroider blanket stitch around edges of hearts. Bind or finish the quilt's edges in the manner you prefer.

Exotic Ring

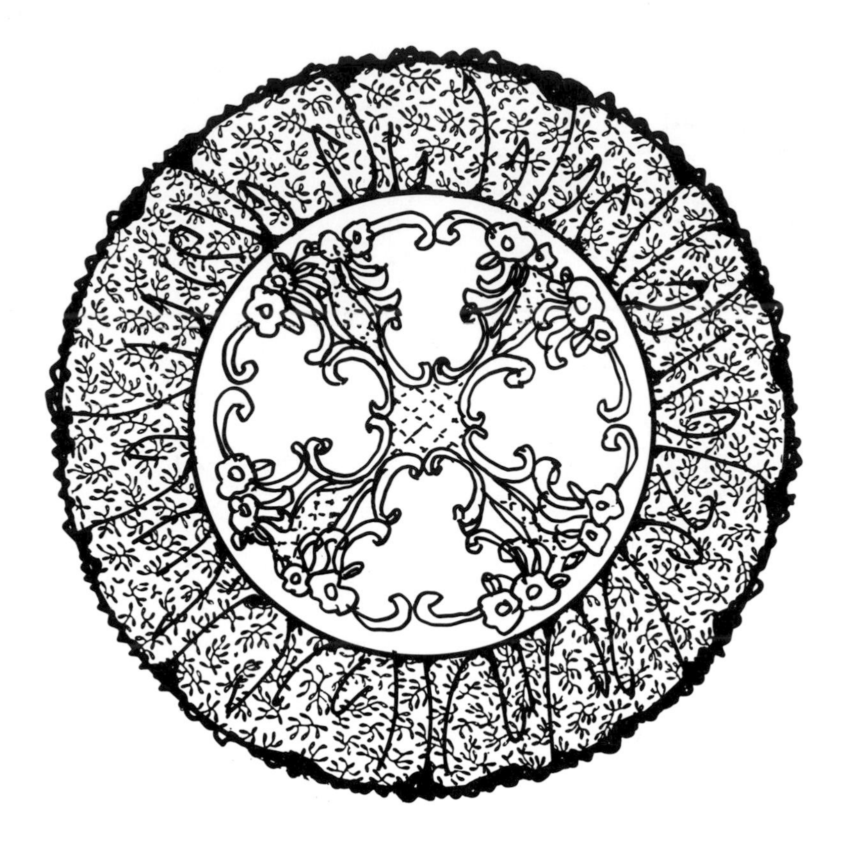

one quarter of design

one half of design

full design

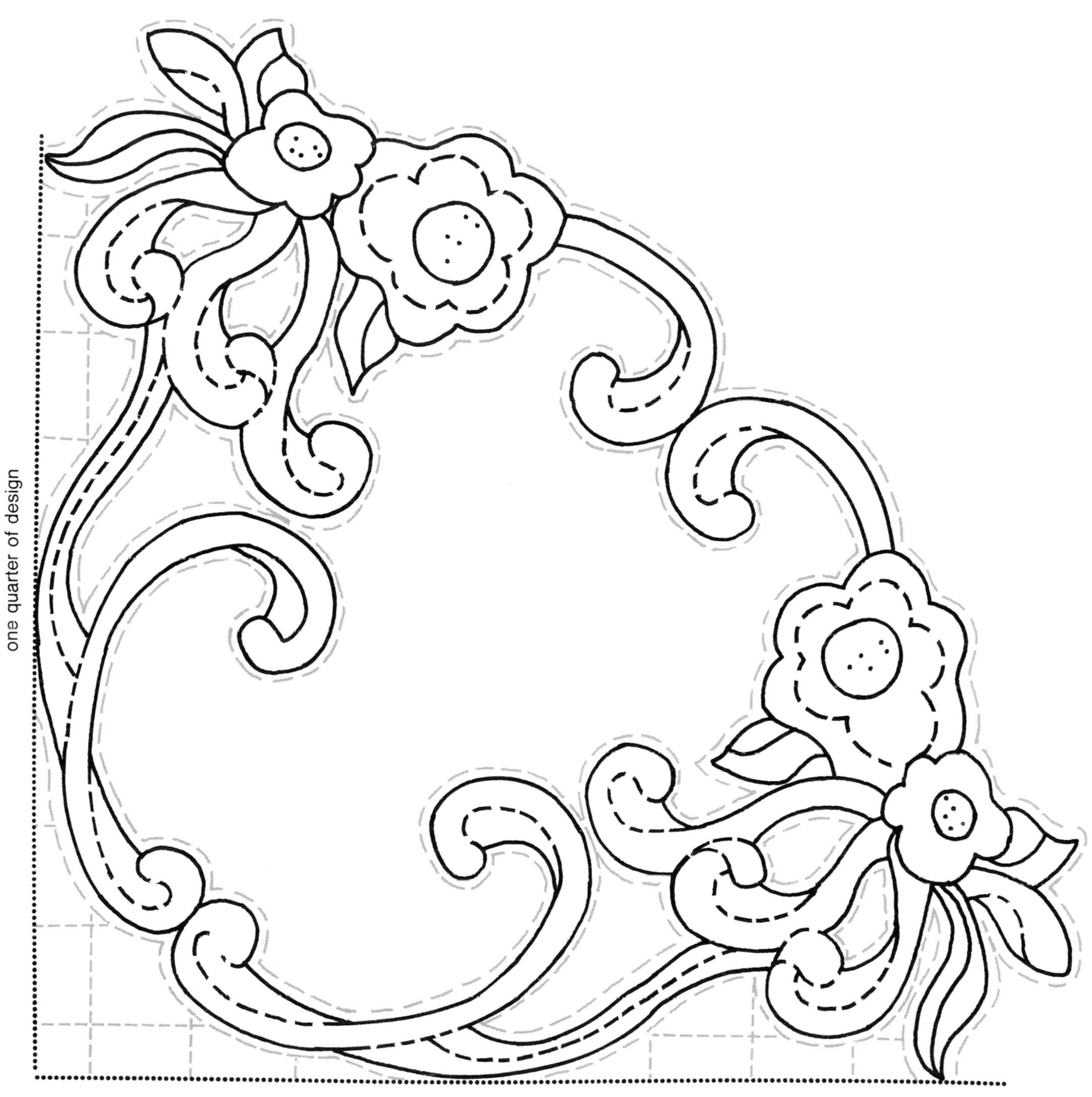
one quarter of design
one quarter of design

Exotica

one half of design

full design

one half of design

Exotic Pastel

one half of design

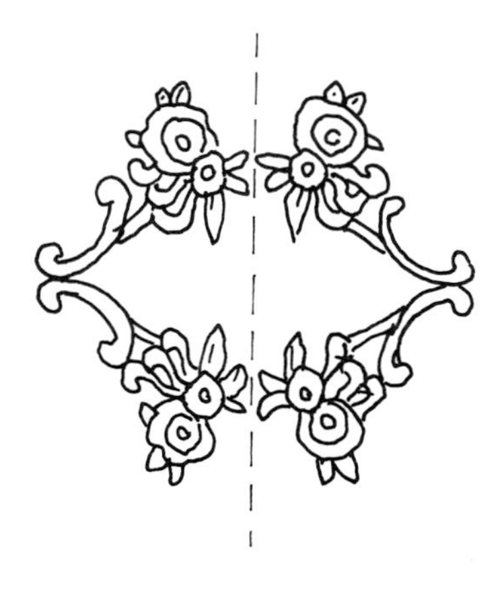

full design

one half of design

Small Bouquet

jewelry pouch

Make this charming "thimble-holder" doll by adding a gathered skirt and kerchief to any small store-purchased doll. Hold the hands and thimble in place by securing them with a loop of ribbon.

Create a sewing basket. Make a pattern for any basket by measuring the length and width across the top edges. Draw onto paper. Center your paper pattern over the appropriate floral-bouquet design.

Twisted Bow

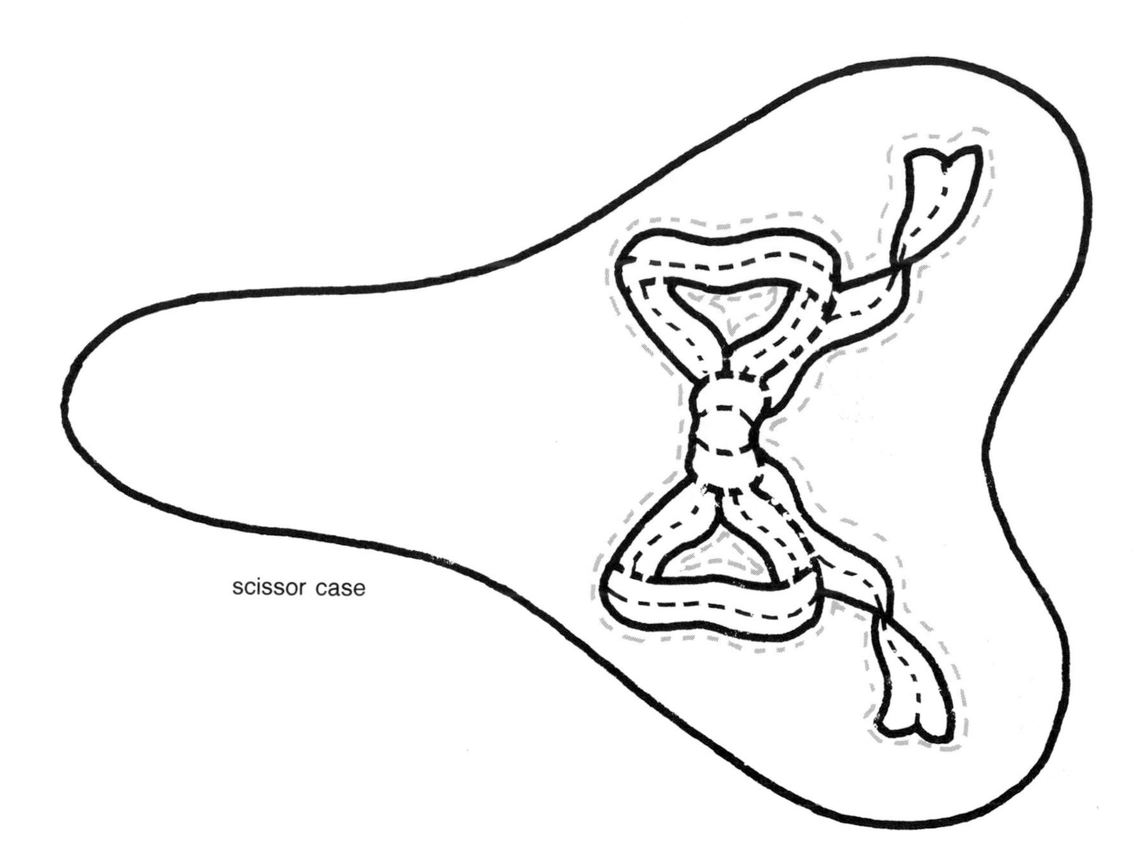

Bows and Bouquets

one section

three sections

Heart of Flowers

Flowing Flowers

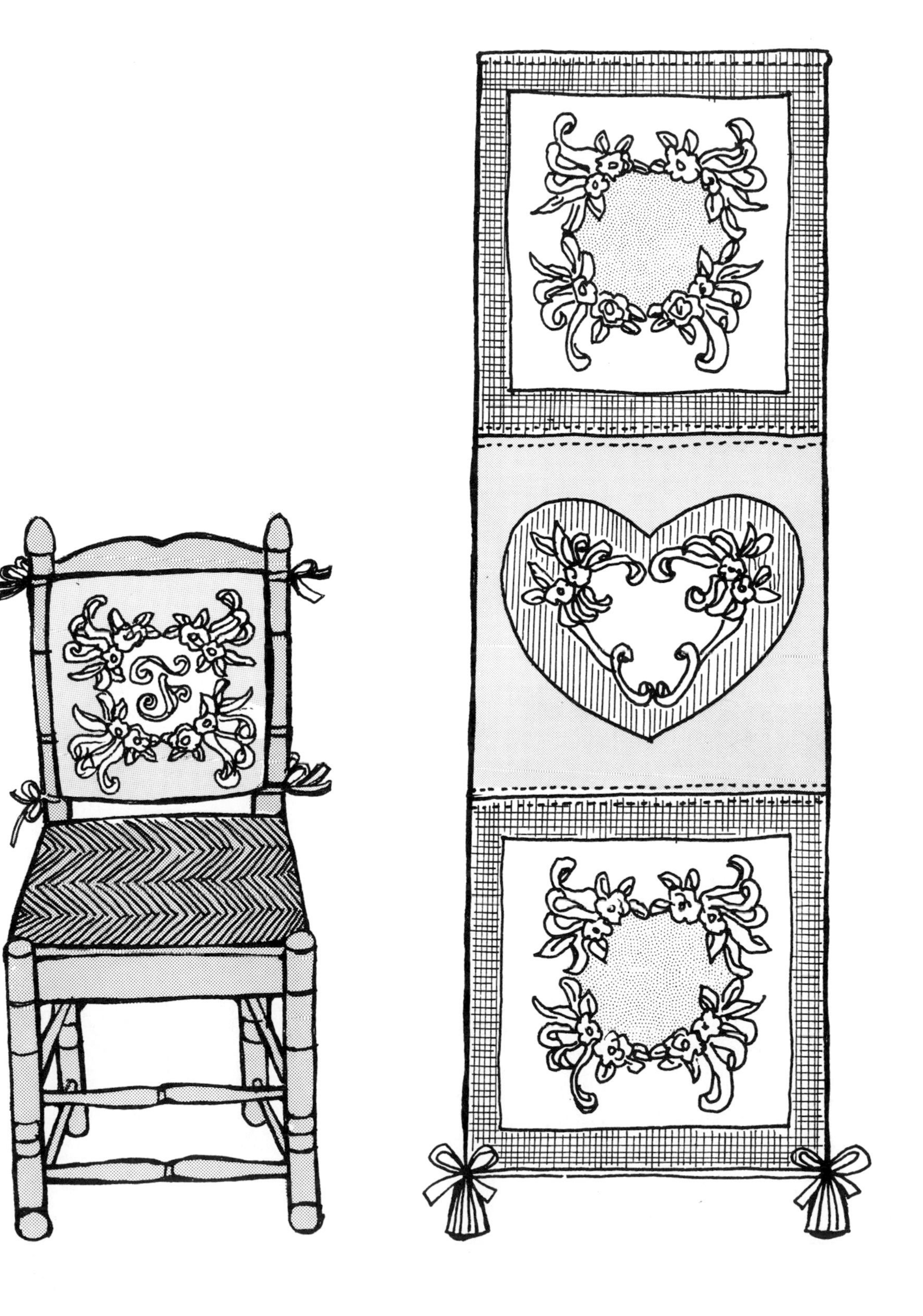

Flowing Border

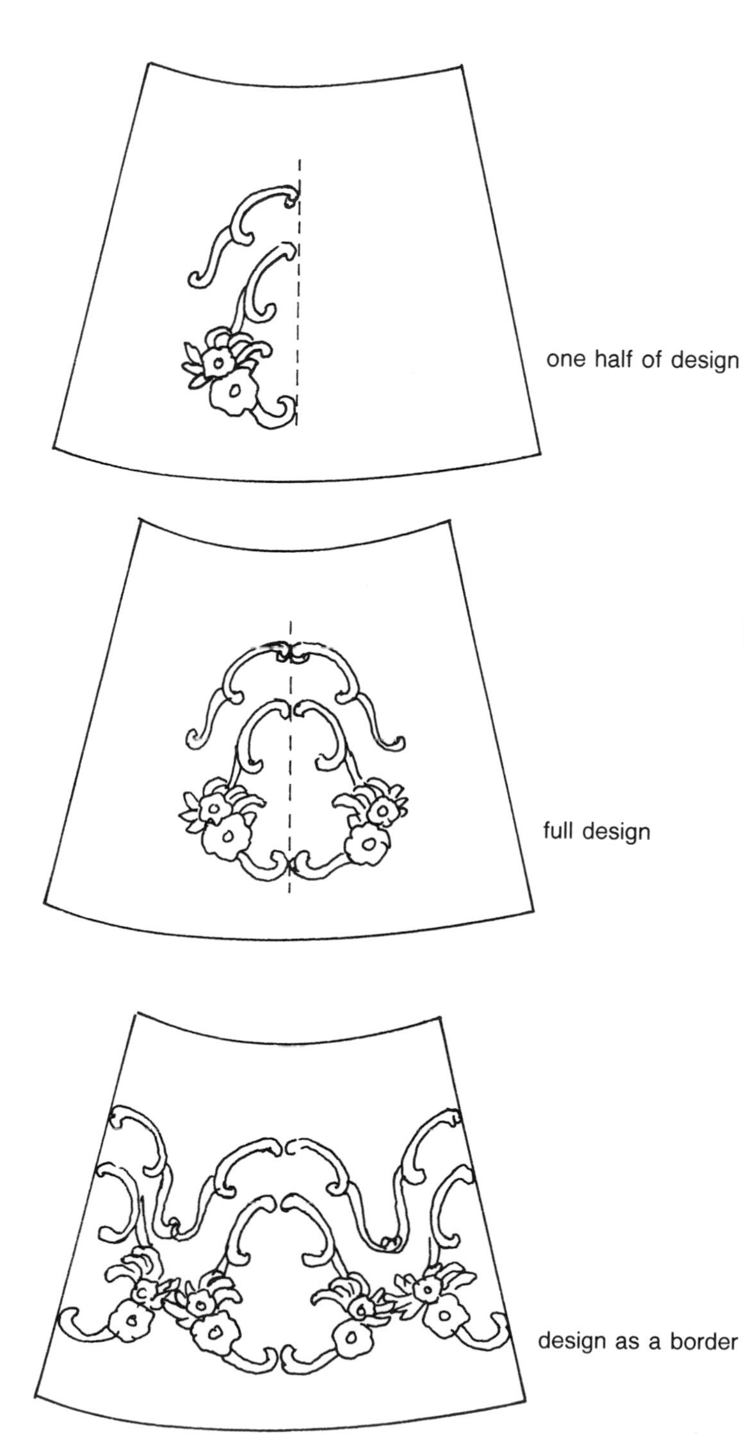

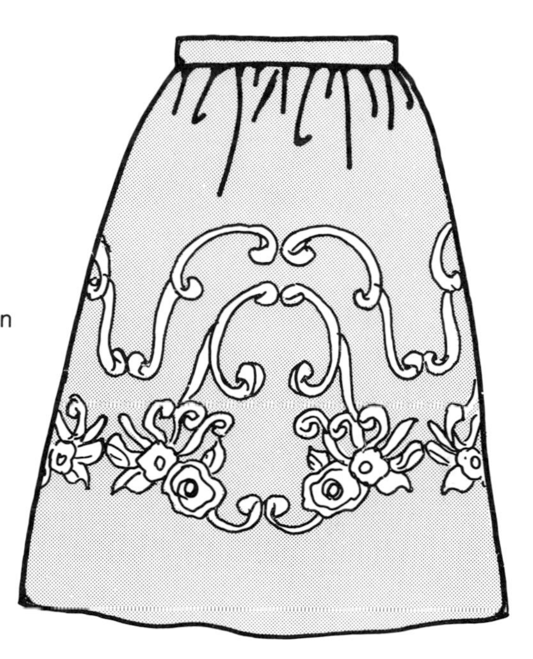

top

one half of design

Soft Flow

one half of design

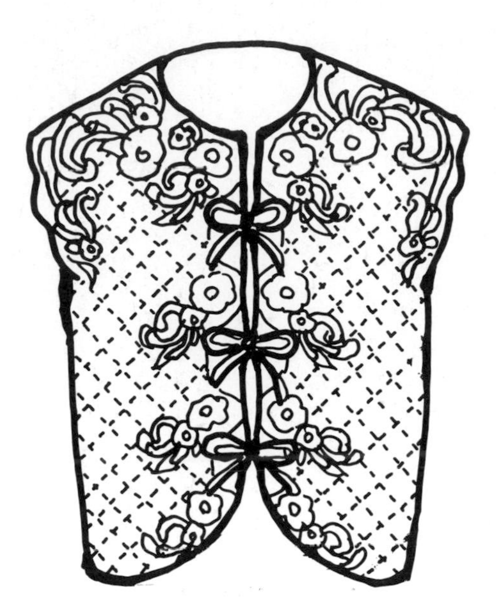

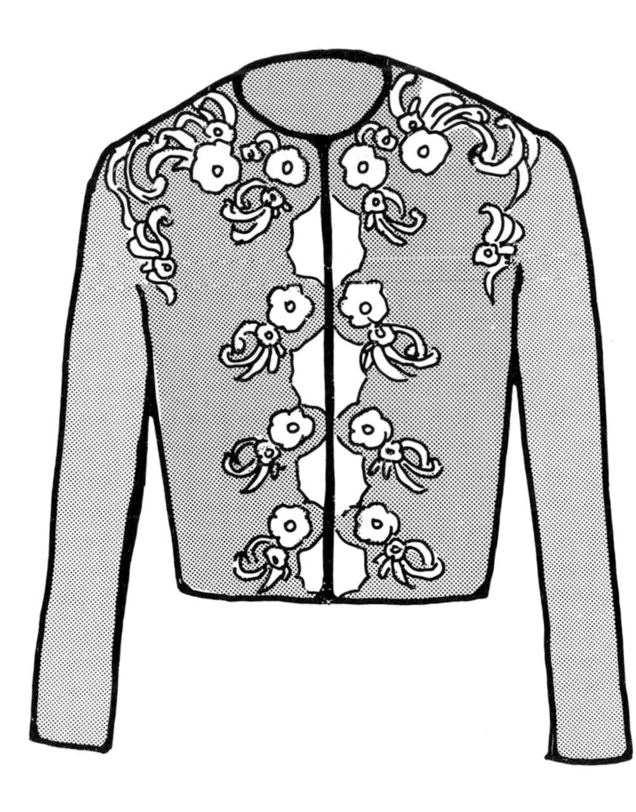

Entwined Hearts

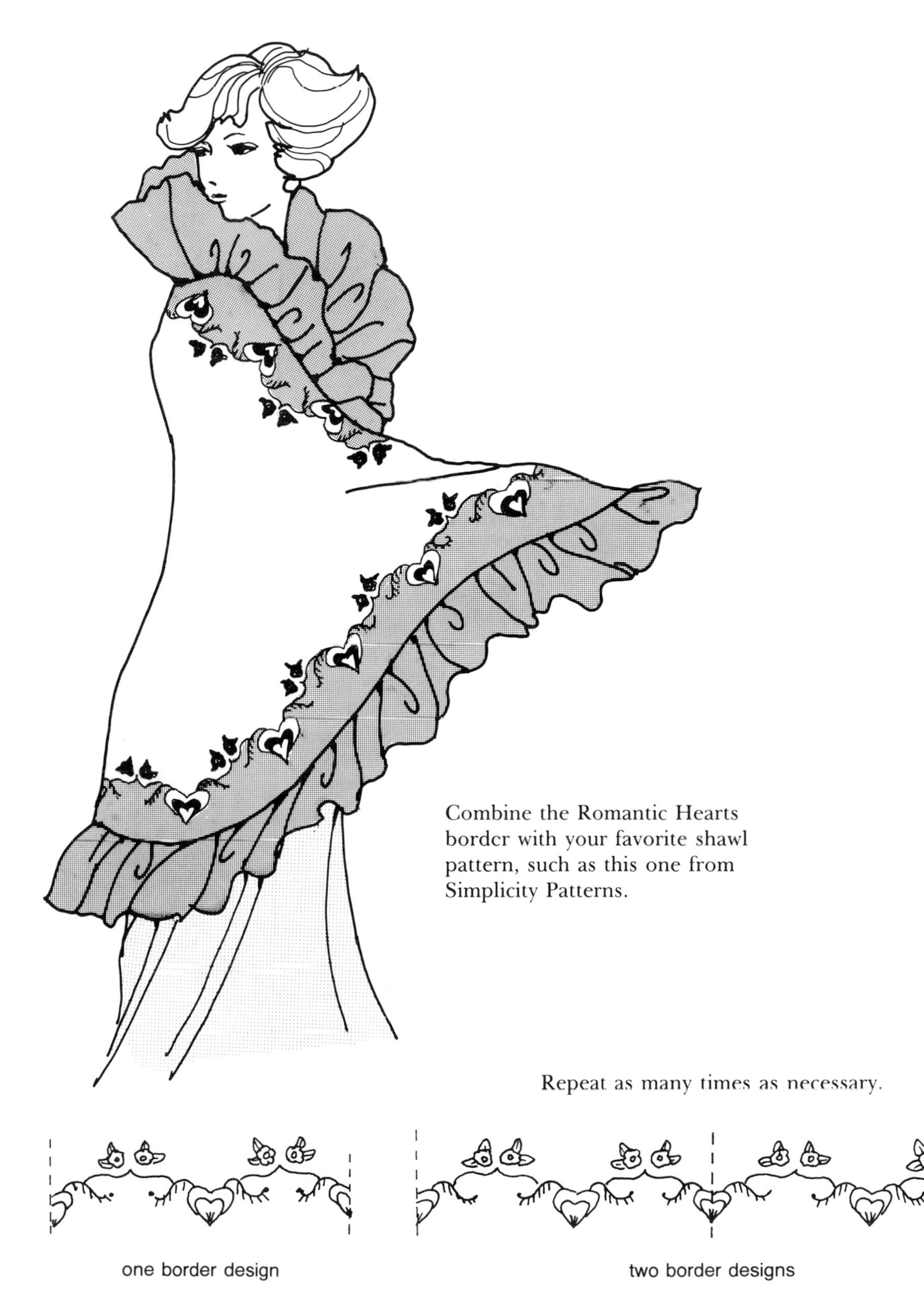

Combine the Romantic Hearts border with your favorite shawl pattern, such as this one from Simplicity Patterns.

Repeat as many times as necessary.

one border design

two border designs

For a continuous border, repeat as many units as needed.

Entwined Flowers and Hearts

For a continuous border, repeat as many units as needed.

Square of Entwined Hearts

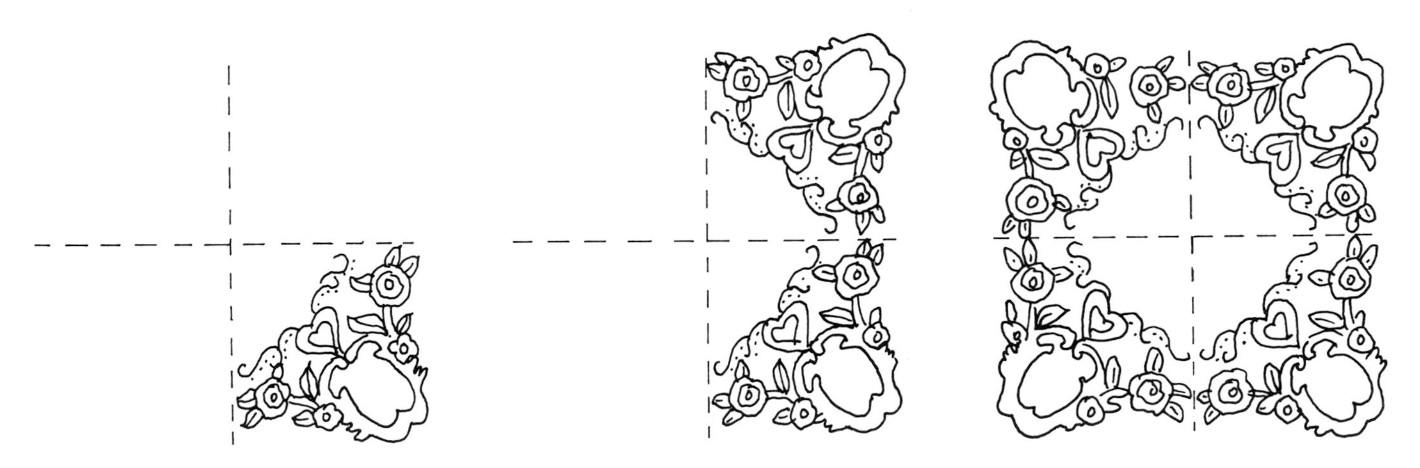

one quarter of design

one half of design

full design

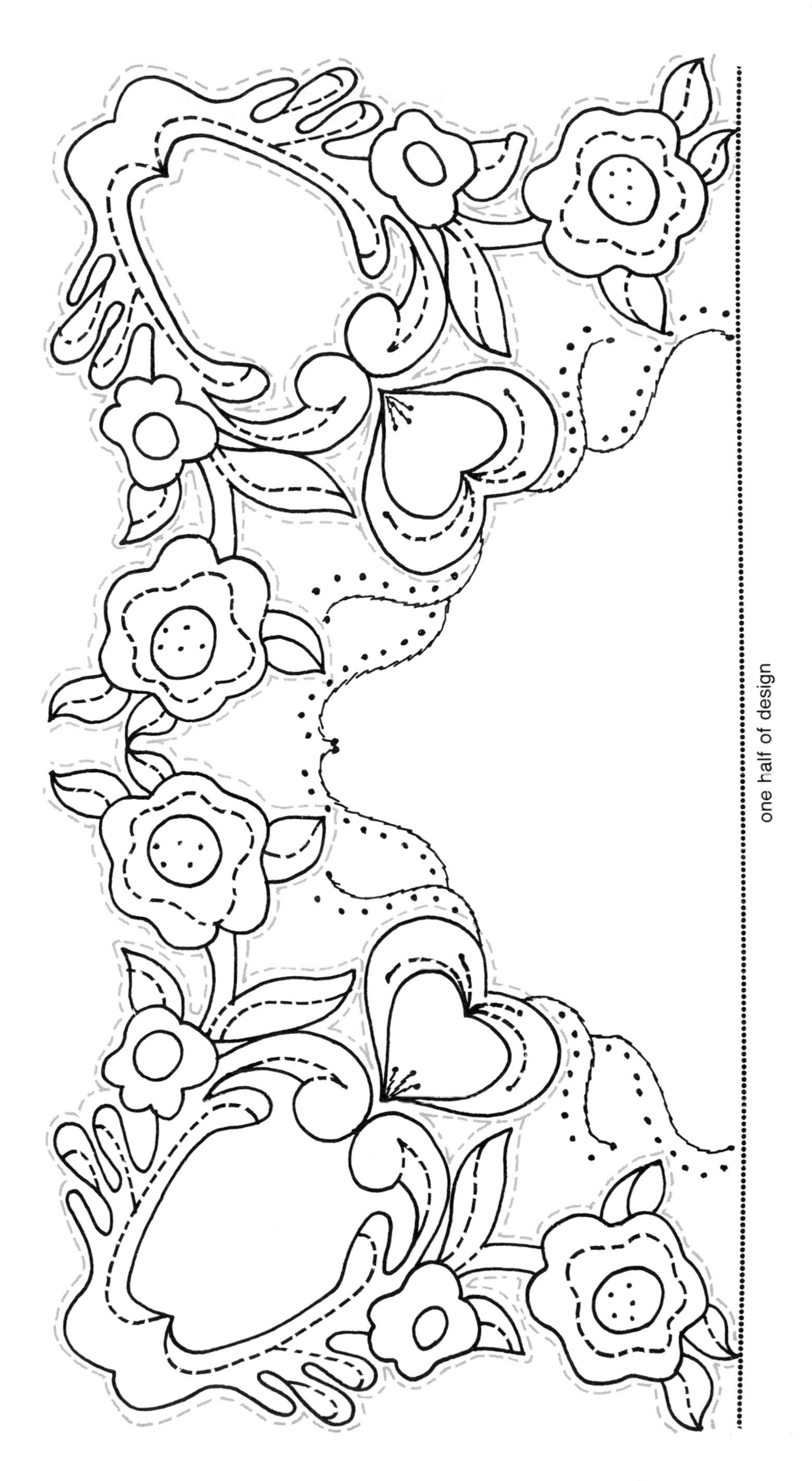
one half of design

Entwined Hearts All Around

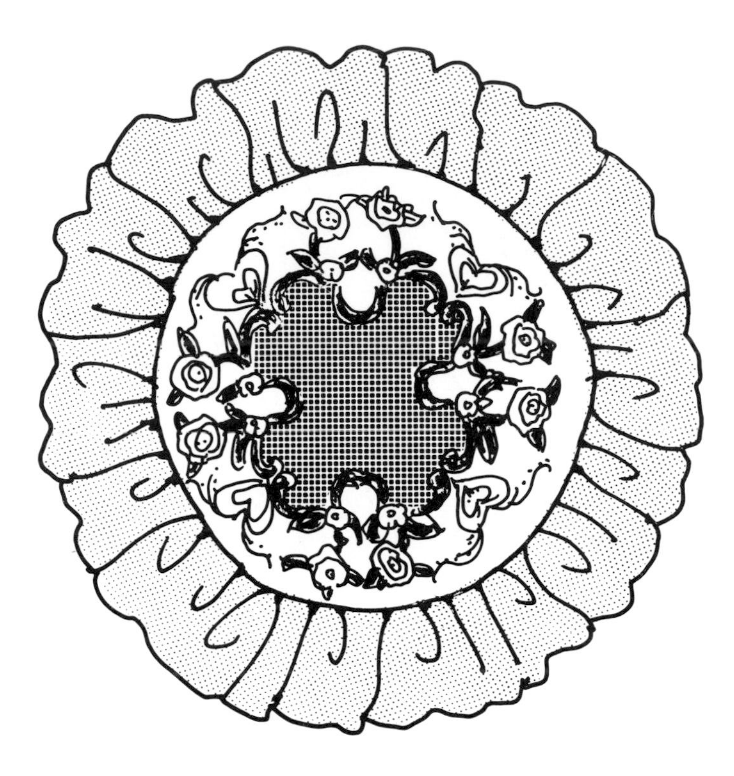

one half of design

full design

one half of design

Flower Checkerboard with Entwined Hearts

one half of design

Heart Cluster

Rabbit with Flower

Curly Lamb

Medley of Hearts and Flowers

Bearthoven

Double Tulips

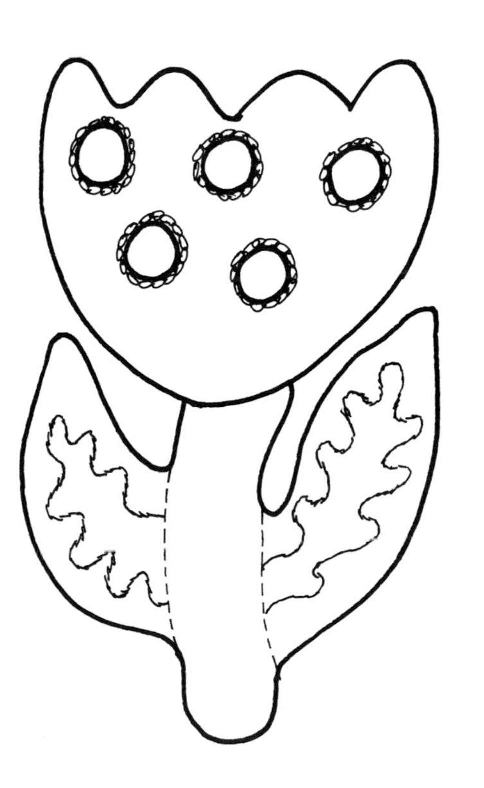

Heart for Heart

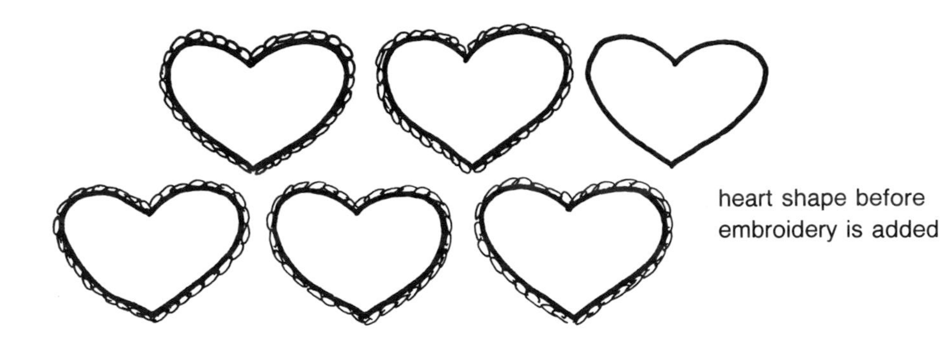

Checkerboard of Hearts

Hen a-Nesting

Not For Animal Lovers Only Quilt

		FINISHED SIZE
Block A:	Cut 4 fabrics 14 × 14 in. (35.5 cm × 35.5 cm)	13 × 13 in. (33 cm × 33 cm)
Strip B:	Cut 12 bands 3 × 14 in. (7.5 cm × 35.5 cm)	2 × 13 in. (5 cm × 33 cm)
Block C:	Cut 9 corners 3 × 3 in. (7.5 cm × 7.5 cm)	2 × 2 in. (5 cm × 5 cm)
Block D:	Cut 8 fabrics 4½ × 3 in. (11.5 cm × 7.5 cm)	3½ × 2 in. (9 cm × 5 cm)
Block E:	Cut 36 fabrics 4½ × 4½ in. (11.5 cm × 11.5 cm)	3½ × 3½ in. (9 cm × 9 cm)
Strip F:	Cut 4 fabrics 40 × 8 in. (102 cm × 20.5 cm)	39 × 7 in. (100.5 cm × 18 cm)
Block G:	Cut 4 fabrics 8 × 8 in. (20.5 cm × 20.5 cm)	7 × 7 in. (18 cm × 18 cm)

Finished quilt size 53″ × 53″ (134.6 cm × 134.6 cm).

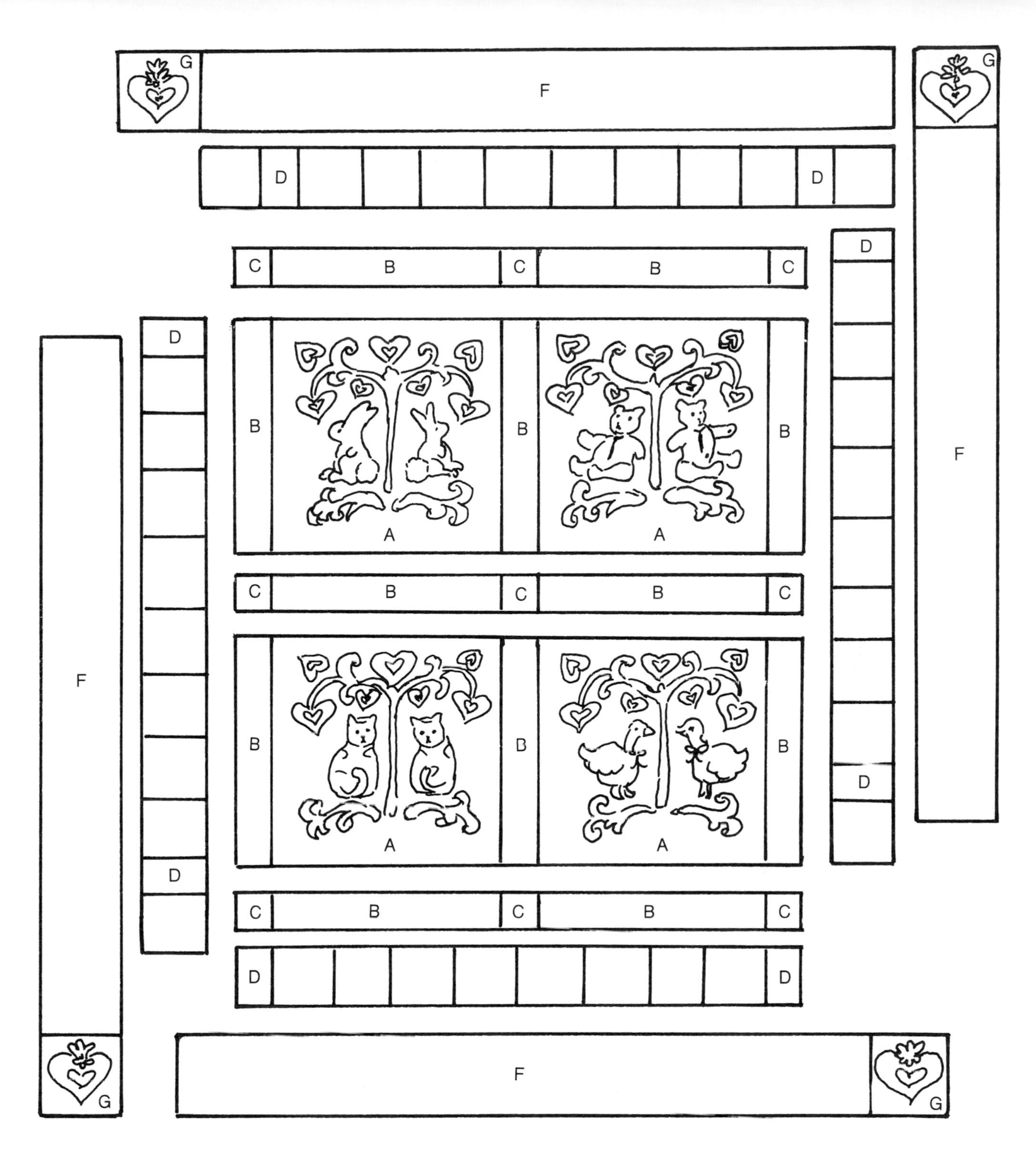

How to assemble the units:

1. Cut the background shapes from various fabrics, following the above chart.

2. Following the illustration, assemble the shapes into a quilt top after having prepared shadow quilting to make shapes A and G. Use ½-inch seams when assembling.

3. Apply bonded polyester sheet batting behind the assembled top, then a lining fabric of lightweight broadcloth behind that. Hand quilt through all the layers, following the suggested lines on the designs or make up your own quilting pattern. Bind or finish the quilt's edges in the manner you prefer.

Cat with a Bell

Tree of Flowering Hearts and Beribboned Goose

Puffy-tailed Bunny

Boysenbeary

Corner Hearts

Sunshine and Hearts

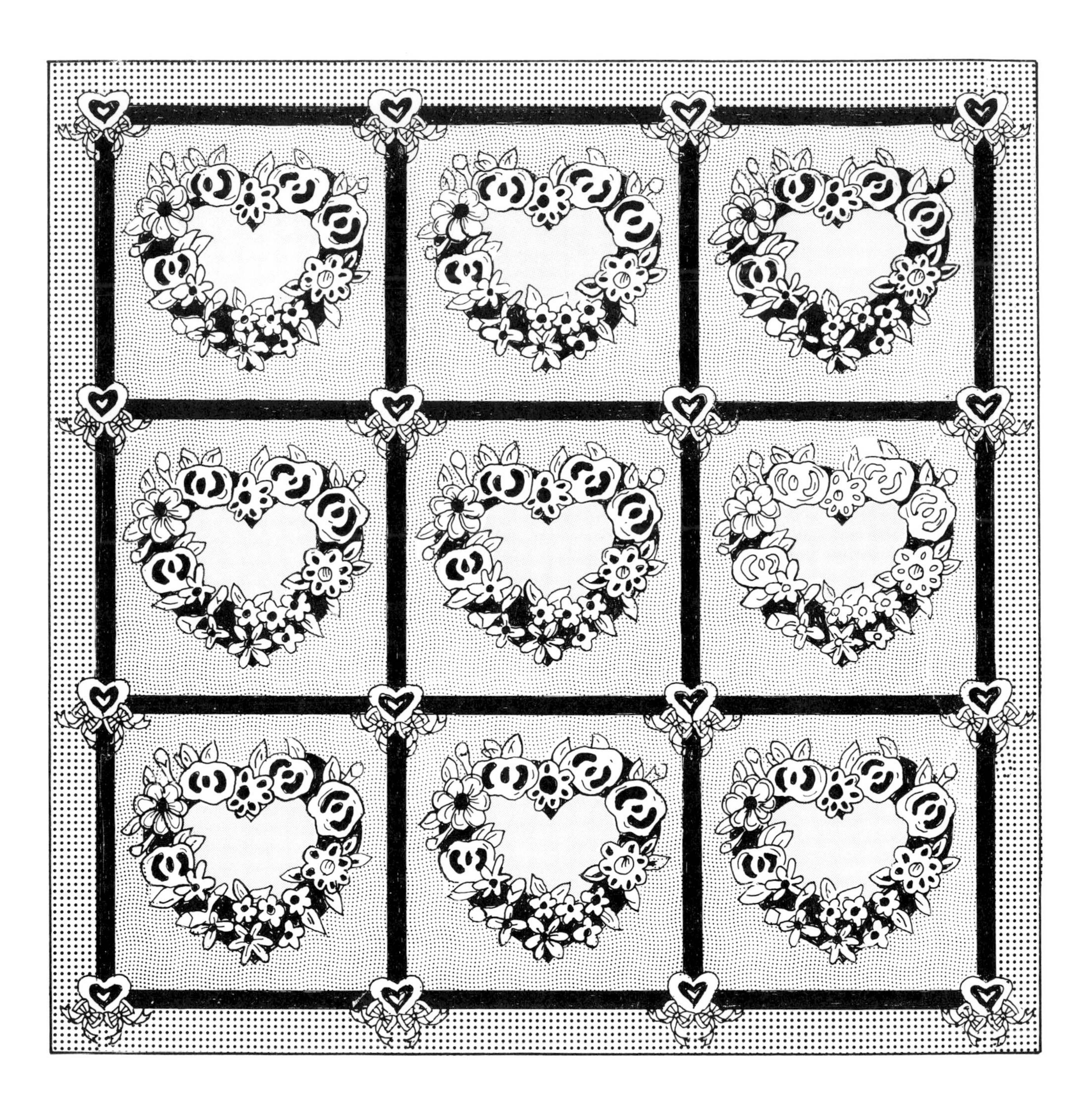

Beribboned Heart

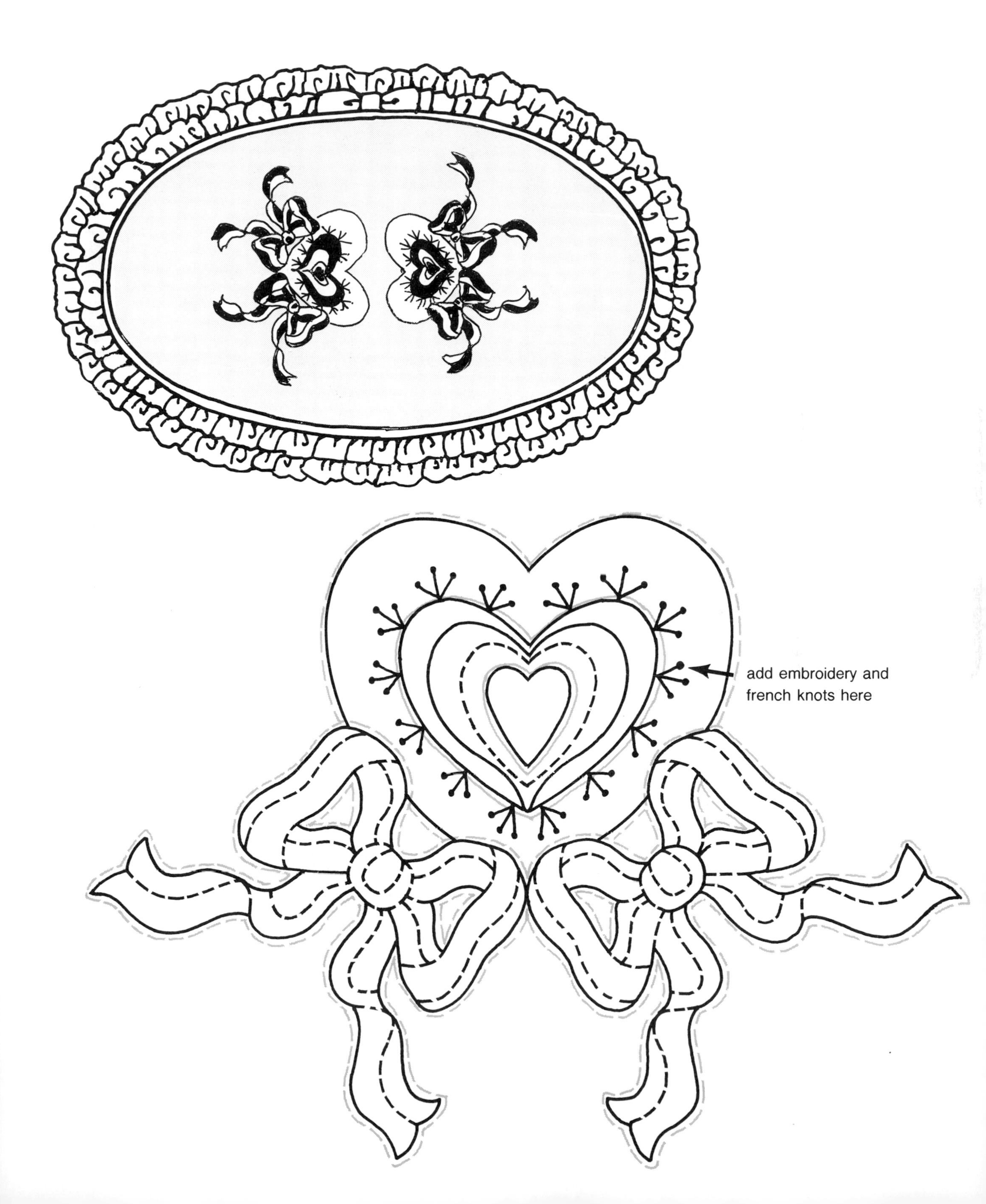

Pig O' My Heart

Combine your favorite commercial animal pattern, such as this one from Simplicity Patterns, with the Flowering Heart design on page 131.

Scribner Cat

Squared Flowers

Add your favorite monogram to this design or Elegant Scroll.

Elegant Scroll

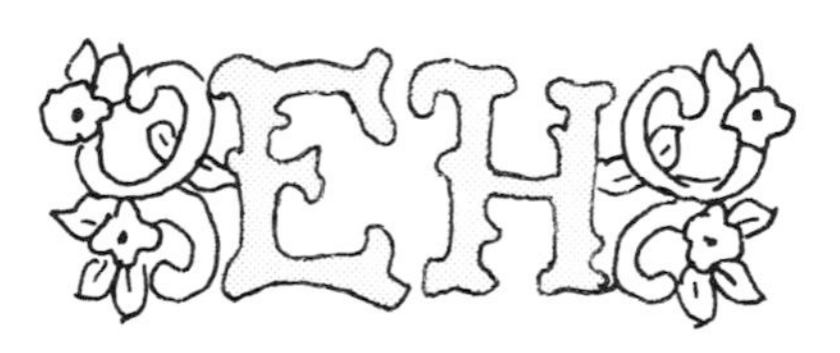

Small Monogram Alphabet

Try different placements of the design with the monogram of your choosing. You can also combine large and small monograms, as shown.

To enlarge or reduce a letter, see the chapter, "Enlarging, Reducing, and Transferring Designs."

STU
VXY
WZ

Entwined Hearts (border on apron skirt), Entwined Flowers and Hearts (apron bib), Square of Entwined Hearts (square pillow), Entwined Hearts All Around (round pillow), Flower Checkerboard with Entwined Hearts (rectangular pillow)

Heart Cluster (row 1, left), Rabbit with Flower (row 2, left), Curly Lamb (row 4, left), Medley of Hearts and Flowers (row 2, middle), Bearthoven (row 3, middle), Double Tulips (row 1, right), Heart for Heart (row 3, right), Checkerboard of Hearts (row 4, right)

Hen a-Nesting

Not for Animal Lovers Only Quilt: Tree of Flowering Hearts, Corner Hearts, Puffy-tailed Bunny (left, top), Boysenbeary (right, top), Cat with a Bell (left, bottom), Beribboned Goose (right, bottom)

Sunshine and Hearts (large repeating motif), Beribboned Heart
(small corner motif)

Pig O' My Heart

Squared Flowers

Elegant Scroll

Christmas Socks

Christmas Tree Ornaments:
Christmas Hearts,
Christmas Roses

Christmas Wreath

Christmas Hoops: Noel, Joy

Christmas Table Top or Tree Skirt

Christmas Socks

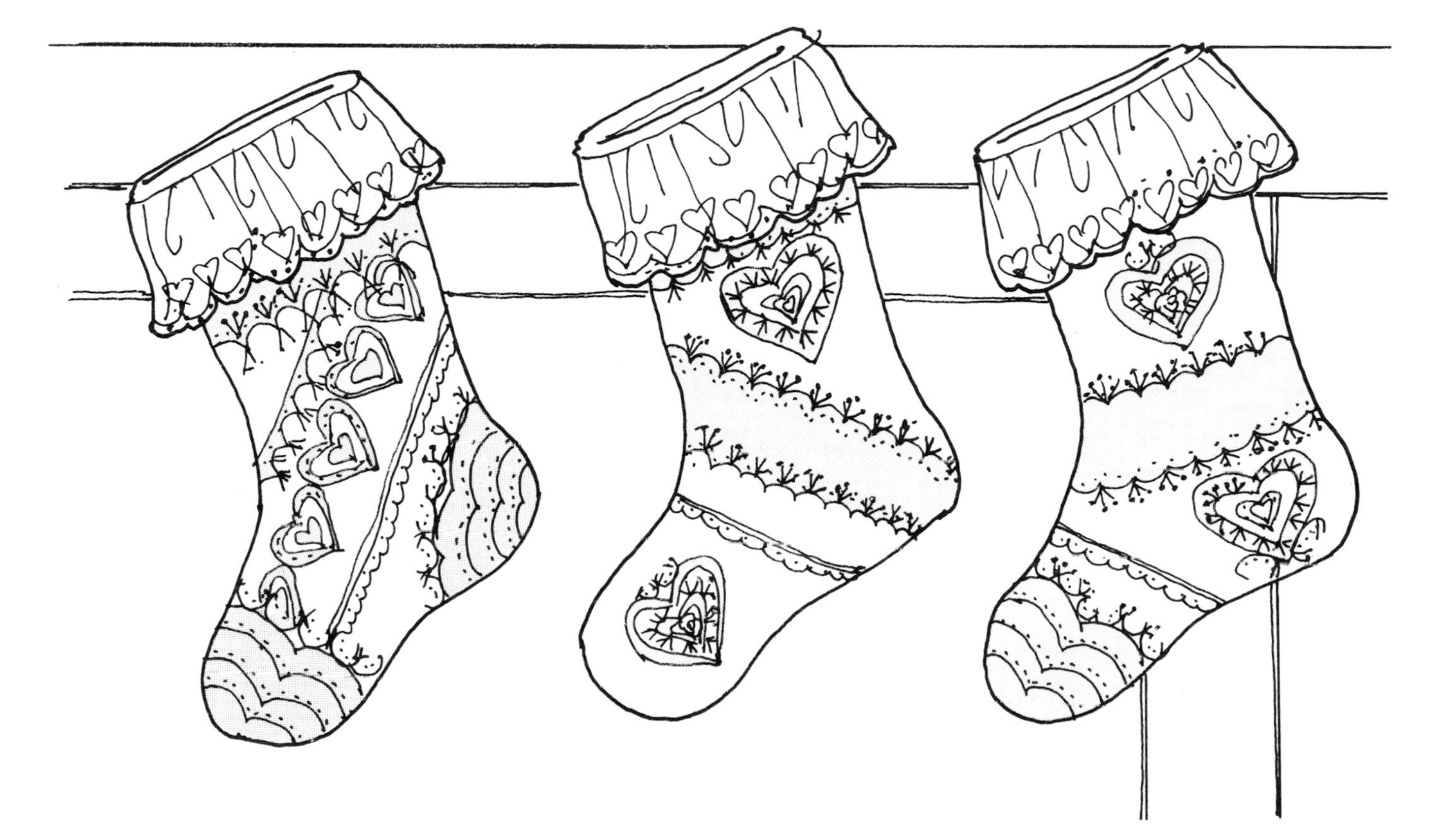

Christmas Tree Ornaments

Christmas Hearts

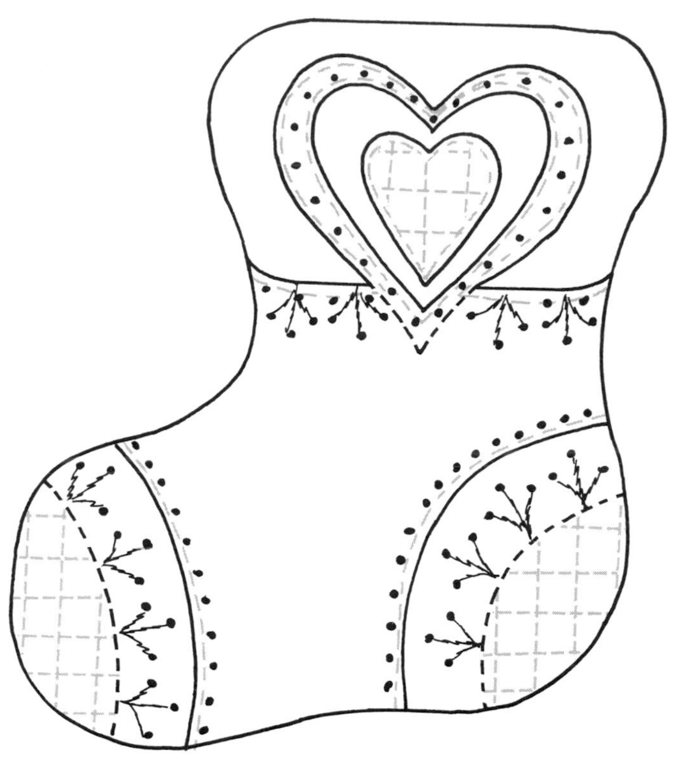

Christmas Roses

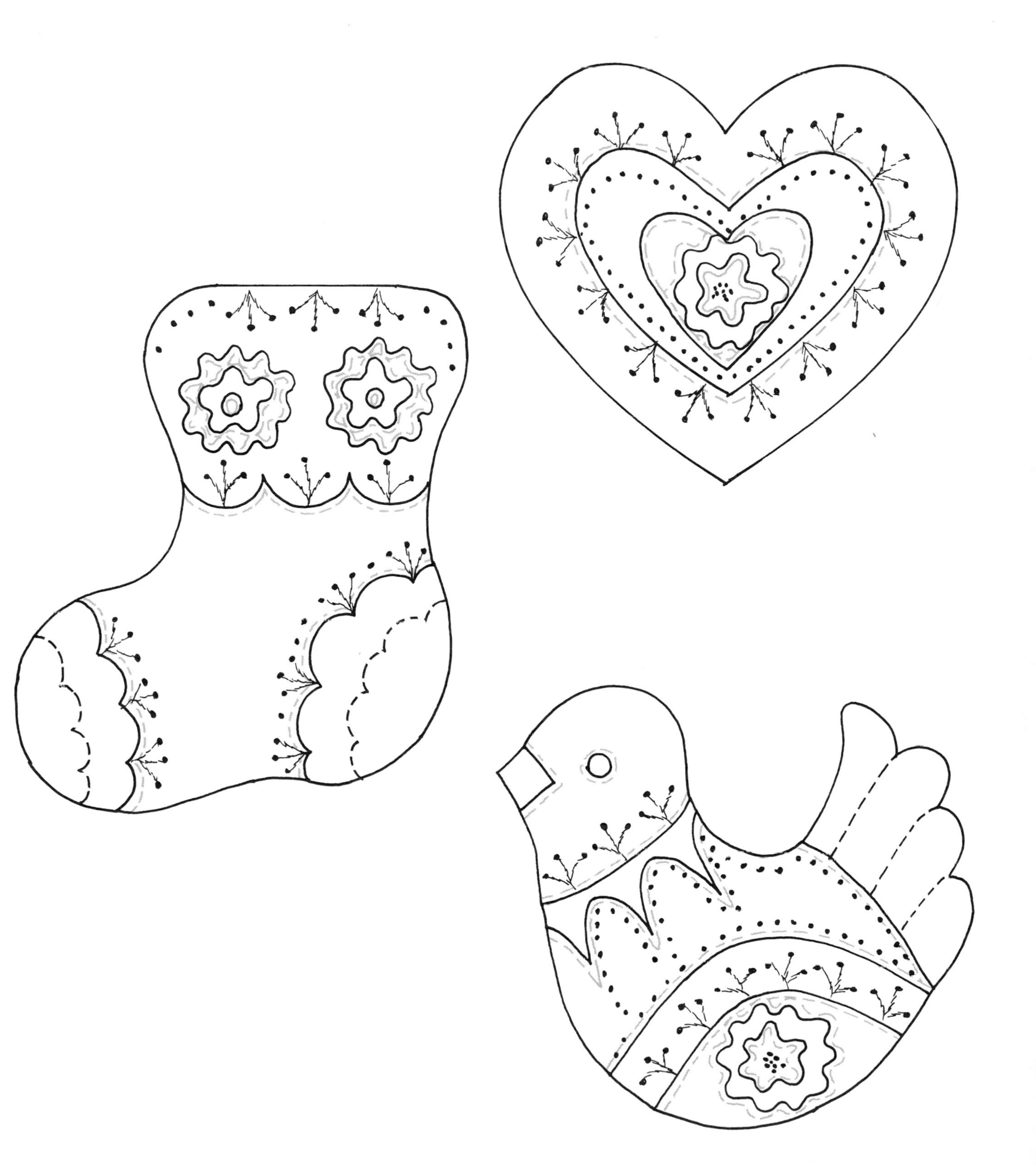

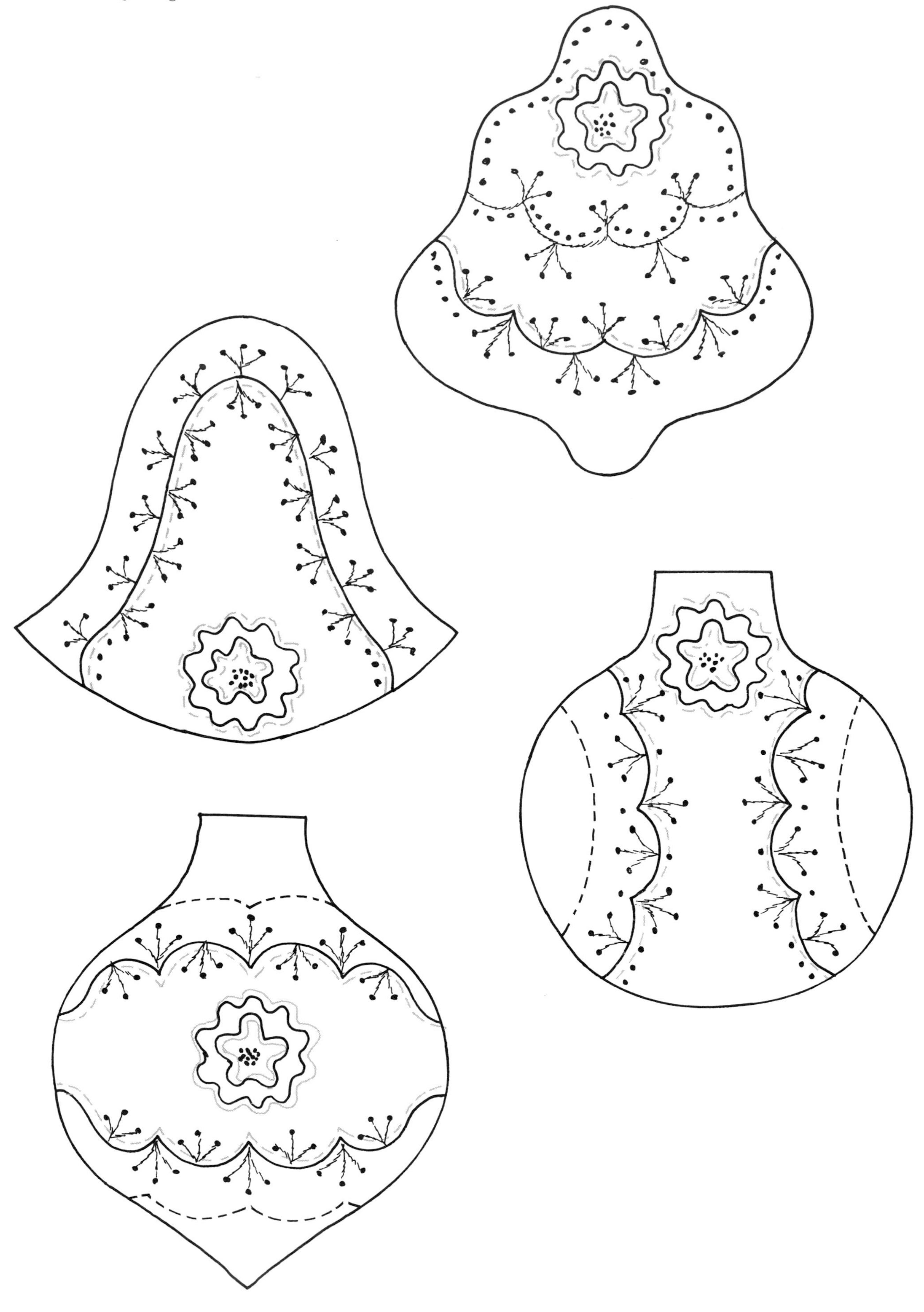

Christmas Wreath

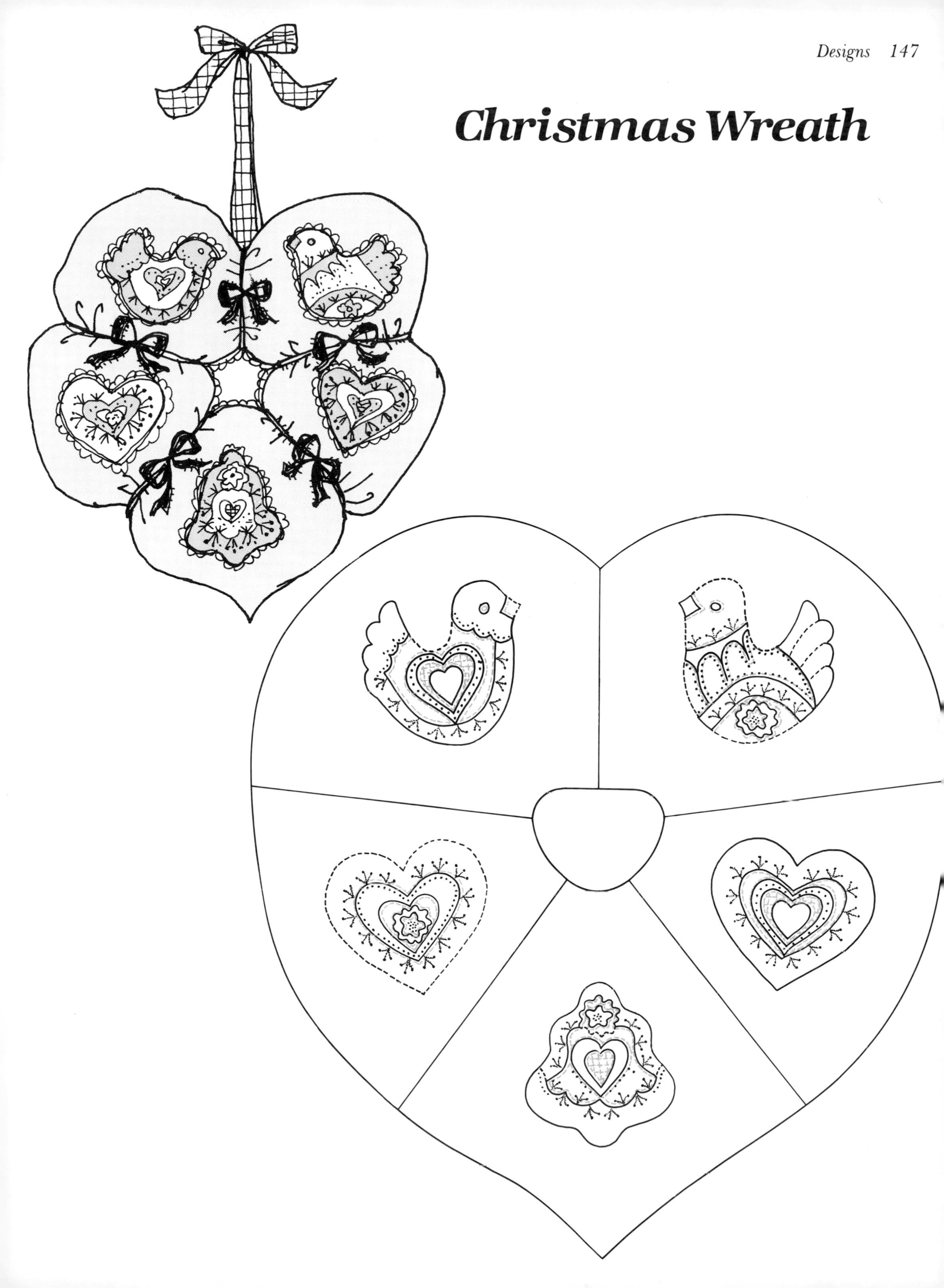

Christmas Hoops

Noel

Joy

Christmas Table Top or Christmas Tree Skirt

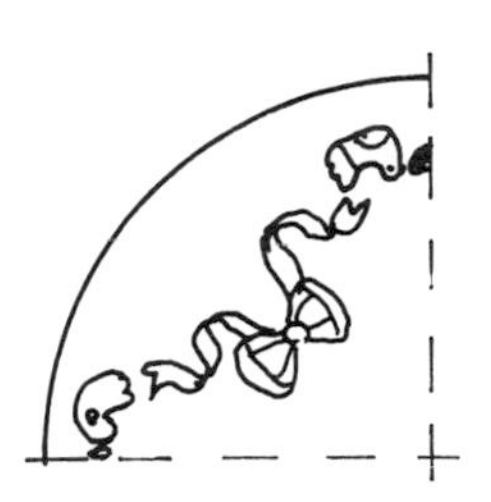

one quarter of design

one half of design

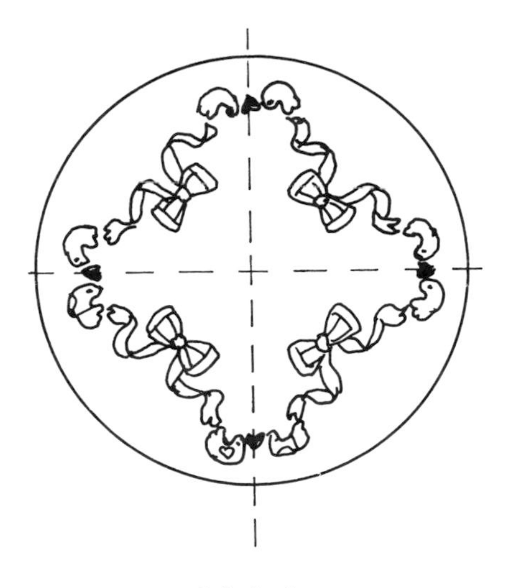

full design

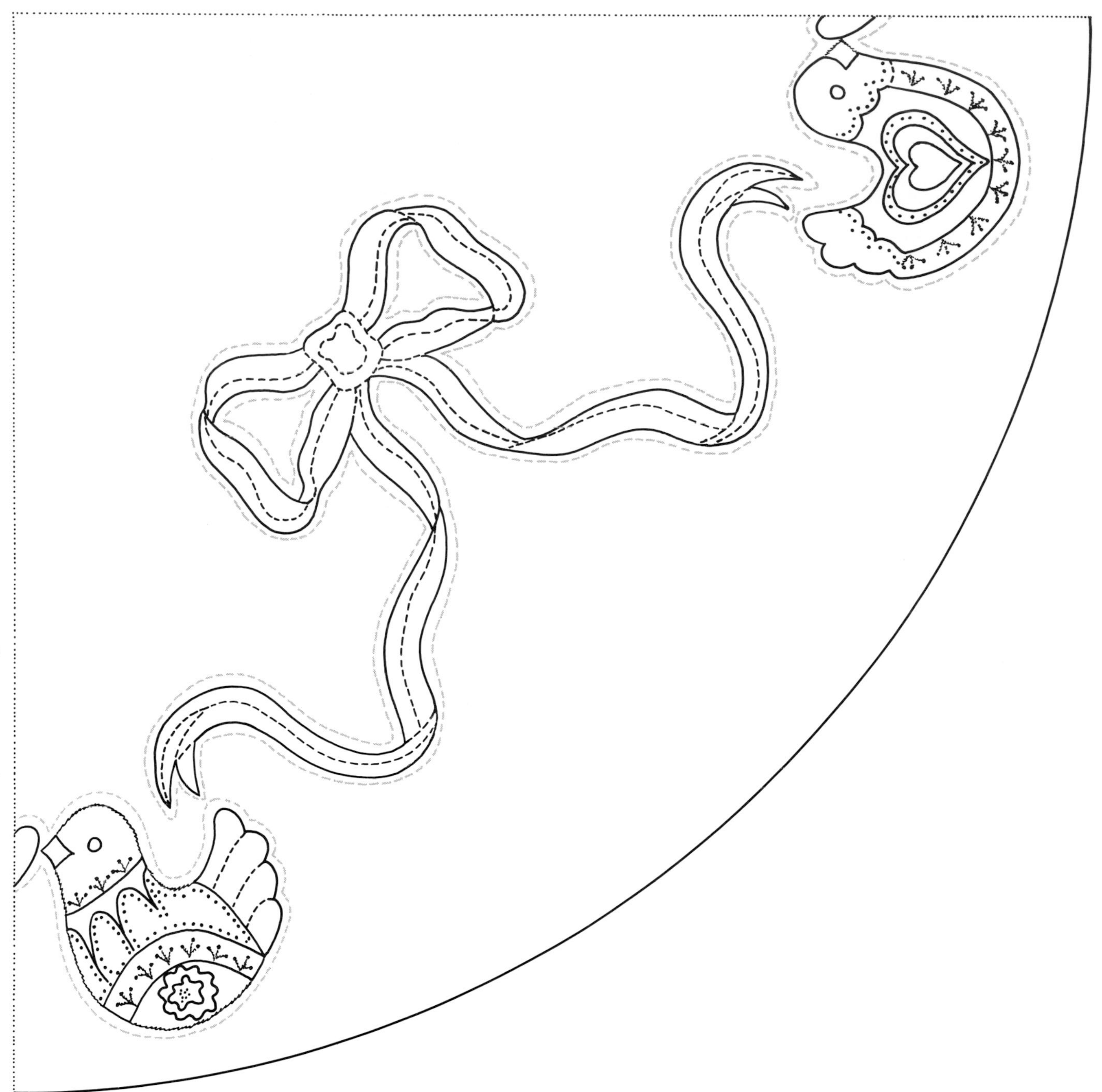
one quarter of design

What to Do When the Thread Tangles and Other Handy Hints

Here is a list of helpful hints that will make your sewing easier and more enjoyable.

1. When hand sewing, avoid using thread any longer than 18 inches (46 cm). This is generally equal to the distance from your fingertips to your elbow.
2. Cut thread for hand sewing at an angle for easy threading through the eye of the needle.
3. When basting, use thread of the same color as the fabric foundation. Thread of a contrasting color might allow fine particles or fibers to show if they break loose or become embedded between the fabric layers of your work.
4. Do not buy fabric just because it's on sale or inexpensive. You usually get what you pay for.
5. Wash your hands before working with fabrics, especially before hand sewing. Light-colored fabrics soil easily.
6. Needles with large eyes make for easier threading.

7. A binding, edging, or ruffle should complement the finished article. It should add to, or assist, the overall design.
8. Be careful when threading your needle that there aren't any lipstick smudges on the thread. These are not always visible until after the stitches are in place.
9. When attaching lace rosettes or small doilies for added surface texture, use french knots or small beads. Also use these to secure ribbon adornments. Try spacing the knots and beads irregularly.
10. To keep stored items free from mildew, a light bulb (protected from contact with clothing or fabric) left burning in the closet is a good safeguard.
11. If you prick your finger while hand sewing and leave tiny spots of blood on your work, a little saliva is the best way to quickly remove the spots before they dry and permanently stain the fabric.
12. Oil, perspiration, hand lotion, and pencil lead can leave unsightly smudges on an otherwise unspoiled piece of needlework.
13. Fabric used to back or line a shadow-quilted project should color-coordinate with the fabrics on the front and be of similar fiber content.
14. Hand stitches made with a contrasting colored thread will show imperfections more readily than those stitched with a less contrasting color.
15. Bay leaves or potpourri can be enclosed in a bag of net or tulle and tied over a garment's hanger for a nice scent. Ribbons, attached to the bag, will allow it to be lowered into the garment.
16. Ribbons used for embellishment add a personal touch to any project. Try to select a variety of sizes, shapes, textures, and colors. Avoid combining only ribbons of a matching color.
17. No hint of a knot or of any fasten-off stitches should be visible from the front side of your finished piece.
18. Never knot your floss or thread when hand stitching is finished. Weave or lace the threads through the stitches on the back side of the piece, positioning them behind colored fabrics if possible.
19. If floss or thread is twisting while you're hand stitching, drop the needle and let it dangle, allowing the thread to unwind.
20. Laces dyed in a strong brewed coffee solution tend to develop a creamy ecru hue. This is true for pale prints and light-colored solid fabrics as well.
21. Use brewed tea, not instant, to tea-dye fabric and trims. Some herbal teas produce a pinkish cast.
22. Light-colored fabric pieces placed over darker fabrics need to be lined or backed to prevent the underneath colors from showing through. A fusible or iron-on interfacing can be used for this. Do your fusing *before* cutting out your design insert pieces.
23. Leave your shadow-quilting project in a protected place and covered when you're not working on it. Dust in the air can collect in the layers. Other hazards include children's inquisitive little hands, which are often sticky; sunlight, which can fade bright colors; and pets with shedding hair and a fondness for curling up right in the middle of your work.
24. Discover the fun of buttons, old and new. Try embellishing your finished work with groupings of overlapping buttons—all of them light, creamy, and delicate. Use the back sides of some of them to capture the iridescence of mother-of-pearl.
25. Keep your finished work smelling fresh. Store it with a small packet of California bay leaves.
26. Never carry, or float, your stitching thread

or floss more than ½ inch (1.3 cm) along the back of your work. A shadow may be visible from the front if you are working with light-colored fabrics.

27. Never leave a needle "parked" in your work. It may rust.

28. When choosing colors, work in white surroundings. A fabric's true color may be slightly altered in a room with green walls or a brown carpet, for instance.

29. Place white fabric, illustration, or mat board over wood or dark-colored surfaces to assist you in your color selection. A temporary white working surface also helps when tracing patterns onto paper or fabric.

30. Check the remnant tables for fabric, but buy only after careful consideration. A remnant may be a much larger cut than you need and can end up costing you more.

31. Contrasting threads, ribbon clusters, bows, trims, metallic threads, ropes, piping, and laces add texture variations, but they need to be used selectively. Shadow quilting is soft and can be easily overpowered.

32. Keep the cut design inserts free of wrinkles, lint, and dust. After they are cut and waiting to be positioned, also keep their edges protected from fraying. Place them inside a folded sheet of heavy white or bond paper. Don't use a large envelope because the design inserts will have to be slid in and out, which may cause their edges to fray.

33. Different sizes and colors of ribbons can be combined to make bows that are elegant and tastefully distinctive.

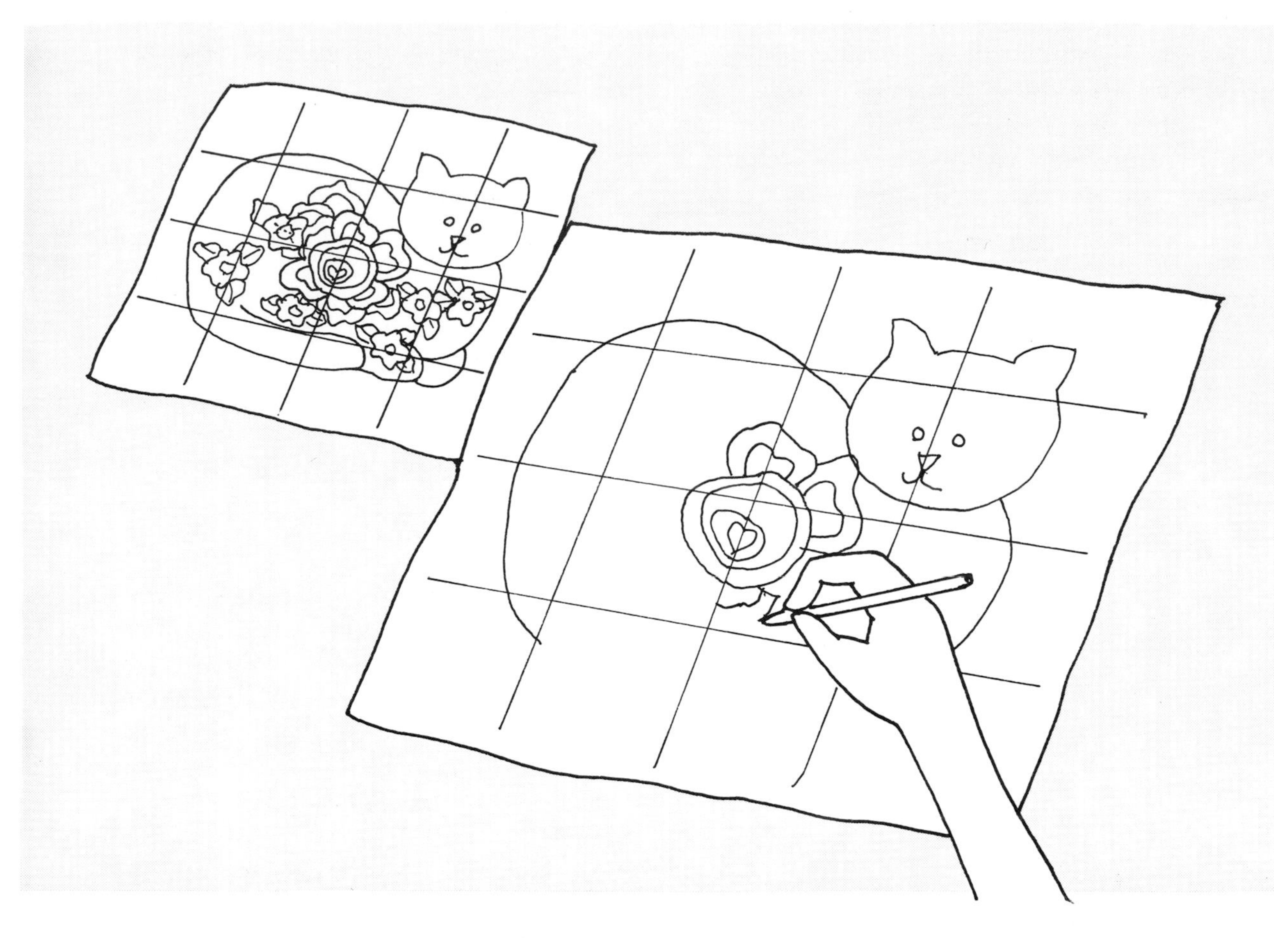

Enlarging, Reducing, and Transferring Designs

Given designs are rarely the exact size you need for the specific project of your choice, so knowing how to enlarge or reduce a design is a great help. Don't hesitate to go ahead and use a design you've selected rather than opt for another that is less to your liking but just the right size. It's not hard to reduce or enlarge designs. You don't need any expensive equipment or training, so come on and try it.

ENLARGING AND REDUCING

Grid Technique

Trace the design you wish to enlarge or reduce onto a sheet of paper that you've marked with a grid pattern of 1-inch (2.5-cm) squares. Pattern paper, sold in most sewing stores, is ideal for this purpose because it is covered with dots placed at 1-inch (2.5 cm) intervals. On a second sheet of paper of approximately the desired finished size of your design, draw the same number of squares as are on the original grid. The squares will be larger or smaller, depending on whether you are enlarging or reducing the original design. Carefully draw the design from each square on the original traced grid to each corresponding square in the second grid.

Photostat

A simpler method is to have a photostat, or PMT (photo mechanical transfer), made to your specifications. This is the technique I use most often for my own work. The cost of a PMT is reasonable if the desired reduction or enlargement is small, say a ten- or twenty-percent change, but the price increases as the size of the enlargement or reduction grows. It is not uncommon to need a design enlarged by 300 or 400 percent. Check the yellow pages of your telephone book under the headings of "Blueprint Services" or "Photo Copying Service" for the photostat or PMT service nearest you. You might also phone first to see if you can wait while the work is being done so you won't have to make a second trip to pick it up in a day or so. I always try to eliminate extra wear, tear, and mileage on my car as well as on myself.

Opaque Projector

An opaque projector can be used to project and magnify your design onto a wall or screen on which you have placed a sheet of paper. The design can then be traced to any larger-scaled proportion you select. Check with your public library or local schools to see if they have a projector that could be made available to you. Some of the needlecraft, quilting, or craft shops are now making opaque projectors available to their customers for either purchase or rental at a very reasonable fee. Several companies selling projectors are listed under "Mail Order Sources for Goods and Services" at the back of this book.

Transferring

The main technique for transferring a design to fabric for shadow quilting is illustrated and explained on pages 21–23.

This technique is suitable 90 percent of the time, but your project may happen to fall into the other 10 percent, usually resulting from the use of a dark fabric that does not allow the design to show through it. If so, there are several solutions that can be used to rescue you.

1. Retrace or darken the lines of the design with a fine-pointed felt-tipped pen with black permanent ink. Tape the design against a window or on a light box, using masking tape across the corners. Position and tape the foundation fabric over the design in the same way. With the foundation fabric stabilized, you will have both hands free to trace onto it, using a white, silver, or pastel marking pencil. The retraced and darkened lines, plus the light coming through the window or the light box, make any dark fabric a cinch to work with. (For how to make your own light box, see number 3, on next page)

2. Dressmaker's carbon can come to your assistance when the fabric that needs the design transferred onto it is dark and the window or light-box technique won't work. Using a fine-pointed felt-tipped pen with black permanent ink, trace your design onto a fresh sheet of paper. Next, pin all four corners of the new tracing over the foundation fabric. A sheet or piece of dressmaker's carbon can then be slipped between the traced design and the fabric. Trace over the design, using a ball-point pen that no longer has any ink in it. The ball point rolls easily over the paper and helps prevent cutting or tearing through, as often occurs with most other marking tools. When I come across a worn-out ball-point pen that has a good roller point, I store it in my supply box with a bright ribbon tied around it to identify it as something valuable that I don't discard just because it's out of ink.

A word of caution. Be sure to test dressmaker's carbon on the fabrics to which it will be applied, checking to make sure that the marks are removable. Many dressmaker's carbons in the home-sewing or needlework market today will not wash out.

3. A light box is a great tool for transferring designs, besides being handy for other design work. Light boxes tend to be expensive at an art supply, stationery, or quilt shop, so I suggest you try to make your own. Start with a large but sturdy corrugated cardboard box, cutting the sides down until they are approximately 6 inches (15 cm) tall. Purchase a sheet of ¼-inch-thick (6-mm) glass large enough to extend 1 inch or more beyond the top edges of the box. Have the glass store sand and polish the edges of the glass; this procedure takes only a few minutes, and the cost should be low. If, however, you bring the glass home unsanded, cover the edges yourself, using masking tape.

Place a cool light source, such as a short fluorescent-tube fixture, onto the bottom of the box. Avoid conventional bulbs, which give off heat that could result in a fire.

I would also suggest that you cut several holes, each the size of a half-dollar and spaced about 4 inches (10 cm) apart, along the two shorter sides of the box to allow for air circulation, therefore helping the box stay cooler when in use.

The advantage of a light box is that it allows you to work with a horizontal surface rather than having to do your tracing up against a window. Also, when you work or trace against a window, you cannot always count on the strength of the light coming through from the opposite side. But the light box provides you with a reliable light source both day and night, and it is portable; it can be carried from one room to another or even be easily transported to another location.

4. If you own a glass-topped coffee or end table, don't overlook the possibility of putting it to double use, as a sometime light box. The same goes for that dining-room table that opens to hold table leaves. A sheet of glass cut to the appropriate size can be set into the opening, giving you the perfect height for a light box. When a lamp is placed on the floor beneath the glass, you become the immediate owner of an inexpensive, yet very practical, light table.

Expanding Designs and Creating Your Own

Have you ever looked at a pattern in your favorite store or at a decorative item your friend has just finished and said to yourself, "I could change a few things and it would look better," or "I can't find what I really want"?

If you have had such thoughts, this chapter is especially for you because in it we're going to explore the wonderful world of creativity. I will help you to experience the heady excitement (and frustration) that goes with achievement as you delve into your inner self, the true source of creativity.

Designing is an extension of yourself. It is an opportunity to create something all your own. Designing allows you to experience the joy and satisfaction of transforming an intangible feeling into a tangible object that you and others can enjoy.

Even if you aren't now planning to design something from scratch, think of how nice it would be to have the ability, should you ever want to change or add something to a design. Think of the pride as you place your own mark on something and give it that extra-special touch.

YOU CAN DO IT

Most of us grow up feeling very inadequate about our ability to create or design. We often think we cannot learn to be creative or that we are somehow lacking in original thought and expression. Too often we have not been encouraged or guided toward improving our creative self.

We will always meet people who have higher creativity levels than ours, but don't let this intimidate you or slow you down. No matter what level you are at now, you can improve your creativity if you have the desire. On the following pages, we will explore ways you can develop your creativity, and you will find lists of sources for further inspiration. They are well worth reading again and again when your creative self-worth needs bolstering.

Age or lack of training doesn't matter. There are people like Grandma Moses, for example, who didn't start to paint until very late in life. Yet she had had dormant talent all those years. Maybe you too can unearth your dormant creative talents and give designing a chance. You may surprise everybody, especially yourself.

I often have people look at my work and exclaim that they simply don't have the natural ability to create such designs. When I hear that type of comment, I paraphrase an old proverb, "Creativity is ten percent inspiration and ninety percent perspiration." Think about it and then let yourself reach out and experiment. Remember, it can only lead to a rewarding experience or a learning experience—and in either case, you win.

FINDING YOUR BEST CREATIVE ENVIRONMENT

An important part of the designing process is that you understand your creative environment. Each of us can benefit from the knowledge of how we work best and the awareness of how creativity is handled. Take a few moments to look over the questions below; then make notes over the next few weeks on your observations about your creative environment.

1. Are you a morning or a night person, or somewhere in between? When is the time that you feel at your creative best, or does it vary? Is it at the break of dawn, when the first rays of sunlight streak across the morning sky, or at the end of day, when your chores are finally laid to rest? Perhaps it is after the family has gone off to work, school, or play. Make a conscious effort to record those very special moments when you feel your "creative juices" come alive and beg to be released. After all, you can handle the daily busyness of life at almost any time, but you can create only when you are in the mood to do so.

2. What type of environment makes your creativity flow? Does music in the background help or hinder? Can you tune out distracting sounds, or do they disturb your psyche? Do you feel that one area or room is more conducive to thinking than another? Do you prefer a dim environment or a bright atmosphere? Do you visualize better in one chair than another?

3. What is your span of creative attention? Is it one, two, or maybe three hours? Is it best for you not to stop for more than a few minutes at a time, or does a twenty-minute break every hour or so refresh and rejuvenate the creative cells? Are you the type of person who prefers to work at a design for only a half hour every day, or do you stick with it as long as you possibly can in one sitting?

As for my creative side, I'm relaxed and freshest, able to flow or move with creative problems, challenges, or dictates, early in the morning. That is why I set aside this time of day for design work, business, new proposals, or any problems that have to be dealt with. I don't use or edge into my creative time by showering or getting dressed, fixing breakfast, making beds, or straightening the house. For me, this prime creative time comes only once, in that first period of my awakened day. Other necessities can wait for the hours when I'm less creative. My creativity cannot wait.

If you were a guest in my home, this is probably what you would see. I get up in the morning between 6:30 and 7:00 A.M., stumble around a little, enjoy a glass of juice and fix a cup of tea, doing just enough to wake up. Then I sit down and begin working. I rarely feel physically refreshed when I first get up in the morning, but the benefits of the night's rest soon become apparent as I start to produce. Design problems left over from the day before tend to find a quick solution. Sometimes with only a little maneuvering, they come to a satisfactory conclusion. It's a lot better than pushing the "dead horse" of yesterday, when my creativity was flagging.

My prime creative time lasts for three to four hours, then slowly tapers off. If several designs need new input, it's important not to devote all my best working hours to only one. Don't assume that I work only three or four hours a day. I put an average of ten to fourteen hours a day into my chosen field, usually seven days a week. These other hours are used in organizing, ordering, planning, and doing the stitching itself, all activities that take less creativity.

At times I get sidetracked and miss my best creative time. Each of us has to see to the other aspects of life, which for me have included driving through the hills looking for one very sneaky dog who thought he'd just wander off and see the rest of the world. And there have been so many other unexpected detours. I remember going to my son's school one morning to hear him explain how a wastepaper basket he was simply standing alongside just happened to explode into flames. It caused quite a commotion that day, postponing his math quiz and wiping out the day for me. Waking up to a leaking roof is always another guaranteed schedule-changer. There will be days like that. When these things happen, you can try later in the day to pick up where a design left off, but it's usually of little use. Creativity can't be pushed. I find that it doesn't help to say, "Hey, I'm ready now, let's get going again."

I feel that it isn't necessary to be a professional designer or needleworker to justify and come to an understanding of what's fulfilling in one's life. Years ago, when my family was still at home and I didn't have an outside career, I sensed that needlework and designing were important to me. The process they encompassed was positive and added something intangible to my life. As one of my stitching friends so aptly said, "It adds hyacinths to the soul." For these reasons, I have always given needlework a firmly established niche in my daily environment.

When I was a full-time homemaker, my creative needs were much the same as today. Therefore I blended my needlework and designing with what might be termed family-oriented activities. The solution was to get up earlier in the morning, two or three hours before the rest of the family, so I could work free of interruption and noise. I quickly learned that a short nap in the early afternoon balanced out the early morning hours. Many homemaking jobs were shuffled to the late hours of the afternoon or to the evening. What you might call conventional housework, such as vacuuming, dusting, cleaning the bathrooms, refrigerator, and so forth, was finished at night.

Each of us is different in the way we work and how we handle creativity. One way of doing design work is not better or worse than another; it is just different. Whatever works best for you is the right way. Remember also that we change and don't stay in an old routine just because "we've always done it that way." Be honest and observant about yourself, get to know and listen to your creative self; you will be far more creative for the effort.

DESIGNING REQUIRES TIME

At some point in my life, I envisioned an artist or designer as someone who sits down and draws or lays things out perfectly, just right, ready to be executed, leaving the designer free to whip on to the next project or design. Well, this isn't the case with me, and after working with other designers, I've found that it isn't the case with any of them either. The designing process is usually slow and drawn out, sometimes actually painful. Unless you experience it, it's difficult to understand how something so exciting and exhilarating can be so frustrating at the same time.

A design will rarely progress to its final form as you thought it would. One aspect of the design may move quickly, while other parts may demand careful developing or refining. This, coupled with adequate time for the designer to get away and reflect on the design, is essentially what the design process is about.

When I begin a design, the basic idea will have been tossing around in my mind for days, weeks, and in some cases, months. The amount of time spent on the physical process is often minor compared to the time required for the developing thought that goes into a design decision. When I'm asked how long a particular design took me to bring to fruition, I can make only a guess. There is no way to accurately calculate the amount of mental sifting that went into a design long before the physical process was initiated.

I start the designing process by identifying the end product, pinpointing in my mind what it will be. Next, I envision the finished product in its final setting, thinking about how and where it will be used. As an example, if I'm planning a pillow, I need to have a feel about the area and the atmosphere of the setting in which it will be placed. This guides me in planning the pillow's size and design area. For instance, I normally wouldn't plan an Art Deco pillow design for use with a primitive country coverlet. If a bolster was being placed on a young boy's bed, I'd most likely avoid thinking in terms of pastel or light colors. Instead, I'd plan to use bold colors, worked from sturdy, washable fabrics.

After the planning and designing are completed, the actual production begins. Necessary changes will become apparent as the work progresses; after all, a design is only a plan to work from, a blueprint, so to speak.

I have never worked on a design that moved smoothly from start to finish. Somewhere along the way, it offered some resistance, and this can be part of the fun of developing a design. I don't look at this as a negative characteristic, but rather as an often-expected occurrence. It's just the nature of the beast.

I frequently tell students that developing a design is similar to raising a child—you need to watch and parent it as it grows. When a design is in its beginning stages, it's too soon to predict how it will flow. When a baby is newborn, you don't really know what its temperament is going to be, although there might be some early indications. As time unfolds, a child's future and success in life can't be accurately predicted; there are still many stages the youngster needs to grow through. Similarly, we also have to parent or nurture a design, expecting a lot from it, hoping for the best and allowing time to assist us as we move through the unpredictable stages. Even when the end is in sight, the difference between a good design and a great design hasn't yet been determined. Remember to allow sufficient time for the design to completely mature.

The next time you see a lovely piece of needlework or a beautiful, well-behaved child, know that it didn't just happen. It took careful planning, skill, and most of all, time.

COPYING VERSUS ORIGINALITY

It isn't unusual to create a design that you feel is original, only to find later on something with a similar motif or feeling. Although I know that all my work is original, I cannot say that there hasn't been another presentation sometime, somewhere, that expressed the same feeling as mine. I see the originality of a design as determined by a combination of (a) the placement of the design, (b) the proportions of the design and its units, (c) the relationship of the design to the less-important motifs blended with it, (d) the inner action of color, and (e) the space that surrounds, or sets off, the design.

I don't feel that the needleworker need be concerned about copying per se because, in truth, copying is fairly impossible to do unless a deliberate attempt is made to copy or imitate. Each person's final design will be unique when any one of the above-mentioned points varies from the original.

When teaching classes, I often suggest to my students that they all start with the same design or motif, then develop it into any end product of their choice. Upon completion of the class, I always find that each finished design appears completely different from the others and is unique, although everybody—and there may be twenty or more students—started with the same design. As an example, one student may have executed her work with strong, intense colors, resulting in a bold statement. Another's design may give emphasis to soft background fabrics, while another student may have added textural stitching over a portion of the design area. One student may have enlarged the design and centered it in the middle of her work, as in a place mat. Another may have a place mat with the same design positioned down one side. Thus each student has used the same basic design but emphasized one part of it while, at the same time, eliminating or playing down other parts. While each student can honestly say that hers is an original design based on a prior work, really it will be an original use of a prior design.

EXPANDING A DESIGN

The simplest design can have an almost infinite set of combinations when you know how to dissect and develop it.

Let's have some fun as we explore some simple changes of position and angle, negative and positive space, the pattern, and so forth. Follow along with these basic exercises to create new designs and arrangements. We are using the designs on page 53 as our example.

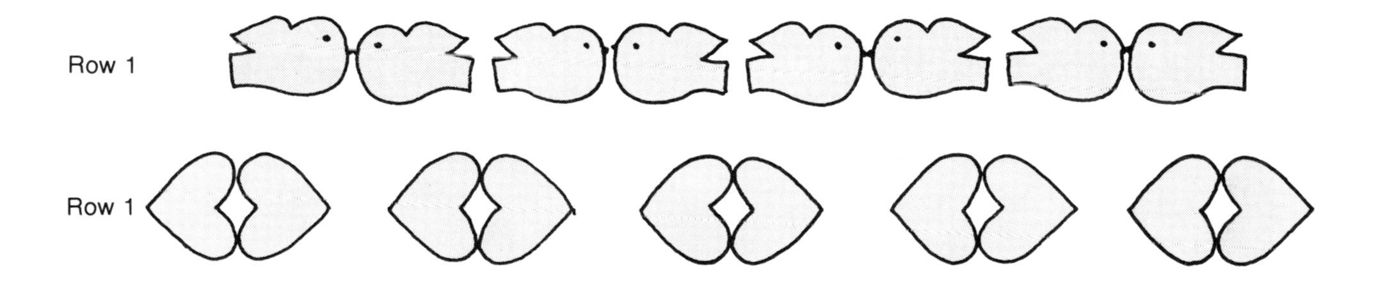

Rows 1 and 2 show how a simple shape can be turned back on itself; this is often described as designing in mirror image. The shape you see is referred to as the positive shape or space. This sets off the background, known as the negative space. Notice the new negative space formed between the wings on the birds in Row 2 and between the hearts in Row 1.

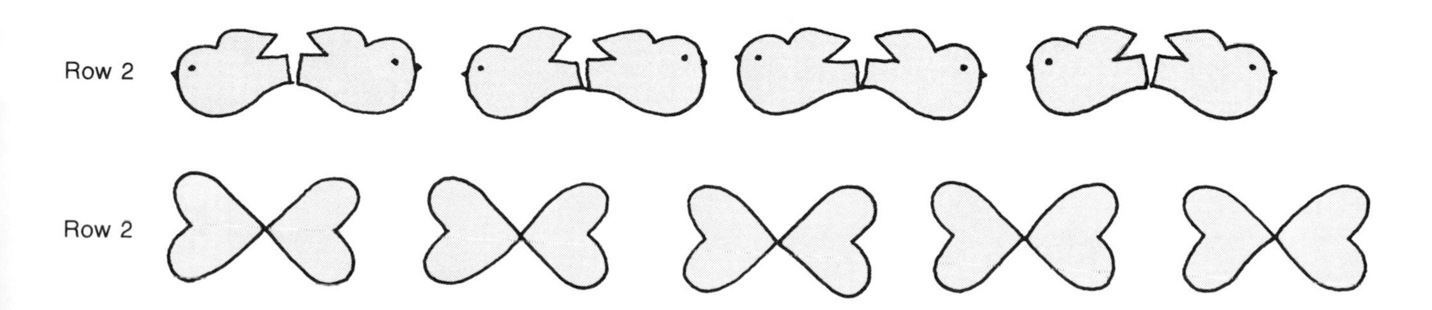

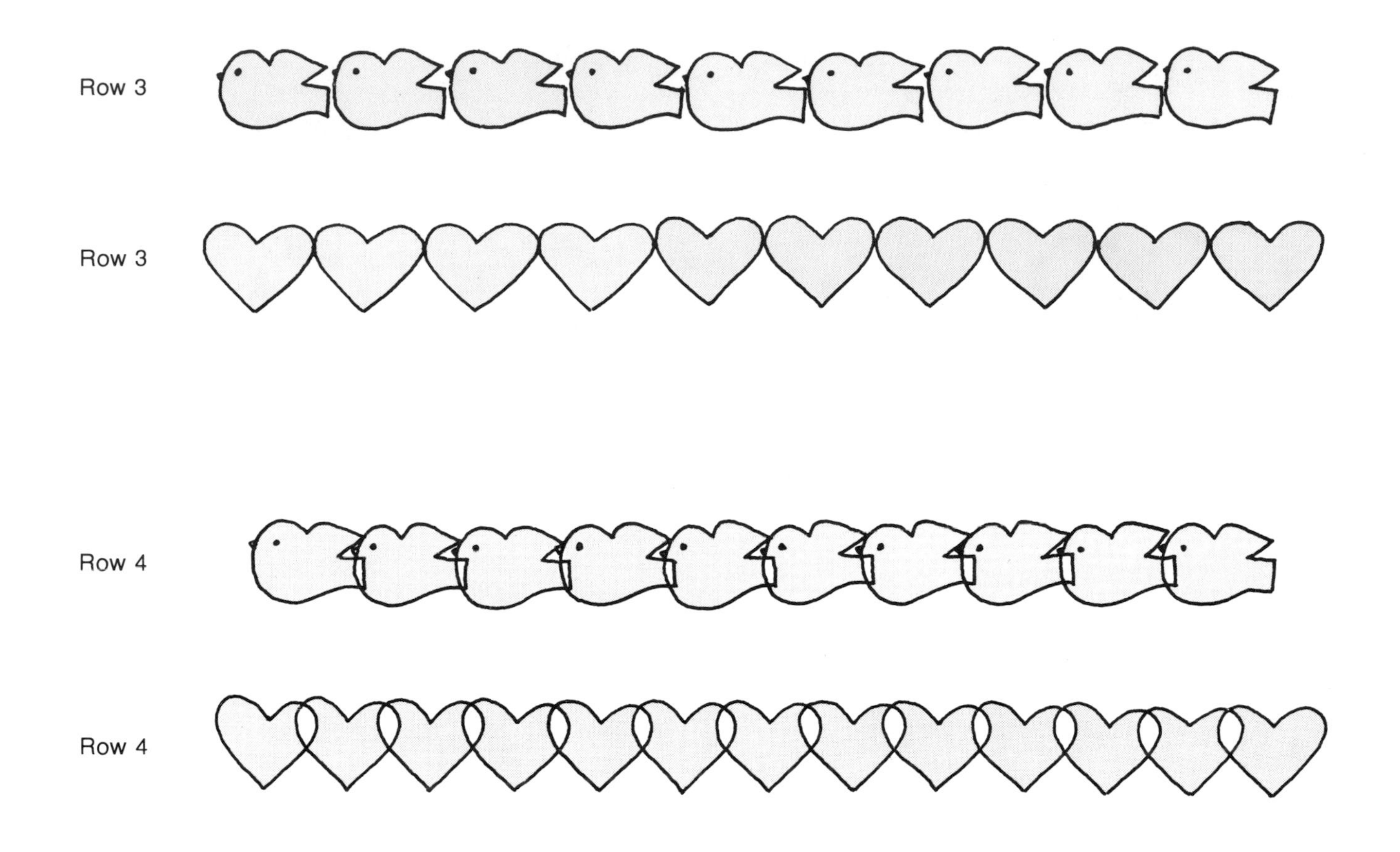

Rows 3 and 4 produce a feeling of strength, of being rigid, disciplined, tight, and strong. Often the shape's arrangement determines the feel of the design. Overlapping shapes can produce strong forms. New patterns, as shown by the white spaces within the shapes, have also been created.

Row 5 suggests the way in which a shape can be positioned at varying heights but with regularity and discipline.

Row 6 illustrates how angling a shape can produce a delicacy of line. Notice how the birds, when worked in pairs, form interesting negative space.

Row 7 returns once again to a feeling of being compact, rigid, and strong.

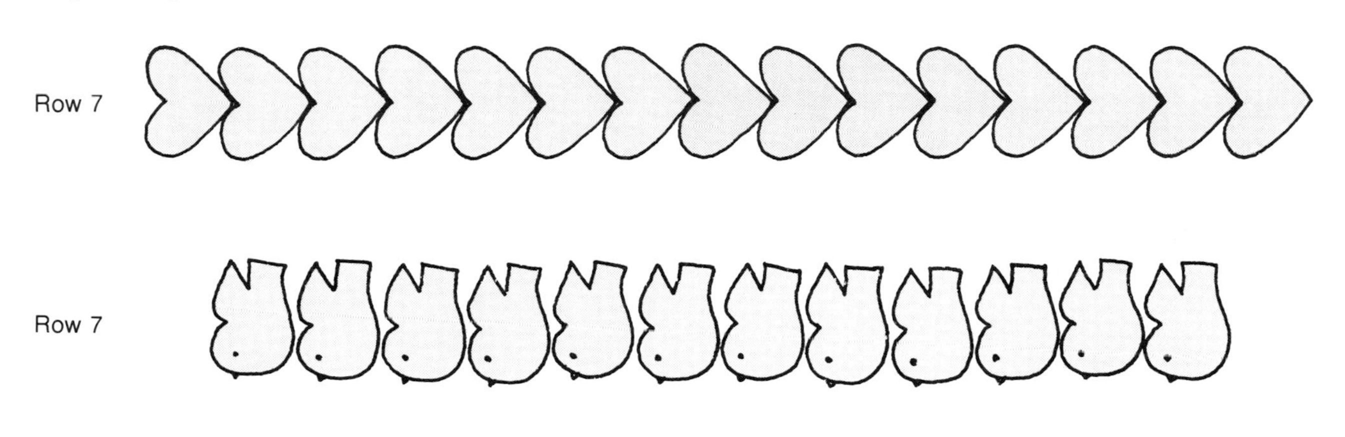

Working with Two Shapes

All six of these designs are produced by using the same two shapes. Which design do you like the best? Why? Which one is the least appealing? Why? Can you expand on this method of developing designs and create three additional ways to combine the bird and heart motifs? Each time a new unit is made or composed, it is repeated so that the developing pattern becomes more apparent. Notice the negative space or background area that the positive space or design motifs produce. Sometimes squinting or standing back from artwork makes this delineation easier to see.

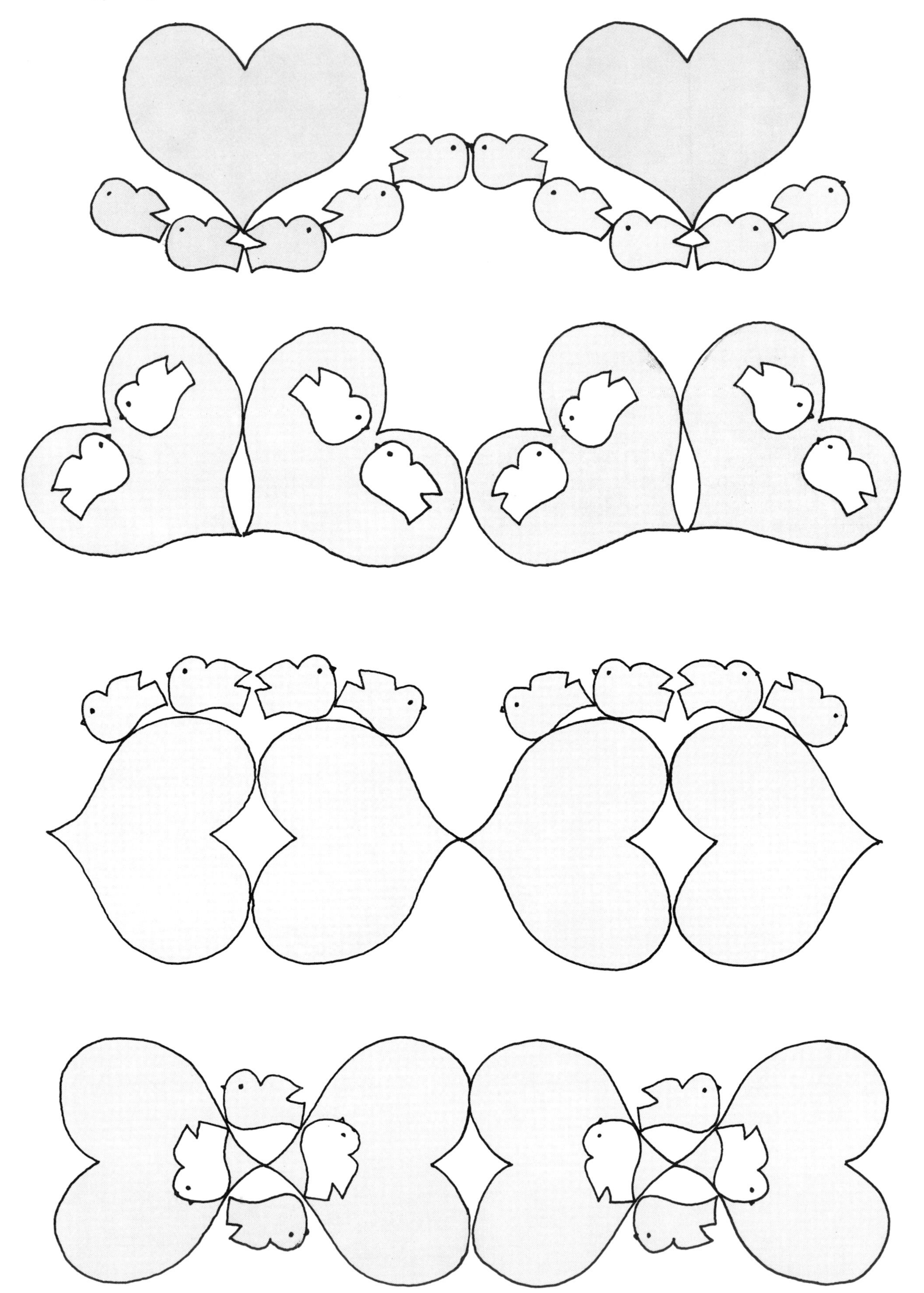

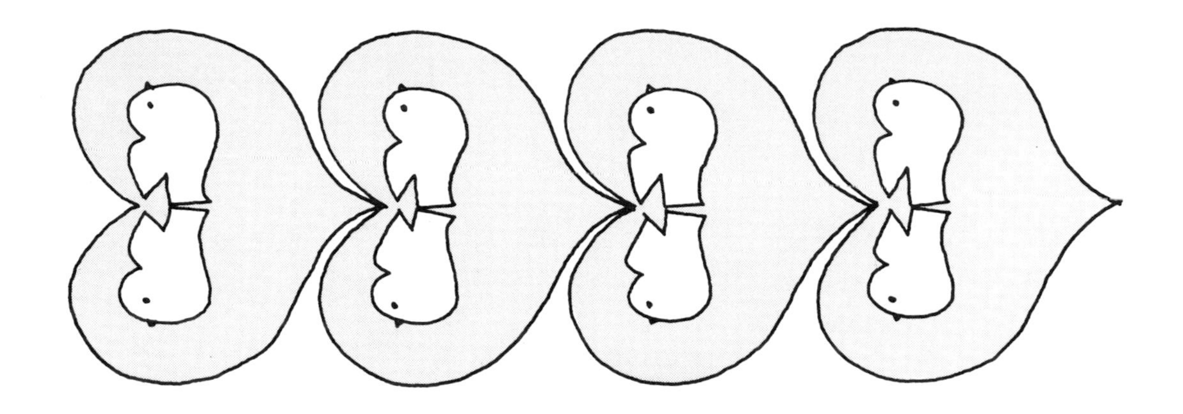

Working with Three Shapes

With the element of the flower added to our two previous shapes, more variations of design and pattern begin to emerge. Try to vary the spacing between the design units. Would the design look as appealing if the units were placed ½ inch (1.3 cm) apart? Would the units work as effectively if they were positioned on a diagonal? Could they be stair-stepped, one slightly above the other? Try overlapping some of the units. What happens to the negative space around the units when you rearrange their position, angle, or closeness to another unit?

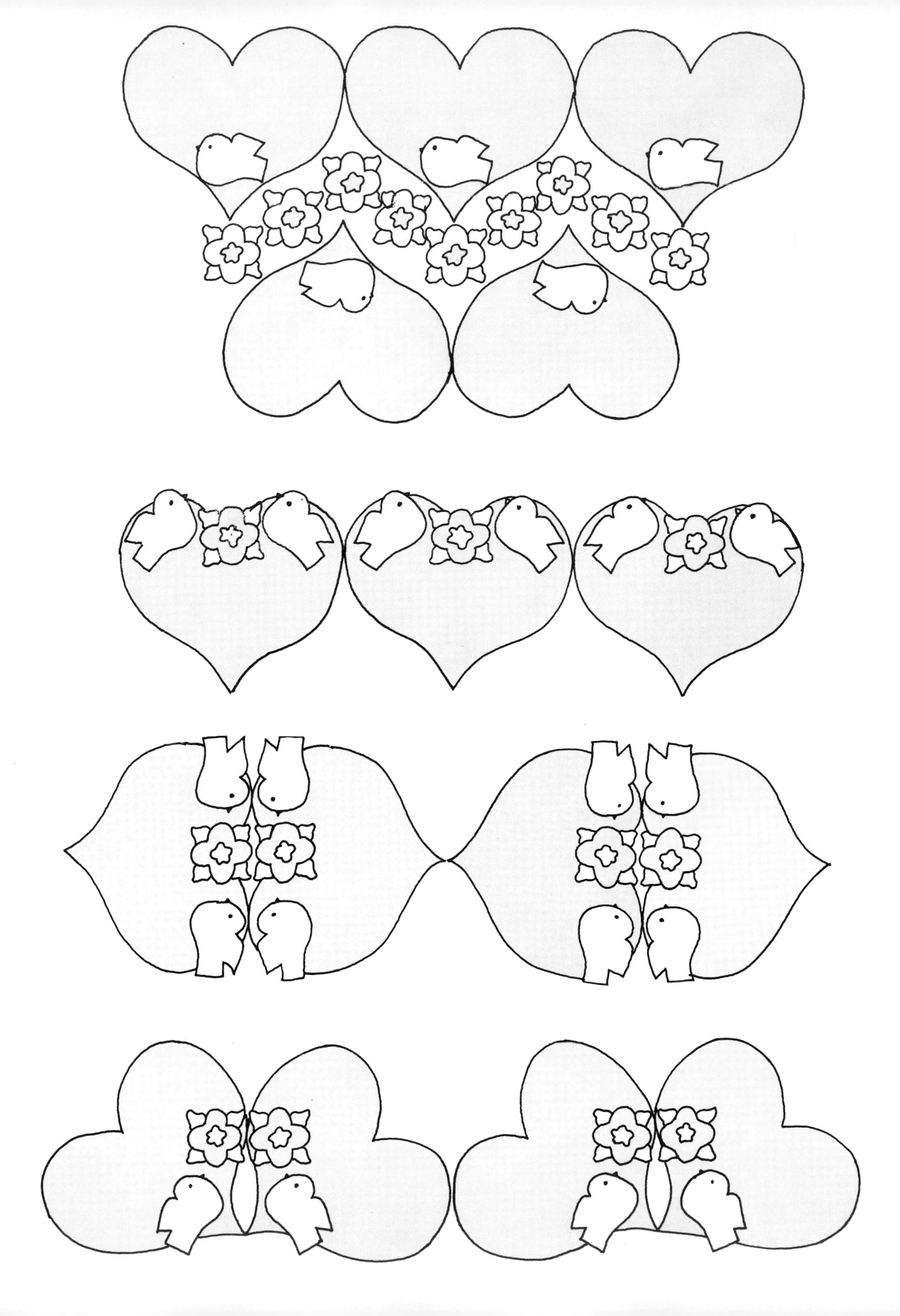

Start with a Design

Take one design and eliminate some of its parts. Reposition the remaining units to create a new composition. Make the new design formal, or symmetrically balanced. Then make an informal, or asymmetrical, arrangement.

Using one design, reproduce it in such a way as to form new units. Try clusters of three, four, five, and maybe even six units. Vary the space between the units. Reposition parts of the design to help the units stay in touch or relate to each other. Study the negative spaces and note how they become very strong, almost competing with the positive spaces.

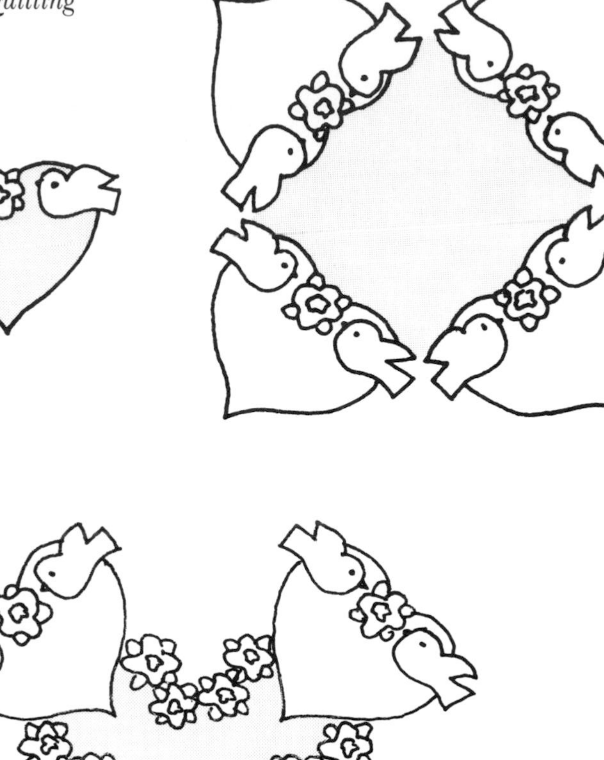

Working with a Pattern

Any area or design can be divided or broken with lines and shapes to develop a pattern. Pattern gives richness and complexity to the design; at times it can even be made the focal point. Shown here are three ways to break up inside space with the use of lines. Some are flowing and parallel to the original design's edges; others are parallel only to themselves, dividing the original shape in half. Try varying the closeness of parallel lines. Can you, through the use of curving lines, make the bottom half of the design appear lighter than the top half? Can you, with the use of lines, divide the original shape into three equal sections? Or four sections? How about making three unequal sections?

When a new unit is formed from one basic design, additional lines and shapes can be applied to produce a pattern. Pattern can be developed within the original design area only, as shown in designs 1, 2, and 3. It can be added to the background or negative space created when the unit was formed in design 4. Pattern can also be developed in both the positive and negative areas, as seen in designs 5 and 6.

These are just a few, simple ways to expand the potential within a design. Every design within this book can be explored similarly.

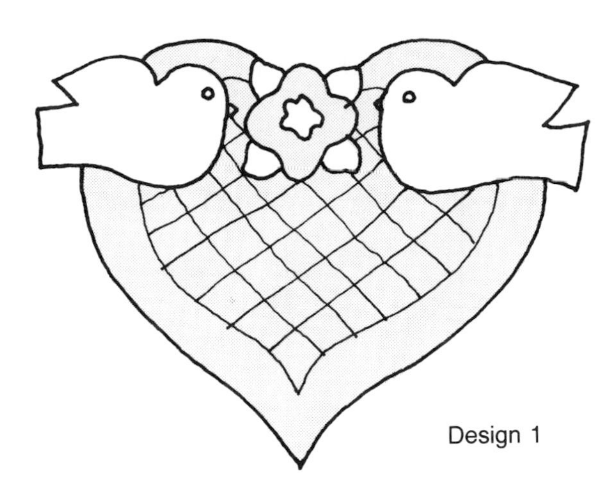

Design 1

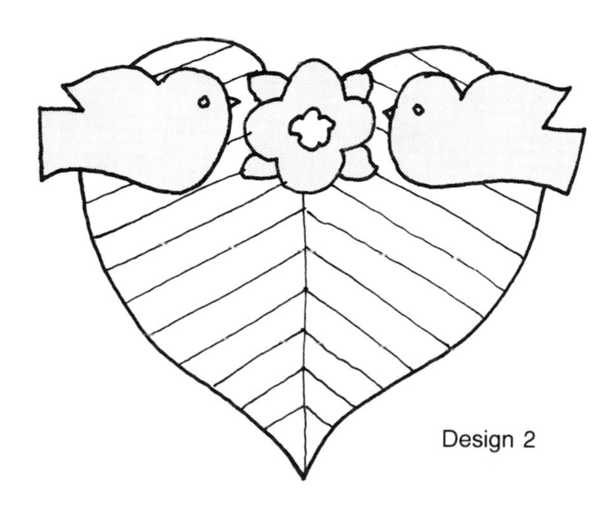

Design 2

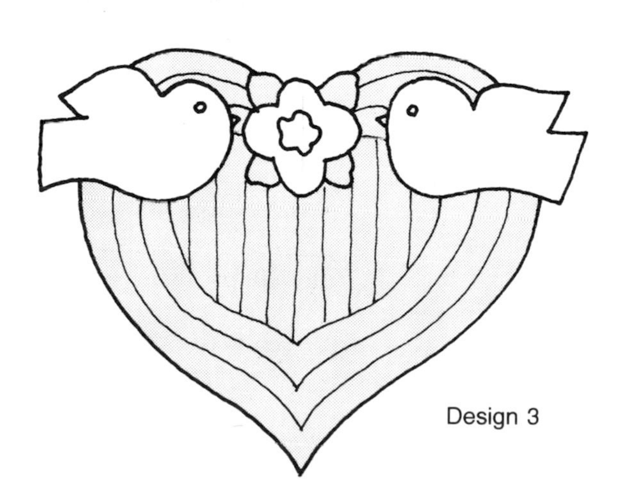

Design 3

Design 4

Design 5

Design 6

SEE, FEEL, THINK—THEN DO

The nature of beauty is a subject argued down through the ages. I am not about to try to define beauty except to say that it is something you feel. No one will argue that a little boy's dirty face as he licks a big ice-cream cone is not something short of exquisite beauty, as is a young girl in her first formal gown. Why are they beautiful?—because they just are. So it is with hand-stitched creations. Shadow quilting often has an unexplainable, but definite, beauty.

We all have had those feelings of "Oh, I just love that" or "Ugly, really ugly." The feelings are there all right, but have you asked yourself "Why?" The reasons that one thing appeals to us and another doesn't are varied. Feelings are often complex and difficult to explain. It is not as simple as "black versus white." When we view something as beautiful, it is a personal preference or prejudice. Maybe you are unconsciously associating a color or pattern with someone or someplace that has strong memories for you. The good or bad memories often transcend to that color or pattern, and you react to the feelings of memory rather than to the actual color or pattern.

Personally, I do not like a particular shade of green. My mother's overwhelming use of the color to decorate almost our entire home is still vivid in my memory. As long as I'm aware of this prejudice, I can work around it. At times I deliberately make myself work with various green fabrics and am usually happy with the beauty that comes from their interaction. One time I even purposely decided to design a quilt that would use two colors I felt would be unattractive together. Of course, I could have predicted that green would be one of those two colors.

Look carefully at your surroundings and be aware of what you see. What is your reaction to that carpet, kitchen tile, or dish design? Learn to analyze your feelings about the color, style, and design of objects around you. Note the clothing and accessories of people you meet; note the calendar on the wall, the pattern and design of the print blouse in your closet. Fall into the daily practice of looking at the world in a very new light and learn to question why you like that planter and dislike the wallpaper in the restaurant. Look beyond your surface reaction to an object and respond to its basic design, pattern, color, texture, and balance. Look deep within and discover why it is appealing to you, or not. Note the sense of order or the lack of harmony in a design. Feel the flow of rhythm or lack thereof in that magazine ad or logo. Plunge yourself into a design and wrap yourself in it. Really be aware of your feelings. Whenever something elicits a response from you, try to feel and listen to what you are seeing and sensing. Dig a little deeper, if you can, to gain fresh insight for the basis of your own development. This type of insight takes practice, but it is well worth your efforts.

You will be rewarded with a storehouse of ideas, both likes and dislikes, that you can build on when designing. You will understand your preferences and attitudes toward a design. You will instantly know what works or doesn't work for you. You will discern patterns, be aware of your feelings toward them, and be able to analyze them quickly for your own benefit. In your projects, you will soon find yourself adding and subtracting ideas until you have just what you want in a design. Look around, see, feel, think, and if you are inspired, don't hesitate to go full speed ahead.

SOURCES OF INSPIRATION

There are many resources and sources that can help to expand your level of creativity, regardless of your income or geographic location.

- Enroll in a class on design. These are offered through some public school systems, frequently in adult education programs, and in art schools.
- Participate in classes and/or workshops that have needlework or other needle-art instruction with emphasis on design. Some good sources for these classes might be the YWCA, your local city park and recreation department, or a private organization. Check your local newspaper and community newsletters.
- Needlework-related businesses often sponsor classes, seminars, or workshops in the field of design. Inquire at your local craft and hobby shops, needlework stores, quilting shops, and fabric stores.
- Organizations such as the Embroiderer's Guild of America and the National Quilting Association are outstanding sources for information. They have ongoing educational and enrichment programs conducted through the mail. Many of these programs lead to certification within the organization.
- Engage a teacher of your own, gathering several other persons with mutual interests to form a private study group.
- Study on your own, with the aid of magazines and other publications. Search out books from your local bookstores or at the library, bookmobile, or from your friends. Don't overlook your local needlework stores, quilting shops, and fabric stores for excellent reference manuals. In the back of this book I have listed some excellent mail-order sources for publications.
- Study every day for a set length of time within your own environment, making it a point to observe and record design inspirations. This is possible whether you are confined to bed, snowed in, obliged to commute into the city every day, or are a full-time homemaker. Here are some suggestions to get you started.

When walking to and from the mailbox, observe designs in:

The mailbox itself, its mountings or stand

Printing styles, placement of printing on letterheads, and line drawings found within the mail

The pattern within the sidewalk, the cracks in the cement, the height of the curbs, the grating in the gutters, the parking-strip widths

The shape the plant beds make around the house or buildings
The style of window treatment, placement of doors and windows, the textures of building materials
The doorknob or knocker; see how the door is decorated with moldings or trims
The style, size, and placement of the house numbers

In your bedroom, observe:

The shape and twists on a coat hanger
Door pulls, moldings, and closet handles
The design on a box of tissue
The proportion of a single tissue, the placement of the fold
The number of colors used for your bed linens. How is the design placed? In even rows, facing up, then down, then up? How many different units or designs are used on the linens?
How lampshades and lamp bases are full of amazing curves, pleats, and ridged lines that contrast with the flowing shapes
How pieces of jewelry are full of design information. Study the way in which a clasp or closure is fitted, shaped, etc.

So what's so important about doing an original design? Why would anyone want to go through hours of frustration, sometimes contemplating, occasionally even verbalizing, bad words? You may find yourself taking out your irritation and anger on others. Do you really need to go through all that? Most of my nonstitching friends would find it ridiculous to add this additional stress to life, especially if all they wanted was a simple design to stitch.

I remember one student who said, almost in a confessional manner, that she was taking the class simply to learn the technique. Basically, she wanted to make one item to show her family. She wasn't attracted to the thought of spending many hours in creating a design that would take only a fraction of that time to stitch. When you think about it, here is a happy person. She knows what she wants. She's using her time in the manner of her own choosing.

Designing isn't for everyone, but once you've been "bitten by the needle," it's a safe bet that you won't be satisfied with anything else.

Making Room for You

START SMALL—THINK BIG

If the creative activity found through sewing or needlework is important for your pleasure and well-being, you need a functional space for it. Don't despair if at first it seems that you have no place in which to work in your home. Remember, "Great oaks from little acorns grow." If you have a very strong, forceful urge to create, a place will appear.

Let's set a plan of attack. Look over your household and decide on the exact space you are going to take over. You don't have to say a word to anyone. But start. Perhaps small, but thinking big. Find a corner, then move outward. In a relatively short period of time, your work can spread beyond your original space. When you find that you are outgrowing the end of the dining-room table or that you have overflowed the small area allotted in the corner of a bedroom, start looking around the house to see if any other areas are available; anyplace seldom used is fair game. Of course none of this will come about until you decide that your work is really important to you and then announce it for all the world to hear, good and loud.

The very first time you manage to leave your sewing machine or equipment out, you have started on your way. There doesn't seem to be a set pattern for taking over space. Some of my friends have resorted to starting only with the dining-room table, then flowed down and around it and soon occupied all of that formerly little-used room.

Take a good look around. Any space is really up for consideration. Ask yourself, "How often is this room occupied?" If it sits empty for a great part of the day, why not use it for your new work area? After all, you pay rent or the mortgage and upkeep payments every day, every week, and every month. Why not use and enjoy that paid-for space?

Here's another issue to settle. Often people let their house dictate how it is to be used. But if you are truly the mistress of your house, you will make sure that it is flexible enough to meet the needs of everyone who lives in it. Sometimes it is not the lack of physical space as much as a matter of studying what you have and determining to make some part of it your very own work area. An extra-wide hallway might be called your "workway." A breezeway might be enclosed and called "the studio." A rarely used attic or basement area might become "high loft" or "lower loft." A huge linen closet might be converted to the "great-beginnings closet."

MAKING YOUR SEWING AREA MORE WORKABLE

If you are fortunate enough to be able to plan or remodel your working-sewing area, here are some points to consider.

A recent national survey showed the U shape to be the preferred floor plan among sewers and needleworkers, closely followed by the L shape. If you look over your own work area, you may find that you have already set up one of these work-efficiency plans. An L shape might be built along a single wall with an ironing board at one end to form the L. Another L shape is formed when two walls meet at a corner.

The U shape is equally easy to visualize. It could be formed from three adjoining walls, or two adjoining walls with a sewing-machine cabinet, ironing board, or freestanding work surface extending out to form the third side.

Now here's another tip I often overlooked in the past, and only when I found that I was running into myself did I discover its importance: Give careful thought to planning a workflow pattern. The placement of your sewing machine and the amount of room available for an ironing board usually determine the flow of work. Most sewers, myself included, prefer a right-to-left work flow. I try to keep the flat work surface to the right side of my sewing machine empty for stacking work that I'm going to begin sewing. I also keep the space to the left of my sewing machine cleared to allow the project I'm working with to lie on a flat surface so it is supported. These two surfaces are already provided if your sewing machine is in a cabinet. A swivel chair placed at the sewing machine puts each part of the sewing process within handy reach, just a twist or pivot away.

Be sure that the height of your ironing board can be adjusted. This will enable you, when working at the sewing machine, to simply swivel your chair to one side so you can press as you stitch.

A portable or rolling garment rack will more than pay for itself through the benefits it provides; finished garments can be placed on hangers, helping to eliminate the need for additional pressing. I like to fold work-in-progress over coat hangers, keeping it out of the way but within my vision. A garment rack can be purchased from most department or variety stores, or you may want to check the mail-order catalogs.

One of the least expensive but most effective remodeling tips I recommend is that you consider painting the walls of your work area in off-white or a light pastel color. When finished in soft, light colors, the ceiling and other horizontal surfaces, such as shelving and storage areas, will reflect more light than dark surfaces. This may assist you in the appropriate color selection of fabrics, besides making your work area appear larger.

Sewing, whether by machine or by hand, requires twice the amount of light as does casual reading. Your sewing center needs general lighting as well as focused, adjustable lighting placed next to often-used equipment; a light behind and slightly to the left of your sewing machine is a tremendous help. In my workroom, I keep a tall floor lamp with casters that allows it to be easily moved to either side of my chair.

Take advantage of all the natural daylight you can. If your sewing center has a window, sit so the light comes in over your left shoulder as you sew rather than face directly into the light of the window, which can quickly lead to eye fatigue.

Rugs and pins do not mix, making smooth floor coverings a wise choice for a sewing area. How often I end up moaning and groaning, silently saying to myself words that shouldn't be heard, when a box of pins accidentally falls and the pins disappear like magic into the deep-pile carpeting.

If you have space for a cutting table, plan on making its surface higher than that of an ordinary table. The top of a dining-room table is generally 30 inches (76.5 cm) from the floor. As you may already know from experience, bending over and working on a surface this low can lead to backache and fatigue. If the table were raised to 36 inches (90 cm), you would be standing in a more upright position, and nagging backache could be greatly reduced. You can elevate any table by placing wooden blocks under the legs. I have found coffee cans to be a handy elevating device; when filled with plaster of paris and allowed to harden, they make wonderful leg lifts. They can easily be removed later, so you haven't permanently altered the height of a special table.

A cutting table or surface that allows you to work from all four sides is ideal. Plan to allow at least two feet of clearance along each side so you can move around without being crowded.

WHERE TO STASH YOUR SEWING STUFF

Take some time to organize the smaller storage units in your work area. Once all your equipment is within easy reach, with a place for everything and everything in its place, you will be able to create instead of wasting time searching for things. It's true that "equipment alone does not a masterpiece make," but it would be difficult to create a masterpiece without the right equipment available, at the right time. Just imagine Julia Child in the kitchen, cameras running as she searches frantically for the right mixing spoon. How about Picasso starting on a new painting only to find all his brushes stiff and hardened with paint?

Depending on your budget and space, plan for storage to hold fabrics. To me, this usually indicates some type of shelving. I prefer adjustable shelving, found at most building-supply outlets, lumberyards, or hardware stores. In my own workroom, a large closet was converted to hold row upon row of shelving. Since my stacks of fabrics tend to look more than a little messy most of the time, I'm happy that I can pull the closet doors shut when a non-needleworking guest arrives. If you don't have a closet in which to set shelving, the shelving can always be placed along a wall, out in the room itself; this area can be closed off with pull-up-style mini blinds hung in front of the shelves. Blinds or roll-down wooden shades look attractive and are fairly inexpensive. When your sewing area is part of a large room, blinds or folding doors can enable you to close off or partition your entire work area. This gives carte blanche for your work-in-progress to be left out, yet closes it off from constant viewing by family members and guests.

Rare indeed is the person who has adequate storage for all her fabrics, and as everyone who knows me will attest, I am not one of them. At present, I store fabrics in five different closets and still need more storage. The interior walls of these closets are painted white, and they contain white shelving and overhead lighting.

The top shelves are cut back 3 inches, making them narrower than the lower shelves. This permits the overhead lighting to fall more evenly throughout the closet.

When storing fabrics, sort and organize them into several categories. All solid-colored yardage to be used for shadow quilting is stored in my largest closet. It takes several shelves to hold the sixty or so shades of red that I've collected. I've accumulated so many blue fabrics that I sort them according to dark, medium, or light. I repeat the process for each of the basic color families.

Clear plastic shoeboxes with flat lids are wonderful for such difficult-to-store items as hem tapes, bias bindings, ribbons and elastics, buttons, snaps, and so on. These boxes are sold at most variety or department stores and can also be found in mail-order catalogs. Plastic storage boxes allow you to see everything inside them, and they are stackable. They also come in a variety of sizes, ranging from those that hold a single pair of shoes on up to those used for bulky sweaters. There are even plastic boxes large enough for storing blankets and quilts.

I store all my Simplicity and other commercial patterns upright in open plastic or cardboard shoeboxes. An oversized pattern can be placed on its side to fit into these same boxes. All patterns are stored by categories or groups. Patterns for decorative items such as pillows, sachets, lampshades, and so on are placed together. Other boxes hold patterns for children's clothing, fashion blouses, skirts, sundresses, and so on. These boxes need no labels because the first pattern in the box is an indication of that box's contents.

To use shallow drawers most efficiently, equip them with cutlery trays or interlocking units such as those made by Rubbermaid. With their narrow compartments, these organizers are ideal for storing scissors, X-acto knives, tweezers, seam rippers, and other sharp-pointed tools, and they help to keep odd-sized items in their proper place. Things that roll around in drawers, such as pencils, will be lodged permanently.

If your work area is without shallow drawers, invest in some inexpensive tackle boxes found at a hardware or art supply store. These have lots of compartments, are lightweight and can be shut, or even locked if needed. Tackle boxes are also easy to carry around.

Stacking rolling carts filled with drawers, sliding bins, or baskets can provide both storage and mobility. I use two rolling carts, each containing eight pullout bins. Set on large casters, they are easy to maneuver from the guest closet where they are stored to either my office or any other room where I may be working. At the end of the work week, they're reloaded with projects and rolled back to the closet. I look forward to this great disappearing act when the work week or a deadline is over.

Spools of thread and wound bobbins can be placed in thread beds. This excellent storage tool can be used flat or hung on the wall near your sewing machine. The largest thread beds available hold around seventy spools of thread and allow easy thread selection. Store the bobbins atop their matching-colored spools of thread on the thread bed. All thread ends should be secured through the notch in the end of the spool.

When shopping for a bobbin box, take along one of your own machine bobbins to make sure it fits the prospective box. Most bobbin boxes are available in clear plastic.

If your storage area is limited, you might need to store fabric and patterns in other parts of the house. Consider using stackable storage boxes that can be placed on shelves in the utility area, kitchen, pantry, basement, or back porch. There are even large but shallow boxes designed to slide under the bed or be placed on those hard-to-reach top shelves in closets. All boxes, if not plastic or see-through, should be clearly marked on the outside as to their contents.

At times I'm known as a "bookaholic," and it's impossible for me to store all my treasured books in one location. Those I use most often, usually reference books with "how-to-sew-it" techniques and books on embroidery and needlework, are kept within arm's reach in my work area. Those I use the least, such as books on primitive art, African art, Italian Renaissance costumes, historic costume design, and so on, are stored on the upper shelves of the bookcases in other rooms. All books are grouped into categories, such as children's art, pattern drafting, color and design, general crafts, flower arranging, and many others.

Whoever invented the modern file drawer is my friend forever. A recent count showed that I currently use fifteen file drawers, besides two large blueprint files with twelve shallow, flat drawers. If you've overlooked the value that this commercial equipment can bring to a work and sewing area, study a catalog at your nearest office-supply outlet. Heavy cardboard files start at about $7.00 each; you can work on up to the $300.00 range for fancier models made of veneers and hardwoods.

In my files I keep all my past business transactions and designs as well as my present and future work. Most of my files, though, are used to house the masses of material needed for design reference. The headings on these file drawers read *Christmas, Moon, Stars and Sun, Hearts, Place Mats, Flowers, Children's Clothing, Vegetables, Dolls, Landscapes, Sea Shells, Lampshades, Butterflies, Vines, Cats, Cherries,* to mention only a few. When I begin to work on a new idea or design, I search through my files, then thumb through my books, collecting all material or information that seems appropriate. Then it's off to the drawing board.

My needle-related product pamphlets are stored in magazine file boxes purchased through an office-supply firm. Besides being handy for holding magazines, I use them for storing teaching materials, lecture notes, and handouts. I also have one file box for all the manuals, information, and guarantees for the equipment in my sewing area, such as the iron, clock, electric pencil sharpener, Steamstress or small, hand-held upright steamer, typewriter, radio, and tape recorder.

If my pamphlet storage boxes are to be left out permanently in a room where they can be seen, I cover them with a self-adhering paper or decorate them with colorful fabrics. This gives them a coordinated look, but of course that lasts only a short time. Soon I need more boxes and I have no time to cover the new ones, or the same fabric isn't available, so they turn into a hodgepodge even though my initial intentions were good.

Coffee cans with see-through plastic lids can be put into service to store lace or trims, pieces of ribbons and, of course, a never-ending assortment of ageless buttons. Simple fabric pockets added to the outside of the cans provide even more space.

Pegboards can hold shallow trays and baskets. Consider installing a pegboard on the wall behind your sewing machine or fastening one over a sliding door. Try a panel of pegboard fastened to the inside of a closet door that swings open. A corkboard hung from pegboard or fastened to a wall puts magazine clippings, photos, and sundry cutouts within easy reach.

Don't forget to get large, washable wastepaper baskets; the bigger, the less need for constant emptying. Beware of small wastebaskets. They can tip over easily when you discard heavy magazines or catalogs in them.

Gift Giving

The possibilities for constructing unique and distinctive gifts are almost limitless with shadow quilting because this needlework form can be applied to such a wide variety of items. There's something for almost everyone, even Fido. While there are satisfaction and joy to be had in doing this kind of needlework, the added opportunity it provides for sharing gives even more pleasure to the giver.

The sudden surge of enthusiasm to share shadow quilting through gift giving may arise following a class given through a needlework shop or guild. Or it may start with the simple purchase of a magazine, only to end up in something slightly less than a million-dollar spending spree. For me, a sewing spree is often brought on sometime before the holiday season. In some cases, three or four days before, but if I'm lucky and organized that year, it may start as much as six months earlier. Whatever the case, here are some tips to make your giving a more enjoyable experience.

1. Never make a present for anyone who doesn't want or won't value or truly appreciate a handmade creation. The members of my family always seem most appreciative of hand-assembled or hand-decorated efforts. A hand-knitted afghan or one-of-a-kind wall hanging is special to them. In return, they always make me feel as though this was the best present they ever received.

I've observed other families and friends who are quite the opposite. If a present didn't come from the finest department store, if it isn't a "purchased" present, it is definitely second class—just making do. Being a slow learner, it took me only a couple of years to catch on to this fact in my own gift sharing. After all, if a piece of crystal or glass would be more appreciated, that's what they will get from now on rather than an item into which I put many hours of work, care, and love.

2. Anticipate the cost of materials and the time it will take to make a proposed gift. Have in mind the amount you would spend if you selected a store-purchased item. Thinking ahead like this will help you from plunging into an ambitious project at an inappropriate time. For instance, would you really want to put ninety-seven needleworking hours into creating a shadow-quilted throw or coverlet for a Mother's Day present when actually it would be a more appropriate gift for Christmas? Perhaps a padded picture frame or a pillow would be a better choice for a Mother's Day or birthday present.

3. Give your handmade gift with pride. After all, it took thought and time and a lot of caring, usually much more so than something you could purchase outright. I like to present my gifts elegantly wrapped in fabric, often using some of the fabric left over from the project itself.

4. You might try giving nonpersonal gifts, something that would be useful and appropriate for each person on your gift list. This helps to eliminate the brain work that can sometimes be aggravating when trying to remember what you gave each person the year before, and it might also help to keep one family member from feeling that the others got something bigger, better, or more special. This would also allow you to consider making the gifts in a manner similar to that of an assembly-line process, undertaking each step on each present at one time, such as doing all the marking, then all the cutting, followed by working the designs, then, finally, all the finishing and assembling.

5. If the gift is to be personal, make sure that the fit is proper, which requires that you know the recipient's size and measurements. After all, we know from experience how body sizes and shapes can change suddenly, often almost overnight. Be sure the colors you select will be appropriate.

6. Gaining a reputation for giving wonderful handmade gifts has its good points as well as, possibly, some bad ones. One bad point might be that you could become known as "the seamstress," able to run up anything on a moment's notice. I have a friend who was asked by one of her relatives, with great sincerity and expectation, if she would please whip up and finish two bed-sized coverlets within the next three days. My friend couldn't imagine how this relative envisioned her. She felt that she must have been seen as a person with nothing else to do but sit by the sewing machine, telephone at her side, just waiting to be asked to sew. My friend also expressed irritation over her relative's indifference to the fact that no one could possibly get those two coverlets, with their intricate designs and piecing patterns, completed in such a short period of time.

7. Another drawback I've experienced in being known as "the seamstress" is that the gift was so well-liked that the recipient asked for three more. It is almost a safe bet to say that every time this happens, you can count on there being *no more* matching fabric. On another occasion, my time was completely unavailable and I ended up feeling guilty by not being able to give a most appreciative person more of the item she asked for. Beware.

8. The good points of becoming "the seamstress'' are in being able to take special and full advantage of the title. It should enable you to make professional requests, such as upgrading your sewing equipment, improving your working area and lighting, buying a better chair, or finding additional storage for materials. It might also enable you to participate in classes or workshops, even some held in another state or county, without feeling guilty lest the money should really be used elsewhere. The title is also a great way of letting your spouse and children know of particular books, periodicals, or items that you would like to have entered on *your* gift-receiving list.

9. Last, be sure to tell the recipients that they can give the gift back if it isn't suitable, although I have never yet found anyone who has taken me up on this.

Panic Situations

What do you do when a design doesn't move for you, when you've reached a real stalemate, nothing seems to be working, you're at your wit's end? As it's being developed, each design will produce some degree of these feelings within you. The following are suggestions on how to cope when this occurs. Each is based on hard-earned experience, although I'd rather they had been gleaned through conversation or reading.

TAKE A VACATION

Try giving your design and yourself separate vacations. Just set the design aside, remove it from your range of vision, and wipe it from your conscious thoughts. Place it in a box or shove it under the bed, entombing it where it will be completely out of sight and out of mind.

This might be next to impossible if you have a schedule that calls for the design to be finished in, say, one week or so. If this is the case, you may have a real headache on your hands (or in your head), and you'll have to work out a solution the best you can, fast. Still, try giving yourself permission to take a three- or four-day vacation from the project. Even this short a time will work wonders. I've found that when I return to a design several days later, magnificent new ideas begin to spring from my head and hands, almost as though my subconscious mind had continued to work on alternative solutions while the rest of me was off doing other things or, as I call it, taking a vacation. Suddenly, with creativity and fresh ideas flowing, the design becomes workable again and begins to move to a smooth, satisfying conclusion.

There are many different kinds of vacation. Their length, their expense, even the amount of pleasure derived from them, varies from person to person. So it is with the designer's vacation. For some, a short vacation might consist of helping out at the school library, going window shopping, meeting a friend for lunch, taking a long walk, or going to the beach for the day, playing a game of golf, junking or antiquing for the afternoon. These are all planned or staged; they're events that make you feel comfortable and relaxed. Each takes your mind and body into a fresh area of vision, touch, and sound.

There are other vacations that fall into the category of "double payoff." I think you'll know what I mean when I tell you about my friend Joan. Her closets were badly crammed, literally jammed, sheltering "better-hold-onto, you-never-know-when-we'll-need-it" stuff. A mixture of who knows what, obviously self-propagating in the quiet darkness behind the forced-closed doors. Joan insists that she had to tiptoe down the hall past her "blue-ribbon-winner closet" for fear the doors would fly open and she'd be found hours later under an avalanche of blue-ribbon "junk."

One day when the project Joan was working on came to a nonbudging halt, she recognized it as her great opportunity for a double-payoff vacation. Thanks to the swap meet or flea market and her ability to convert her own "junk" into other people's treasures, three weeks later she had extra money in her purse—to reinvest in needlework, of course. She received high praise from her family and friends, who thought she was undergoing a "better-late-than-never" change in her scavenging habits. To top that off, she was delighted to have newly acquired space in her half-filled closets for her new purchases. She was no longer in fear of having to do battle as she passed the now easy-to-shut doors. Following this double-payoff vacation, flush with money and fame, Joan returned to her design with enthusiasm (but I forget whether the design benefited or not).

Designers and artists will often work on several designs at one time. This automatically allows their attention to leave a particular piece and their minds to take a rest or vacation, so to speak. I used to be very impressed by magazine layouts showing the working studios of painters and designers. There would be numerous works in process, scattered magnificently about, adding artistic clutter and color to the setting. Oh, yes, the magazine's stylist may have shuffled things around, doctoring up the setting more than just a little, but in reality, this juggling of several projects at one time is the natural way to work when developing designs.

If you're fairly new at designing, you'll soon realize that it's difficult to work on only one design at a time. Try to work on five or six different pieces simultaneously, giving to each its full share of attention for as long as the design or work flows. When you reach a point where you no longer feel inspired or you can't quite decide what the piece needs next, it's time to set that design aside and turn to another.

Some people I've encountered have put forth various reasons for not being able to work on more than one design at a time, even though they professed to want to do so. The reason most commonly given is that "my work space at home is so limited that I can work on only one piece." The second reason I hear most often is, "I can't begin something new until I finish what I've already started."

The first statement of having limited space is a complaint of almost everyone. Actually, when have you ever heard someone say she had enough room? A strong determination to improve your storage or working area may be what's needed. I'm a firm believer in the theory that we can achieve almost anything once we set our mind to it. After reading the section "Where to Stash Your Stuff," make a list of ten inexpensive storage ideas that you can put into immediate action. Set a time limit in which to accomplish your ideas, aiming for three weeks or less. With this achieved, you'll be free to enjoy the difference that better storage can make, and at the same time, you will have gained some momentum to move on to bigger things. Before the excitement cools down, consider redesigning closets, installing shelving, purchasing files or storage units, putting in better lighting, even expanding an existing room or area.

Meanwhile, clean out closets, or have a garage sale. Store those "no-longer-used-but-want-to-keep" items in well-marked boxes in out-of-the-way areas such as the basement or garage. Most of us have more room than we realize if only we would selectively use it.

People who fall into the second category—those who can't begin working on something new until they've completed their first project—are making a statement about lack of permission, not lack of ability. If you find this is your niche, try asking yourself, "Why? Is it really a good rule for me? Can it be changed slightly, moderately, or completely eliminated? Do I want to continue to accept this idea or rule?"

You may identify this feeling as similar to having an old dinghy in tow, something you acquired in your mind as you were growing up that you're still pulling along, no matter whether it's needed or not. Perhaps you've even passed the rule along to your family and offspring in an attempt to help them develop what you considered to be good work habits. Only you can make the decision to cut the dinghy loose.

MOVE YOUR DESIGN TO ANOTHER LOCATION

Another technique I find essential while building a design is to move it to the location in which it will ultimately be placed. For example, when working on something that will be used in the kitchen, put it into the kitchen and see how it relates to its surroundings. It may suddenly take on an appearance of delicacy and seem to be out of place among the large, rigid appliances. Your "oh-so-perfect" design may fade into the woodwork, so to speak, when having to compete with tiled counter tops or the bold flooring patterns often found in kitchens today. It's better to find out early in the planning stage that changes are needed rather than later, when the design is completed in fabric and fiber.

If the finished design will be used in a child's room, study it there. Is it too large in scale for the smaller-sized furniture and accessories? Does it need refining before being placed on small articles of clothing? Is it too bold in color to be used next to a young infant's delicate skin tones?

Too often when we're developing a design, we don't take the time or trouble to move it from the flat, horizontal surface of a table to a vertical position. Consider how different the design might appear if it were to be positioned along the hemline or bottom edge of a floor-length table skirt. Would it be lost in the fullness of the gathers? Should it be opened up or simply repositioned a little higher? Perhaps it needs to be made thicker, given more bulk or beefed up in certain areas in order to keep it visually flowing.

Even with all these changes, you may find that your design still doesn't work properly around the hemline. You may have to begin over again, moving the motif to the top of the table and allowing it to cascade down the sides. This design that seemed to be lost when placed low suddenly comes to life when placed high. Similarly, a design that you developed to wrap around a bouffant sleeve on an evening top might appear entirely different when centered over a photo-album cover or positioned on the corner of a pillow top.

ASK OPINIONS OF OTHERS

Don't overlook the wonderful resources to be found in other people's opinions and their points of view. Because each of us sees through different eyes, another person's insight can help give new input. Learn to use this to your advantage. I have one friend who asked her son and some of his playmates to quiet down, gather around her design work, and tell her what they saw. Their comments, besides being outrageously funny and relieving her tension, left her with six different unabridged and fresh viewpoints. Probably some she would never have visualized herself. In the end, none were really useful, but positive communication took place. The children felt very important while my friend had relaxed and become less uptight about her project.

It might take several attempts at asking other people for their opinions on a design you're developing before you find someone who gives back a piece of information you can build upon. I have a friend whose opinion I often seek. She will usually throw out some small, fresh insights that help the design take off once again. Then there are the others whom, I already know from experience, it is better not to ask.

KEEP A SENSE OF HUMOR

Seriousness sets the concrete
Of rigid thinking
And reflexive activity,
Etching behavior
And feeling
Into pathways
Of stone and mortar. *

Humor is one of the ingredients essential to creativity. A sense of humor is the stuff that gets us through and the key to the old saying, "Tough times never last, but tough people do." It's easy enough for all of us to recognize the stress in our lives today and see how often it can stifle a sense of humor.

There can be emergencies, sometimes serious and other times downright ridiculous. A child who has discovered one shoe missing from his school locker and needs another brought to school immediately so he can resume the day's activities. A dead car battery that leaves you begging your good-hearted neighbors to let you borrow their car so you can keep an appointment, only to have a flat tire along the way. Perhaps, you say to yourself, it was meant for you to stay put that day. While we can usually control our work and our schedules, there are times when we are literally at the mercy of others.

A serious commitment to a design as it develops usually means that you will have limited time to enjoy other aspects of life. A certain amount of isolation is necessary. For myself, I'm serious about my chosen field of work. It requires long hours, and I frequently work seven days a week, sometimes for weeks on end. During these stretches, I find that I have to work at maintaining my normally limited sense of humor. Besides telling myself that distractions aren't really important and reminding myself that no matter how much I might want things to be different, the wind will blow me around just as it pleases, so I'd better relax and go with the flow.

I recall a story about a student who was told by his guru that he would know he had mastered life when the day came that everything was right, just perfect, and he, the student, was able to say aloud, "And this too shall pass."

Beware the seriousness of others.
It is contagious and addicting.

In seriousness
You automatically lose concern
For mutual growth
And become entrenched
In an impoverished insular identity.

Laugh whenever possible
*And play at being serious.**

LEARNING FROM DISASTERS

When a project doesn't turn out as well as you had envisioned, your initial reaction will probably be disappointment, even discouragement. You've put in valuable time and effort, and probably you've found it necessary to purchase special materials. You had great expectations for that project, but now, as it comes to a finish, it looks less than desirable, really terrible.

A failure is not fatal. Try to look upon it as an unexpected opportunity to learn, even if the lesson is one you'd rather not have to take. It's usually a failure that gives us the impetus to go out and do better, to do things we otherwise wouldn't have needed to do or thought of doing before the disappointment. A failure gives us one of the best learning opportunities of all because of the commitment we've already invested.

Nor are delays deadly. See a delay as an opportunity to do better next time, as a time to plan for greater things. Use a delay as the appropriate moment in which to excavate yourself, to move yourself out of the thought patterns you've settled into. So often we become overly preoccupied with a design. We gear ourselves to look for "perfection" as we move from out-of-order toward order itself. Use an unexpected pause to reevaluate your goals.

Understand that delays are only that. Nothing more.

And if you find yourself anxious about pressures, know that they are not permanent. Nothing stays fixed forever. Don't give pressure a permanent home; learn to dismiss it. A disaster often brings pressure with it, but try to recognize it for what it is and don't build on it. Know that it will pass.

Whatever you put into your mind will manifest itself in the world. Don't think "disaster;" think instead of the opportunity with which you are now presented. You can work out brand-new dimensions. Anything you can conceive, you can achieve. Designing is simply "seeing beyond." As it says in Romans 8:19, "The creation waits with eager longing for the revealing."

*Anthon, Robert M., and J. Digby Henry. *When the Butterfly Rests in Your Hand, Do Not Close It.* Pierce Publishing Co., Santa Ana, CA 92707-1979. Used by permission of the author.

A Footnote on "Finish-O-Phobia"

Do you have a serious case of the dreaded affliction "finish-o-phobia"? Do you begin new projects without finishing, or even hoping to finish, the old ones? Do partially completed needlework projects get set aside for long periods of time, maybe forever? Do you have cut-out and stitched but unassembled projects hiding away in the dark crevices of closets? Do your friends ever ask, "Whatever happened to that such-and-such you were so busy with last week?" Do these questions bring about a feeling of guilt within you? This is the affliction I identify and label as "finish-o-phobia," known to be chronic in needleworkers of all ages. Here are some tips to help you begin again with a clear slate and conscience.

Some of the reasons for this affliction might be the "put-it-off-until-tomorrow" habit, which is more than just procrastination. Maybe you find that you dislike the details of assembling and finishing the remaining projects—details that might seem boring when compared to the more exciting and creative aspects of the design. For myself, I find that when I've been literally chained to one project and I've had to devote large segments of time to it, I tend to sour on that design. Or perhaps you find that you feel very confident about your ability to do the needlework areas but less so when it comes to the final machine sewing and assembling techniques. You just seem to fall apart. Do you fear you are going to ruin the project into which you have put so many hours, that it's going to come out looking like an old and well-worn housedress?

Perhaps it's a case where finishing a project may mean that you have to buy additional elegant trims, exquisite ribbons, laces, buttons, or other costly notions. This can put pressure on your pocketbook and at times can cause you to shelve a project until cash is more readily available or spending money is not so dear.

Hand needlework generally requires considerable periods of time, and this can, unfortunately, sometimes mean that your project has become obsolete. Do you perhaps find yourself working on designs developed around brown carpeting for a particular room, but now that six years have lapsed since you first began, the faded brown carpeting has been replaced with cherry red and the half-completed designs no longer seem appropriate?

If you suffer from the annoying ailment of "finish-o-phobia," here are some suggestions that might help. Try to pinpoint your pet needlework or sewing peeve and then select a project that will avoid it. Don't pick a project that requires hours and hours of intricate finishing and construction if that is what you dislike to do or tend to get uptight over. There are plenty of terrific projects available that don't require these skills. I have two friends who traded work with each other as their solution to this problem. One woman loved to do handwork and was able to stitch away during her lunch break and while commuting to and from work. The other woman was at home, raising her young children, and didn't have a moment to spare during the day. When all the children were tucked away at night, this woman found blissful solitude and fulfillment in working with her sewing machine. So one friend did all the handwork and traded it with the other, who did the assembling and finishing. When they compared the time each spent on a given item, they found that it averaged about half-and-half. From that point on, they just traded their skills and their time straight across.

I find it helpful to purchase and gather all the supplies necessary for the completion of a project at the time I'm ready to begin working on it. This helps to eliminate trips back to the store with half-completed work in hand. I feel better organized and lucky if the pieces only get wrinkled or a little soiled compared to the ultimate disaster of actually losing some of them in all the to-and-fro.

Every once in a while, perhaps every six months or so, I'll go through my storage cubbyholes and remove all the stashed-away, half-completed projects. After not having seen them for a period of time, some of them look refreshingly interesting. Others, seen again in the light of day, are definitely no longer appropriate in my life, making them easier to dispose of. Mary Ellen Hopkins, a well-known quilting lecturer and owner of The Crazy Ladies and Friends in Santa Monica, resorts to the wonderful practice of turning her various half-finished projects into desirable "giveaways." She wraps each uncompleted project in fresh tissue paper, puts it into a lovely gift box from a fashionable department store or boutique, and wraps and seals it with lots of ribbon and glittery stickers. These boxes are then ready to give away at Christmas or on other special occasions as projects to inspire others to complete them. The packages look enticing from the outside, while their partially completed contents give many a reluctant future needleworker the "shot in the arm" to try something new. And just think, each recipient of one of these wonderful packages is receiving a present that will take only half the ordinary time to complete.

You might try to look upon your unfinished treasures as your chance to become philanthrophic too. If you know someone who is a housekeeping nut, or someone who falls into the category of "show me a clean house and I'll show you a boring person," this may be your chance to help mankind. Present the person with a beautiful gift box of a half-finished project, and know that you may be the one responsible for showing her there is more to life than a spotless home.

And then there's Mary, who suggests that when things really become desperate, she will simply move into a new house, a bigger house, with twice as many closets. Only firm reasoning from her spouse keeps her where she is.

Another trick that I've found helpful in dealing with uncompleted projects is to wait until I am terribly enthusiastic about beginning a new project. Then I pull out the old half-completed projects and line them up across my bed. I have to admit that at times there have been as many as twenty neatly stacked piles. With the new masterpiece to look forward to, I find it easy to bulldoze through the old piles, eliminating some and quickly finishing others. Sometimes I'll begin my day by working for a couple of hours on an unfinished item and then reward myself for such meritorious effort by spending the rest of the day on the new masterpiece. It's amazing to see how quickly time can fly and the old piles can be completed if there's a brand-new project waiting in the wings. In twenty short days or less, the twenty unfinished piles are gone, mission accomplished, while I have had the enjoyment of beginning the new project as well.

You might consider holding a "finish-o-phobia" swap meet, inviting your friends in to contribute their incomplete projects to the swap. Of course you don't want to belittle your own swapping projects; rather, build them up like a Paul Bunyan-type of story: "How fantastic this would be in your family room, Betty, over by the fireplace." Watch out, though, you may so inspire yourself that you end up holding the item back for yourself.

About the last piece of advice I can give is that you have a party and give the projects out as booby prizes.

RECOMMENDED READING

MACHINE SEWING, HAND ASSEMBLING, FINISHING, AND MOUNTING

Designers Guild. *Soft Furnishings,* New York: Farrar, Straus and Giroux, Inc., 1980 (in Great Britain, Fakenham Press Limited, Fakenham, Norfolk)

Dickson, Elizabeth, and Margaret Colvin. *The Laura Ashley Book of Home Decorating.* New York: Harmony Books, 1982

Finch, Karen, and Greta Putman. *Caring For Textiles.* New York: Watson-Guptill, 1977

Hoover, Doris, and Nancy Welch. *Tassels.* California: Uno Graphics, 1978

Ireys, Katharine. *Finishing and Mounting Your Needlepoint Pieces.* New York: Thomas Y. Crowell, 1973

Lawson, Donna. *If You Can't Go Naked—Here Are Clothes to Sew on Fast.* New York: Grosset & Dunlap, 1973

Lindahl, Judy. *Decorating with Fabric, an Idea Book.* Portland, Oregon: Self-published, 1975

Rode, Janet E. *Fabric Decorating for the Home.* Birmingham, Alabama: Oxmoor House, 1976

Simplicity Sewing Book. New York: Simplicity Pattern Company, 1985

Wiener, Joan, and Sharon Rosenberg. *Son of Hassle-Free Sewing.* San Francisco: Straight Arrow Books, 1972

DESIGN AND COLOR

Beaney, Jan. *The Young Embroiderer.* New York and London: Frederick Warne, 1966

Bridges, Ann, ed. *Alphonse Mucha.* New York: Harmony Books, 1980

Chapman, Suzanne E. *Historic Floral and Animal Designs for Embroiderers and Craftsmen.* New York: Dover, 1977

Cox, Doris, and Barbara Warren. *Creative Hands.* Science Edition, New York: John Wiley & Sons, 1966

Gaber, Susan. *Treasury of Flower Designs for Artists, Embroiderers & Craftsmen.* New York: Dover, 1981

Gillon, Edmund V., Jr., *Art Nouveau: An Anthology of Design and Illustration from the Studio.* New York: Dover, 1969

Goldstein, Harriet, and Vetta Goldstein. *Art in Everyday Life.* Fourth Edition, New York: Macmillan, 1966

Harrison, Elizabeth. *Self-expression Through Art.* Second Edition, Peoria, Illinois: Chas. A. Bennett, 1960

Hornung, Clarence P. *Allover Patterns for Designers and Craftsmen.* New York: Dover, 1975

Howard, Constance. *Embroidery and Colour.* New York: Van Nostrand Reinhold, 1976

———. *Inspiration for Embroidery.* London: B. T. Batsford, 1966

———. *Needlework School.* Foreward by Constance Howard. Chartwell Books

Karasz, Mariska. *Adventures in Stitches and More Adventures—Fewer Stitches.* Revised and Expanded Edition, Funk & Wagnalls Company, 1959

Laury, Jean Ray. *Applique Stitchery.* New York: Reinhold, 1966

Liley, Alison. *Embroidery—A Fresh Approach.* London: Mills & Boon, 1964

Masini, Lara-Vinca. *Art Nouveau.* Secaucus, New Jersey: Chartwell Books, 1976

Messent, Jan. *Embroidery and Nature.* London: B. T. Batsford, 1980

Mirow, Gregory. *A Treasury of Design for Artists and Craftsmen.* New York: Dover, 1969

Nichols, Marion. *Designs and Patterns for Embroiderers and Craftsmen.* New York: Dover, 1974

Proctor, Richard M. *Principles of Pattern for Craftsmen and Designers.* New York: Van Nostrand Reinhold, 1968

Rush, Beverly. *The Stitchery Idea Book.* New York: Van Nostrand Reinhold, 1974

White, Kathleen. *Design in Embroidery.* London: B. T. Batsford Ltd., 1969

MY ALL-TIME FAVORITES

Anthony, Robert M., and J. Digby Henry. *When the Butterfly Rests in Your Hand, Do Not Close It,* Santa Ana, California: Pierce, 1979

Bank, Mirra. *Anonymous Was a Woman,* New York: St. Martin's Press, 1979

Brookes, John. *The Garden Book,* New York: Crown, 1984

Cooper, Patricia, and Norma Bradley Buferd. *The Quilters,* New York: Doubleday, 1977

de Conceicao, Maria, and Nancy Grubb. *Wearable Art,* New York: Penguin, 1980

Dewhurst, C., Kurt, Betty MacDowell, and Marsha MacDowell. *Artists in Aprons,* New York: E. P. Dutton in association with the Museum of American Folk Art, 1979

Douglas, William Lake, and Susan R. Frey, Norman K. Johnson, Susan Littlefield, Michael Van Valkenburgh. *Garden Design,* New York: Simon and Schuster, 1984

Emmerling, Mary Ellisor. *Collecting American Country,* New York: Clarkson N. Potter, 1983

Gibran, Kahlil. *The Prophet,* New York: Knopf, 1923

Hailey, Elizabeth Forsythe. *A Woman of Independent Means,* New York: Viking Press, 1973

Hall, Eliza Calvert. *Aunt Jane of Kentucky,* Boston: Little, Brown and Company, 1907

Hemphill, Herbert W. Jr., and Julie Weissman. *Twentieth-Century American Folk Art and Artists,* New York: E. P. Dutton, 1974

Hymes, James L., Jr., *Behavior and Misbehavior,* Third Edition, Englewood Cliffs, New Jersey: Prentice-Hall, 1955

Laury, Jean Ray. *The Creative Woman's Getting-It-All-Together at Home Handbook,* New York: Van Nostrand Reinhold, 1977

Moulin, Pierre, Pierre Le Vec, and Linda Dannenberg. *Pierre Deux's French Country,* New York: Clarkson N. Potter, 1984

Otis, Denise, Ronaldo Mais, and Ernst Beadle. *Decorating with Flowers,* New York: Harry N. Abrams, 1978

Peck, M. Scott. *The Road Less Traveled,* New York: Simon and Schuster, 1978

Stewart, Martha. *Entertaining,* New York: Clarkson N. Potter, 1982

Thompson, Flora. *Lark Rise to Candleford,* New York: Crown, 1983

Verey, Rosemary, and Ellen Samuels. *The American Woman's Garden,* Boston: Little, Brown & Company, 1984

Waites, Raymond, Bettye Martin, and Norma Skurka. *American V.I.E.W.,* New York: Harper & Row, 1984

Walker, Alice. *The Color Purple,* New York: Washington Square Press, 1982

Wilkinson, Elizabeth, and Marjorie Henderson. *The House of Boughs,* New York: Viking Press, 1985

MAIL ORDER SOURCES FOR GOODS AND SERVICES

GENERAL

United States

CABIN FEVER CALICOES
P. O. Box 6256
Northwest Station
Washington, DC 20015

Send $2.75 for mail-order catalog. Three hundred swatches of fabrics for $2.75. Accepts Visa and Mastercard. All orders processed next day. Huge selection of books, notions, left-handed scissors, opaque projectors, and light boxes.

CLOTILDE
237 SW 28th Street
Ft. Lauderdale, FL 33315

Free catalog. No credit cards. Orders processed in 2 days. Extra-special products.

THE COUNTERPANE QUILT SHOPPE, INC.
Mallard Square, Hwy. 64
P. O. Box 1484
Highlands, NC 28741

Lovely full-color catalog for $2. One hundred-fifty fabric samples available for $2. Carries everything for the quilter. Their specialty—"Quilters Fabric Service"™, monthly mailings of color-coordinated 4″ × 4″ samples.

JOSEPH'S COAT
26 Main Street
Peterborough, NH 03458

Free catalog available. Orders processed within 72 hours. Large stock of books. Has left-handed scissors, voile, and a large assortment of solid-colored fabrics.

ORANGE PATCHWORK PUBLISHERS
P. O. Box 2557
Orange, CA 92705

Send SASE and $1 for full-color catalog. Largest supplier of publications on shadow quilting and a variety of other patchwork books.

OSAGE COUNTY QUILT FACTORY
400 Walnut, Box 490
Overbrook, KS 66524

Catalog for $1. Send check for payments on orders. No credit cards. Special platinum needles, silk quilting thread, voile, many fabrics.

THE QUILT PATCH
1897 Hanover Pike
Littlestown, PA 17340

Catalog available with samples for $2. Accepts Visa and Mastercard. Processes orders in 1 to 2 weeks. General supply of sewing notions and quilting supplies.

TREADLEART
25834 Narbonne Avenue, Suite 1
Lomita, CA 90717

Catalog is $1. Visa and Mastercard accepted. Will ship COD. Two days to process orders. Specialty—sewing-machine supplies and sewing notions. Light boxes. Send fabric swatch and they'll match.

TUMBLEWEED
99 Mt. Auburn Street
Cambridge, MA 02138

Catalog and fabric samples available for $1.75. Accepts personal checks. Carries all quilting supplies.

Canada

GINA BROWN FIBERCRAFTS
2207—4 Street SW
Calgary, Alberta
Canada T2S 1X1

Visa and Mastercard accepted. Processes all orders in one day. Scissors, D.M.C. embroidery floss, glue sticks, air- and water-disappearing markers, voile, chiffon, organza, and many solid-colored fabrics.

QUILTS AND OTHER COMFORTS
1560 Bayview Avenue
Toronto, Ontario
Canada M4G 3D8

Visa and Mastercard accepted. Processes orders in 2 to 3 days. Huge selection of books, patterns, and notions. Fabric swatches upon request.

Australia

PATCHWORK & SEW ON
184 Canterbury Road
Heathmont, Victoria
Australia 3135

Accepts Visa and Bankcard of Australia. Processes orders in 2 to 3 days. Comprehensive range of general quilting supplies. Wide selection of solid-colored fabrics, voile, fine iron-on interfacing.

PATCHWORK PALACE
91 Woniora Road
Hurstville, N.S.W.
Australia 2220

Has free catalog. Accepts Visa, Mastercard, and Bankcard of Australia. Processes all orders in one day. Fabric samples available for $2.50. Left-handed scissors. Specializes in supplies for patchwork, quilting, and appliqué.

England

THE PATCHWORK STUDIO
2 Church Lane
Old Stevenage, Herts
England

Has free catalog. Fabric samples available. Specializes in designing patchwork quilts besides carrying all essential supplies. Send SASE for more details.

SPECIAL PRODUCTS

Left-handed Scissors

FISKARS MANUFACTURING CORP.
Attn. Customer Service
7811 Stewart Avenue
Wausau, WI 54401

Opaque Projector

KOPYKAKE
3701 West 240th Street
Torrance, CA 90505

SPORTY'S TOOL SHOP
Clermont Airport
Batavia, OH 45103

Space Organizers

HOLD EVERYTHING
Williams-Sonoma Mail Order Dept.
P. O. Box 7456
San Francisco, CA 94120

Surgical Tweezers

BROOKSTONE
127 Vose Farm Road
Peterborough, NH 03460

Wood Accessories

SUDBERRY HOUSE
Four Mile and Colton Roads
Box 895
Old Lyme, CT 06371

EDUCATIONAL ASSOCIATIONS

AMERICAN INTERNATIONAL QUILT ASSOCIATION
P.O. Box 79126
Houston, TX 77279-9126

Membership is open to any dedicated quilter, quilt collector, or person involved in the quilt business. Association was founded to allow dedicated quilt lovers the opportunity to work toward increasing the prestige, artistry, creativity, professionalism, and recognition of quilts.

NATIONAL QUILTING ASSOCIATION, INC.
P.O. Box 62
Greenbelt, MD 20770

Members receive a quarterly newsletter, calendar of events and coming attractions, and book reviews. The association offers a Teacher's Certification Program, Judges Certification, and Masters Guild.

INTERNATIONAL QUILTERS EXCHANGE
c/o Lindsay Guy Moss
720 Cheatham Hill Trail
Marietta, GA 30064

Source to exchange information between groups or individuals around the world.

EMBROIDERERS' GUILD OF AMERICA
200 Fourth Avenue
Louisville, KY 40202

Provides members with correspondence courses; conducts regional and national seminars.

NATIONAL STANDARDS COUNCIL OF
AMERICAN EMBROIDERS
P.O. Box 8578
North Field, IL 60093

Offers a national correspondence school; conducts regional and national seminars.

INDEX